PATIENT CAPITAL

PATICIENT CAPITAL

THE CHALLENGES AND PROMISES
OF LONG-TERM INVESTING

Victoria Ivashina and Josh Lerner

PRINCETON UNIVERSITY PRESS
PRINCETON AND OXFORD

Requests for permission to reproduce material from this work
should be sent to permissions@press.princeton.edu

Published by Princeton University Press
41 William Street, Princeton, New Jersey 08540
6 Oxford Street, Woodstock, Oxfordshire OX20 1TR

press.princeton.edu

LCCN 2019932655
ISBN 978-0-691-18673-3

British Library Cataloging-in-Publication Data is available

Editorial: Joe Jackson and Jacqueline Delaney
Production Editorial: Kathleen Cioffi
Text Design: Leslie Fliss
Jacket Design: Faceout Studio, Spencer Fuller
Jacket Texture: Shutterstock
Production: Erin Suydam
Publicity: James Schneider
Copyeditor: Jennifer McClain

This book has been composed in Arno and Penumbra Sans Std

Printed on acid-free paper. ∞

Printed in the United States of America

1 3 5 7 9 10 8 6 4 2

CONTENTS

PREFACE: PRIVATE CAPITAL 101

The focus of this book is on long-term, risky, and illiquid investments. These may involve the provision of funds to individual projects, from developing a new drug to building a highway, but often such investments are also in companies, whether a Minneapolis-based provider of microorganisms for clinical tests or a Hong Kong–based satellite communications specialist.

The growing and thoughtful debate on long-term investments has been focused on ideas: Is the world running out of good ideas? Why have companies found it seemingly harder to become more productive? Our agenda is to make progress in a different but essential direction: *how to make sure that when good ideas arise, they are funded and nurtured by patient capital*. Building on recent academic research, our own work, and many discussions with investors, this book outlines the key challenges facing long-term investments and suggests ways to address them. Before diving into the details, however, a few brief definitions are in order.

Throughout the book we often use the term *private equity*. Over the past several decades, private equity has been the primary way in which longer-term illiquid investments have been made. In the traditional structure of private equity, the money is raised and allocated through funds managed by specialized intermediaries known as general partners, or GPs, such as Sequoia Capital or the Blackstone Group. Some of these groups focus on start-ups—a style of investment known as *venture capital*—while others focus on mature firms undergoing transformations (*buyouts*). Yet another group focuses on firms that are in between, which are often already profitable but need capital and advice (*growth equity*). The sourcing of the deals, due diligence process, valuations, and sources of value creation following the investment are substantially different in these three segments of the private equity industry.

General partners raise funds from investors, which may be families, insurers, pensions, university endowments, or long-term pools that governments set aside, known as *sovereign wealth funds*. The capital providers are collectively referred to as limited partners, or LPs, and the funds are known as *limited partnerships*. The funds typically have an eight- to ten-year life span, sometimes with extensions.

Private equity investors typically manage several funds at one time, with various degrees of remaining maturity and sometimes with different areas of focus. But for a large part of the industry's history, private equity investors typically did just what their name promised: they invested in privately held equity (as opposed to debt). For venture capital and growth equity, the investments were typically made in the form of complex preferred shares. For growth equity and buyouts, investors often used, in addition to their equity, debt borrowed from banks and other investors (together referred to as *leverage*). After the investment, the general partners would hold the entity for five years or so, typically guiding its progress through one or more board seats. Once the investments were sold—whether to a corporate buyer (in what is known as a *trade sale*), an IPO (initial public offering) of publicly traded shares on a stock market, or even to another private equity group—the fund was wound down.

In exchange for their services, the general partners received a "management fee," an annual payment often in the range of 1.5%–2% of the total amount of funds raised (also known as *committed capital*), as well as a 20% share of the ultimate profits (*carried interest*) and sometimes additional "transaction fees." But this model in recent years has begun to undergo change, with funds having longer lives, new structures, and including new types of investments.

This book draws on lessons from the past to make suggestions for the future. So we consider not only traditional fund models, as described above, but other ways to pursue concentrated and illiquid investments in risky projects. That said, in the interest of space we shy away from the challenges facing investors in publicly traded securities or those pursuing investment strategies with shorter horizons, such as the ones hedge funds and activist investors employ.

As we move through the chapters, we introduce several advanced concepts concerning long-term investors and private equity. These include asset allocation, performance measurement, compensation, governance structures within institutional investors, the incentives (or "agency") problems introduced by the fund structures, and so on. While this book is not intended as a textbook on the private equity industry, we explain the relevant concepts as we bring them up. We ultimately hope this book will be engaging to not only the industry participants but, more broadly, people who are interested in innovative ideas and how to bring them to life.

ACKNOWLEDGMENTS

A book like this one, which seeks to draw together work in many arenas over the past several decades, makes it challenging to acknowledge contributors. Most directly, it draws on academic work with coauthors. The most relevant of these collaborators are Shai Bernstein, Paul Gompers, Anna Kovner, Lily Fang, Antoinette Schoar, and David Scharfstein. We thank them for permission to use here some of our jointly developed ideas, as well as for many conversations that shaped our own thoughts.

The volume also draws extensively on some of the frameworks that were developed by Josh with Felda Hardymon and Ann Leamon in the many case studies they wrote together for the Venture Capital and Private Equity class at Harvard Business School, as well as the associated textbook and casebook. Similarly, several ideas build on the cases and notes developed for the Private Equity Finance class taught by Victoria. The case protagonists were generous with their insights, many of which have found their way into this volume.

The various endeavors on long-term investing we have tackled under the aegis of the World Economic Forum also directly addressed many of the issues in this volume. This work also draws on insights from real-world projects that Josh has done with long-term investors and private capital groups through his advisory firm, Bella Private Markets. A number of chapters draw on writing that Ann Leamon did for these projects, as well as conversations with many thoughtful practitioners as part of this effort. Especial thanks go to Peter Cornelius, Nori Gerardo-Leitz, David Swensen, and Alison Tarditi for their many helpful conversations throughout the process and comments on the manuscript.

We also owe a debt of gratitude to the several research associates who helped with the development of this book: Luting Chen, Austin Milunovich, Kaveh Motamedy, Alexey Tuzikov, and Lucy Zhang. Kathleen

Ryan of Baker Library provided great help, as usual, with the researching of various facts and figures. Our assistants, Victoria Koc and Maryna Zhauniarovich, helped the effort in innumerable ways. We also gratefully acknowledge Harvard Business School's Division of Research, which provided financial support for the project.

PATIENT CAPITAL

CHAPTER 1

The Need for Investing Long-Term

Long-term investing has never been more important than today. Many of society's most intractable problems—from addressing the environmental ills of the planet, to revitalizing decaying infrastructure in developed and developing nations alike, to ensuring national security, to the hunger for innovation to stimulate economic growth—resist easy solutions. Rather, they can only be addressed with the thoughtful application of time and money.

Moreover, it is increasingly clear that the "investor" who has traditionally stepped up to address many of these problems—the government—is unwilling or unable to do so in much of the world. In Europe, many ambitious efforts have been pared back or have proved ineffective. Consider Spain, for instance. Its landscape is littered with "ghost airports" whose construction was funded by the European Union and the national government, despite the absence of demand for them.[1] Some of these airports failed to attract a single commercial flight in the first few years after their construction.[2] Meanwhile, the nation's efforts to encourage alternative energy have been a victim of inconsistent policies. Numerous Spanish renewable energy companies teeter on the edge of bankruptcy, a consequence of the government's abrupt shift from the promise of extended generous subsidies to a "solar tax" and draconian regulation.[3]

In the United States, the ideology of small government appears to be resulting in a reduced role of public investment in areas such as environment technology and innovation more generally. Even in areas targeted by the current administration, such as President Trump's much-hyped infrastructure plan, prospects are uncertain and the government anticipates playing a limited leadership role: the program seems to depend critically on private sector spending. And in defense research, since 9/11 the trend appears to have favored short-run projects with well-defined end points, rather than the kind of expansive projects that characterized earlier decades and led to computing and communications breakthroughs.[4]

If the long-run needs are to be addressed, it seems clear that another set of actors will need to take the lead. Those best positioned to address them are likely to be the pools of capital in the hands of pensions, insurers, sovereign wealth funds, endowments, and families. These organizations are given the responsibility of holding capital for many years, or even forever, in the case of universities and families.

In addition to their long time frames, these institutions command enormous sums of money. The Organization for Economic Cooperation and Development (OECD) estimates that pensions in the nations under their purview alone held over $35 trillion in assets in 2015. They also estimate that the life insurers in the same countries had close to $15 trillion in assets in 2015.[5] As we seek to estimate the amount of investible assets held by sovereign wealth funds, endowments, and family offices, the task becomes progressively harder, but these run into trillions of dollars.[6]

The hunger of these parties—which we henceforth refer to as investors—for opportunities to invest long-term is greater than ever. Public pensions and social insurance programs are facing huge shortfalls, which are unlikely to be made up with traditional stocks and bonds. For example, Moody's estimates that US federal, state, and local pensions had a shortfall of $7 trillion in 2017 (not including the "big kahuna" of $13 trillion of unfunded social security obligations).[7] The same report suggests that the situation was little better in many other nations. Similarly, sovereign wealth funds are being rapidly depleted in many nations as governments spend their resources faster than they can garner returns, in hopes of avoiding crippling recessions and social unrest.

In this era of depleted resources, generating attractive returns is a priority. But the challenge of doing so with traditional assets in an environment where stocks worldwide are anticipated to be modest performers over the coming years[8] and interest rates are slowly being ratcheted upward is substantial. As a result, in the past two decades investors have been increasingly lured to approaches such as the Yale model or the Canadian model, in which long-term assets such as private equity and real estate play an essential role. For instance, Yale—for many years a poster child for this kind of approach—over the past two decades (through the end of the 2016 fiscal year) earned only 5% annually from its bond holdings and a more attractive 12% annually from its domestic equities, but 14% and 16%, respectively, from private equity and real assets, such as timber and farmland. Meanwhile, Yale has earned an almost unbelievable 77% annual return from its venture capital investments over the last two decades; by way of perspective, had someone invested a thousand dollars and gotten such a return over twenty years, it would have grown to $91 million![9] To be clear, that is only true if one can continuously reinvest all cash flows at the 77% rate of return.

Intuitively, the appeal of investing in the long term is clear. History is full of examples of savvy investors who went "against the grain" and enjoyed fabulous returns as a result. John D. Rockefeller Jr.'s investments in Tokyo real estate beginning in 1946, Warren Buffett's investments after the purchase of Berkshire Hathaway in 1965, and Charlie Lea's decision to support Federal Express through a half dozen rounds of disappointments and earnings shortfalls have been justly celebrated.

So investors are looking beyond traditional stocks and bonds, in the hope of garnering more attractive returns by turning to stickier, longer-term investments. The *Wall Street Journal* estimates that the amount raised in US private markets, including private placements of debt and equity directly to investors, totaled $2.4 trillion in 2017, more than the $2.1 trillion raised in public markets.[10] Even if investors wanted to stick to public markets, the supply of firms has shrunk, at least in the United States. Craig Doidge, Andrew Karolyi, and René Stulz document that the number of domestic exchange-listed firms has fallen by about one-half over the last two decades.[11] (In the rest of the world, the number of new listings continued to grow until recently, when the number appeared to level off.) Instead, investments in categories as diverse as young and restructuring ventures, highways and bridges, farmland, and wind farms have come into favor. In an ideal world, these disciplined investors would fill the capital gaps, simultaneously generating attractive financial returns and addressing social needs.

Yet in many cases, despite these substantial needs, investments in these areas have been problematic at best, plagued by distortions of many types. Far too often investors have taken a "quick and dirty" approach to complex investments, and then been surprised when this approach did not work. The result has been a lot of wasted money and little real progress.

A dramatic example is the notorious "cleantech bubble."[12] In the years between 2008 and 2011, venture capitalists—newly awakened to the potential risks of global warming—plowed over $15 billion in firms working on areas such as solar, wind, and biofuels. In many cases, the investors, in their hurry to deploy capital into the next big thing, funded technologies that technologists had been unsuccessfully struggling with for decades. In others, such as the notorious Solyndra, inexperienced management, flush with cash from governmental and private investors, made a series of mistakes reflecting their lack of understanding of the market and the nature of the competition. Bad luck played a role as well, particularly the rapid fall in the price of natural gas as fracking spread like wildfire in the United States, the decline in government subsidies for cleantech firms after some well-publicized failures, and the financial pressures brought about by the Great Recession.

Within a few years, it was clear that these investments were struggling, and the enthusiasm for all things cleantech began to wane considerably in the venture community. Before long, social media and its myriad applications had emerged as the new next big thing for these investors. As a result, early-stage funding of cleantech firms fell from $1.4 billion in 2011 to about $100 million in 2014. While some qualified successes may have come out of this investment boom—the emergence of Tesla and the electric car industry would be one case—it is hard not to feel that this was an expensive and largely unsuccessful effort to address extremely complex issues that was abandoned when some seemingly appealing but naive initial approaches did not work out.

As a result of this and many other disappointments with their long-term investments, investors are increasingly seeking out fresh approaches to investing long-term. To cite three recent examples:

- In 2017, the then chief investment officer of the largest US public pension, Theodore Eliopoulos of the California Public Employees Retirement System (CalPERS), urged the $323 billion pension to begin a direct private investment program. This initiative would take a stake in privately held companies in areas such as life sciences, rather than investing through funds. In this way, CalPERS could help reduce the $800 million it paid in fees to private equity managers in the prior year, as well as holding the investments for more extended periods. Questions were raised as to whether the pension could pay the staff of this effort enough to attract top talent, even if they segregated the direct investment staff in a separate legal entity.[13] At the end of that year, the pension instead requested bids from major financial institutions to serve as a strategic partner for its private equity program.
- The Public Investment Fund, one of several sovereign wealth funds owned by the Kingdom of Saudi Arabia, made two massive commitments to new private funds. While the PIF has existed for decades as a slow-moving holding company, in recent years it has been given a huge influx of public funds, with the promise of more to follow from the proceeds of the proposed Saudi Aramco privatization. Yet even by the standards of its often free-spending sovereign wealth fund peers, its actions have been striking. In the first move, it committed up to $45 billion to the Softbank Vision Fund. The Softbank fund, which had come very close to reaching its $100 billion goal in early 2018, was thirty times larger than any other venture fund ever raised, and ten times the largest technology-focused buyout fund. In the second move, it tentatively committed to provide half of Blackstone's

proposed $40 billion infrastructure fund. The proposed fund was twice as large as any that Blackstone had raised before. The move was particularly striking in light of Blackstone's decision to abandon raising a $2 billion infrastructure fund in 2011 (though of course in a very different political climate). But as the *Financial Times* reported, the inexperience and governance structure of the Saudi fund raised concerns about the wisdom of this course both within and outside the Kingdom.[14]

- The investment office of a wealthy Asian family (whose name we cannot disclose) was ripped by dissension, as the professional investors complained about the casual approach taken by the family patriarch. In particular, the staff felt that the chair of the family office—the grandson of the founder who had sold his retail business to a global conglomerate for several billion dollars—was taking a far too undisciplined approach to investing in projects and companies. Their data suggested that the track record of the family's investments over the past decade had been quite mixed. In turn, the patriarch argued that the family office staff was seeking to constrain his ability to respond quickly and flexibly to the opportunities that his global network were presenting to them.

These three episodes illustrate some of the critical land mines that long-run investment programs face. However desirable from an abstract perspective, the success of these programs in execution has been repeatedly hindered by the same issues. Thus, we are not great fans of investors simply diving into the pool of long-run investing, as so many are today. Indeed, the pursuit of long-term investments is no longer a focus of just the largest institutions: our work shows that, between 2008 and 2017, all pension funds aggressively expanded into alternative investments; a pattern that holds for funds of all sizes, including those with only $50 million in assets under management.[15] There is an urgency to think carefully about the major pitfalls that others have encountered and to strategize about how they will overcome them. These barriers are not impossible to overcome—we will highlight numerous successful examples—but without proper attention, they are certain to appear. The goal of this book is to identify these pitfalls and to propose actionable solutions to avoid them.

WHAT IS LONG-TERM INVESTING AND WHY IS IT NEEDED?

A natural starting question is, What exactly is long-term investing? In many discussions, the definition is left quite vague, reminiscent of US Supreme Court Justice Potter Stewart's memorable delineation of obscenity ("I know it when I see it"[16]). For instance, the World Economic Forum defines long-term investing as "investing with the expectation of holding an asset for an indefinite period of time by an investor with the capability to do so"[17]; while the Focusing Capital on the Long Term Project, an august body of industry elders, defines long-term investing as "a multiyear time horizon for value creation."[18] Both definitions seem close to tautological.

For our purposes, we take a more prosaic definition of long-term investing: investments with typical holding periods exceeding five years that, in recent decades, have been typically pursued in private partnerships. This categorization includes investments in cutting-edge technologies, fast-growing private firms hungry for capital and more mature restructuring ones, infrastructure projects, and more esoteric categories, such as farmland and water. As we already indicated, main investors that primarily do long-term investing (whether directly or through intermediaries) include private and public pension funds, family offices, endowments, insurance companies, and sovereign wealth funds.

Meanwhile, short-term investing involves liquid assets that can be readily bought and sold, such as stocks and bonds. While few people boast about being short-term investors, there are a lot of them! The World Bank calculates (based on statistics from the World Federation of Exchanges) that the mean holding period of a stock has dropped from over five years in 1975 to under eight months in 2016; worldwide over a similar period, the decline has been from about four years to nine months.[19]

Our focus on long-term investing should not obscure the fact that short-term investing conveys important benefits as well, providing liquidity to capital markets.

In fact, the shortening of public equity holding periods may beg the question, Why do we need long-term investors at all? If a series of short-term investors each makes the decisions that maximize the value of the company they hold, wouldn't we get to the right place, despite the multiplicity of owners? In other words, how can patient capital create value?

One answer is that assessing potentially innovative new products and services can be very hard. What appears to be a disastrous misstep in the short run can ultimately turn out to be an overwhelming success in the long term. This can be illustrated by considering some of the most revolutionary product introductions of the last half century. Apple's initial foray into mobile devices, the iPod, sharply undersold estimates after its 2001 release in the face of critical skepticism.[20] (*Wired* suggested that the name might be an abbreviation for "I Prefer Other Devices" or "I'd Prefer Owning Discs," while the *New York Times* snarked that "'Breakthrough digital device' might be pushing it."[21]) As sales lagged projections, the company's share price fell by 25%. Rather than reversing course, the board supported Steve Jobs. And by the time Apple stopped breaking out iPod sales in 2014, the firm had sold 390 million of these devices.[22] The Boeing 747 and IBM 360 are similar examples of products that ultimately proved to be wildly successful—and to have much broader societal implications, at least mostly for the better—despite delays, cost overruns, and extensive criticism by stock analysts.[23] And these same issues also face organizations that are simply trying to adopt technologies developed elsewhere.

The intuition behind these observations is formalized in a line of work on the myopic behavior of public markets started by Jeremy Stein.[24] While Apple, Boeing, and IBM may have had the deep pockets to ignore the suspects and finance their "troubled" projects, these may be more the exception than the rule. Stein depicts a world where the market rewards firms for having higher earnings, anticipating that more profits today presages even more next year. Managers, knowing this, feel compelled to boost today's earnings, even if it means not funding long-run projects that will ultimately create value. He argues that even though the investors know that the managers are doing this (and consequentially, the investors discount the price of the company's shares), managers continue this behavior because all the other managers are doing the same thing. Thus, the managers are trapped in what economists call a "prisoner's dilemma," referring to a setting where two inmates inform on each other, even if they would be better off staying mum. In a similar vein, firms may cut long-run expenses to impress the market, even though the world would be better off had they collectively decided not to do so.

While Jeremy wrote this model in the 1980s, its depiction of the world is even truer today, given the proliferation of activist hedge fund investors such as Bill Ackman and Dan Loeb, who have successfully agitated for cost-cutting and restructurings at many "underperforming" firms. The academic finance literature has argued that in many cases interventions by hedge funds have boosted shareholder value and long-term firm performance.[25] But it is hard not to be suspicious that in some instances the single-minded focus of these activists on returning cash to investors leads to detrimental outcomes.

Private patient markets may have powerful advantages in this setting. In today's world with its emphasis on big data and continuous measurement, we might be inclined to think that the feedback provided by the public markets would always be a good thing. But practitioners frequently argue the very fact that the investment is privately held can insulate management from the pressures to "do the wrong thing" to please the markets. Outside of the public spotlight, it can be easier to undertake the riskier product development plan, the painful restructuring, or the substantial but slow-to-bear-fruit investment.

These claims about the virtues of private markets are intriguing but hard to prove. For the decision to go public is not a random or casual one. Firms that go public are disproportionately the more successful and promising ones. Shai Bernstein illustrates some of the virtues of private markets in an ingenious way: by comparing post-IPO behavior of companies that go public with companies that filed to go public but were unable to complete the offering because the stock market fell in the months after their filing.[26] (Because the market for new offerings is so fickle, an extended downturn may make it next to impossible to go public.) The companies that go public experience a relative decline in the quality of new ideas being generated by the firm. In this case the shortfall appears to result from the facts that many of the key inventors depart the firms (doubtless to other start-ups) and those who remain become less productive (presumably distracted by the joys of their newly acquired wealth).

Not only may public markets push managers to do the wrong thing, but they may not be very effective at providing oversight in the first place. In many cases, it is very hard for investors to discern what private information and incentives the entrepreneurs and their cronies may have. For instance, when a firm raises equity from outside investors, the managers have an incentive to engage in wasteful expenditures (e.g., lavish offices) because they may benefit disproportionately without bearing the entire cost.[27] In the context of long-term investing, entrepreneurs might invest in strategies, research, or projects that have high personal returns but low expected monetary payoffs to shareholders. As an example, consider a biotechnology company founder who chooses to invest in a certain type of research that brings him great recognition in the scientific community but provides little return for the investors. Consistent with this observation, Ilan Guedj and David Scharfstein have shown that the success rate of the pivotal clinical trials involving cancer drugs for cash-rich, young biotech firms is only 3%, as opposed to 35% for pharmaceutical companies.[28] They suggest that in many cases the managers proceed despite clear indications of problems, eager to hold on to the role of CEO for as long as possible.

If entrepreneurs and investors could write detailed contracts covering every contingency, these problems might be avoided, but this is impractical. Even if the investors strongly suspect the entrepreneur has followed a certain action that was counter to their original agreement, they cannot prove it in a court of law. As a result, investors often shy away from these situations, making patient capital hard to find.

We have highlighted two things that can go wrong with public market investing: the market may push the manager to be too short-term, and managers may promote their own agenda at the expense of the investors. A third difficulty is more prosaic. There may be misjudgments of the size of the opportunities. The difficulty of discerning which projects will be winners in the long run is not just confined to stock market analysts or the general public. Even those who specialize in investing in such projects can struggle to discern their potential. An example of the difficulty of determining long-term value is demonstrated in the context of Bessemer Venture Partners, a top-tier venture capital firm that has made its reputation investing in young firms. On its website, the organization has a long list of failures: terrific companies that it failed to invest in, and why. (Of course, Bessemer has also chosen many winners, or else it would not be around to put such a list together!) For instance, the organization reveals it declined the opportunity to invest in eBay when it was first founded because the investors could not see the value in a platform for trading comic books and Pez dispensers.[29]

Making this point more systematically, our colleagues Bill Kerr, Ramana Nanda, and Matt Rhodes-Kropf examined the ultimate investment outcomes of a single large and successful venture capital group.[30] This firm routinely asks its team to score the deals that it undertakes at the deal closing. The striking finding that emerges from over a decade of transactions is that the initial ratings of the deals that ultimately turned out to be superwinners, moderate successes, and outright failures were essentially identical.

These three challenges—the pressure for short-run performance, the need to oversee managers, and the difficulty of determining which opportunities are greatest—suggests a role for a different type of strategy than investing short-term. Long-term investors who are actively involved in managing an investment may be able to contribute a lot of value. Although they cannot predict up front whether the venture is going to be successful, they can work really closely with the companies and projects in which they have a stake. Ideally, long-run investors may be able to steer the investments in the right direction as well as limit the kinds of distortions discussed above.

In an increasing number of cases, as already suggested, long-term investors have adopted private investment partnerships as their vehicles of choice. These partnership investors employ tools—the screening of investments, the sophisticated transaction structures, the staging of investments, and the provision of oversight and informal coaching—that help ensure project success. If things are going poorly and cannot be altered, they may sometimes cut off funding to avoid throwing good money after bad. In addition, private equity firms' high-powered compensation schemes give these investors incentives to monitor companies more closely, because individual compensation is closely linked to the firms' returns.

Of course, long-run investing and private partnerships are not synonymous. Berkshire Hathaway, for instance, has made a series of highly successful acquisitions out of a public fund structure. TIAA, which manages pensions for academic and medical professionals (among others), is well known for its active stances regarding the governance of particular public companies. These activities can have what economists term *positive externalities*: all investors benefit from the increase in value when they improve the operations of the firm.[31] As has been well documented in the finance literature, the active involvement of the investor can help improve the outcome of the firms being financed.

But this process is not an easy one, and many organizations do not have the skill set or structure to successfully select and oversee investments. For instance, banks seem poorly designed to do these tasks. Bankers often do not have the necessary skills to evaluate projects with few tangible assets and significant uncertainty, or to provide intense monitoring after the capital goes in. They are also often severely limited in their ability to take risks. Moreover, banks (as well as corporations) have found it difficult to replicate the compensation schemes of private partnerships. Organizations without high-powered incentives have found it difficult to retain personnel once the investors have developed a performance record that enables them to raise a fund of their own.[32] So even in countries where the financial sector is centered on the banking system, such as Germany and Japan, policymakers today are seeking to encourage the development of a private capital industry to ensure more adequate financing for risky entrepreneurial projects.

At least in theory, the willingness to take on investing long-term—and the consequent need to assess opaque projects, provide oversight, and face the danger of not being able to readily liquidate investments—should be rewarded. If profitable opportunities cannot be funded by traditional short-term investors in public markets, we anticipate that other ways would be developed to provide them capital. A long body of work on financial innovators has highlighted their energy and creativity in addressing the major financial challenges of the day, whether the need for funding sailing ships to travel from Europe to Asia for trade or to build the railroad networks of the United States.[33] The explosion of private capital firms over the last three decades can be understood precisely as such a response. And indeed, a substantial body of evidence suggests that venture capital–backed firms have greater innovation and job creation than their peers,[34] while those funded by private equity experience increases in product safety, productivity, resiliency in economic downturns, and innovation, as well as decreases in workplace injuries.[35]

THE CHALLENGES OF LONG-TERM INVESTING

In theory, therefore, investing for the long term provides important benefits to companies and the economy. These investors allow projects that otherwise would not be funded to receive funding; they provide oversight and protect companies and projects from the potentially distorting pressures of public markets. Moreover, because the investors should be rewarded for their willingness to make these investments, the ultimate beneficiary groups—whether pensioners, citizens, or students—should also benefit. This all sounds terrific!

This begs another question: If it is all so wonderful, why is there a need for this book? Of course, it is not so simple and pretty a picture. There is undoubtedly a confluence between a plethora of opportunities crying out for long-run investment and the desire on the part of many investors for higher-performing investments. But, as the cleantech story earlier suggests, many forays by investors into long-term investing have had limited success. What accounts for these disappointments, which have been more the norm than we might like to believe?

Despite the appeal of long-term investing, and the potential for outsized gains, the experience for many investors has been mixed. The returns in aggregate from many classes of alternatives as a whole have barely matched the public markets in recent years, not even providing compensation for the greater risks and illiquidity that these investments bring along with them. In many cases, investors have approached long-term investments in a stop-start pattern, jumping in when markets are hot and dropping out when returns decline. And in all too many cases, the managers of the funds doing these investments have done well, even as the individuals and institutions providing funding have suffered.

Consider, for instance, the experience of the state of Alabama, which has seen a substantial series of reverses in its pension investments, almost to the point of being comical, were it not for the state's desperate need for resources.[36] For decades, the Retirement Systems of Alabama has been under the purview of David Bronner, who had extensive powers to invest in assets of any type. Bronner sought to make long-term investments that ranged from purchasing office towers to buying large equity stakes in firms.

So far, so good. But many of these bets ended disastrously: in 2003, for instance, he invested $240 million into US Airways, an investment that netted eight board seats for the retirement system and the title of chairman for Bronner. The company ended up filing for bankruptcy in 2004. Other forays, such as ones into broadcast media and newspapers a few years after, also encountered economic headwinds as digital media gained traction. The pension did not hesitate to invest in local projects as well, such as the RSA Tower in Mobile and the Robert Trent Jones Golf Trail, many of which had questionable economic logic. The return on the $200 million investment by state pensions in the golf course was reported to be about 1.5% annually between 2011 and 2014, at a time when public equity markets were booming.[37]

But doubtless the biggest failure was what was supposed to be a $350 million investment in 2007 into a new railcar facility in Barton, Alabama, which promised to create 1,800 jobs.[38] Apparently, during the due diligence process, the pension missed the facts that the facility would cost almost twice as much to build as the entrepreneur estimated, and that the entrepreneur had misrepresented his indebtedness and assets. Ultimately, the project ended up in bankruptcy in 2010 before any railcars were produced. The pension took possession of the property and invested another $275 million to complete it.

The ultimate losses of the investment are hard to compute. The pension did succeed in leasing the plant to Navistar, which in turn has subleased portions of the facility to other firms. But this was hardly an arm's-length deal. Navistar had received substantial investments from the pension to encourage it to construct diesel engine facilities elsewhere in the state, and as part of the transaction, the local economic development authority gave generous subsidies to Navistar based on jobs created at the facility.[39] (The employment thresholds for these payments were subsequently revised downward when Navistar did not meet these targets.[40]) The CEO of the company reimbursed $21 million to the state pension as part of a deal to avoid criminal prosecution.[41] But even Bronner acknowledges that the losses on the project have been in the hundreds of millions.[42]

As a result of these miscues, as well as the more typical challenges of overly generous benefit promises to employees, Alabama is critically underfunded. While the pension claims its unfunded liabilities are $16.7 billion, calculations by Josh Rauh suggest a fairer estimate would be $46.3 billion (one of the largest discrepancies in percentage terms of any state).[43] This puts Alabama in the bottom quartile of state pensions both in regard to assets over liabilities (about 40%) and in the ratio of state pension liabilities to state tax revenue. The Alabama Policy Institute indicates that payments to cover pension shortfalls were already the largest expenditure by the state after education in 2015, and projected that they would rise sharply in subsequent years.[44] Given the lagging performance and shaky finance of Americans' public pensions, Alabama's performance is akin to finishing at the back of the marathon—painful for the participants and painful to watch.

If this was just the experience of one of the fifty states, it might be easy to dismiss. But, unfortunately, it is easy to find many others. Kentucky, for instance, has gained notoriety for being home to the worst-funded pension plan in the US.[45] The Kentucky Retirement Systems (KRS) unfunded pension liability was $32.8 billion at the end of the 2016 fiscal year, and under more conservative assumptions this number could be as high as $84 billion, or about $26,000 for every adult residing in the state.[46] The perilous state of KRS does not just have problematic implications for state employees. The shortfall caused national bond-rating agencies to lower Kentucky's credit rating, making it more expensive for the state to build schools, roads, and other public infrastructure projects. Indeed, the pension obligations were at the heart of the accounting firm PricewaterhouseCoopers rating of Kentucky as the state with the next-to-worst financial position, ahead only of basket case New Jersey.[47]

How did Kentucky reach this unfortunate condition? A wide variety of systemic problems created its funding gap, but long-term investments were again a magnet for problematic behavior. For instance, a 2011 investigation by state auditors revealed $11.6 million in fees paid or committed to "placement agents" acting as intermediaries between KRS and private investment firms that needed help selling their products, a number of whom were close to the chief investment officer at the time.[48] (Although the US Securities and Exchange Commission (SEC) opened an inquiry into the matter, no charges were filed.) To cite one egregious consequence of this alleged "pay to play" decision-making, in 2009, KRS allocated more than $24 million to Lawrence Penn's $120 million Camelot Acquisitions' Secondary Opportunities fund. KRS was one of the fund's biggest and earliest investors.[49] An SEC investigation subsequently revealed that Penn diverted $9.3 million from the investment vehicle to fuel his luxurious lifestyle, buying jewelry, a fancy car, and other lavish goods.[50]

Nor is this a problem confined to south of the Mason-Dixon Line. Similar stories could be repeated in New Jersey, New York, Illinois, California, and on and on. But beyond these tales of shenanigans, a broader lesson is clear: simply undertaking investments in long-run, illiquid assets is not a magic potion for high returns.

Some of the problematic issues can be laid squarely at the feet of the families and institutions who ultimately control the funds:

- Inadequate incentive schemes to reward staff members for making the right choices for long-term performance;
- Poor processes for selecting investments, based more on the safety of a familiar brand name or the fashionable nature of the area rather than the nature of the investment, often driven by boards and advisers who do not steer in the right direction;
- A lack of tools for measuring their own financial position, whether the extent of their need for future capital, the amount of risks they are exposed to, or even in some cases how well they are doing and the extent of their holdings; and
- A failure to effectively communicate what they are doing to stakeholders or potential partners, which in turn creates a cascading series of difficulties.

Other issues, though, must be laid at the feet of the investors who are managing funds seeking to undertake long-run investments:

- Inappropriate incentives that lead to the temptation to increase assets under management relentlessly, even if it translates into lower returns for the investors managing the funds (albeit not to the fund managers themselves).
- The gaming of performance, which makes traditional performance metrics—at best, often limited and flawed—even less revealing.
- The exploitation of market power by established private capital groups and a lack of coordination among investors who, desperate to access an attractively performing fund, bypass many of the principles of good governance (ironically, the same governance

principles that fund managers insist on in the companies in their portfolios)

- In many cases, concentration of power among the founding partners and a broader lack of fairness within the partnerships, leading to defections and attenuation of investment success over time.

Ultimately, the differing perspectives of capital providers and investors lead to a paradox. While long-run investors are all about funding change, the way in which these funds are organized has been remarkably noninnovative, despite the evident problems with the current model.

The issues with the current model of long-term investing are straightforward to describe but harder to fix. Because at its heart, patient long-run investing is hard and is characterized by infrequent information about how well things are going, due to long gestation periods and lack of market feedback. It is thus hard to assess risk and reward and, consequentially, to incentivize managers and govern funds.

But as vexing as these problems may seem, their solutions are not as remote as may first meet the eye. Around the world, a variety of approaches have been undertaken to address these concerns. These range from time-honored strategies by established family and endowment investors, to fresh approaches being taken by institutions newer to long-run investing, to new fund architectures being explored by intrepid managers. From these best practices, a set of potential solutions can be identified.

ROAD MAP FOR THE BOOK

In this book, we explore this seemingly remote and challenging territory. Thus, while we do not hesitate to diagnose problems, much of our attention is devoted to promising solutions. We argue that the world of institutional and high-net-worth investors, despite their seeming distance from the daily existence of most of humanity, has profound impacts on our lives and those of our children. Understanding why investors go wrong, and how they can do a better job, is therefore important to all of us.

After setting the stage in this introduction, in chapters 2 through 4 we look at the challenges and opportunities facing the individuals and institutions who provide the long-term capital.

In chapter 2, we begin with the history of long-term investing. We feature vignettes that capture some of the key historical moments, beginning with the John Maynard Keynes formulation of an investment strategy for King's College at Cambridge, which established many of the principles that long-term investors follow to this day. We then fast-forward to the pioneering family offices, focusing on the experience of the Rockefellers and their movement from opportunistic direct investing to an embrace of private capital funds.

We then highlight the diffusion of these ideas. These investment strategies were first adopted with gusto by a small group of families and university endowments, who initially operated in obscurity and later to great acclaim and interest. These approaches to long-term investing then spread to a much broader array of pension funds, sovereign funds, and other players. But this process of diffusion also saw evolution, most noticeably in the twenty-first century. In particular, while large institutions frequently invested in the same types of funds as the endowments and the family offices, they also sought to exploit their size to get more favorable economic terms and to build their own direct investment capability.

In chapter 3, we explore the set of problems that afflict these investors. We first highlight the fundamental challenges that long-term investing poses. It is hard to determine, for instance, whether private capital is worth the trouble: not only are the data ambiguous but the main yardsticks used to assess performance are flawed. Second, determining which individual groups are the top performers, and whether they are likely to remain on top in the future, can be extraordinarily hard.

These challenges can be exacerbated by the special status of many long-run investors, in particular, the heavy representation of nonprofit or public (or quasi-public) institutions. In many cases, these investors have been plagued by a lack of resources, insufficient (or inappropriately designed) rewards to the investment team, and overconfidence in their ability to select investments.

At the core of these issues lies a challenge of governance of these investors. Firefighters may have challenging jobs, but the kind of skills and training that prepare them to rush into a burning building to save a child are not necessarily linked to success on an investment committee overseeing the firefighters' pensions. Similarly, the president of a local bank may be vital to the economic life of a small college town, but that individual may not be the best person to oversee the school's endowment. Yet many institutions are characterized by inexperienced, politically connected, or parochial boards, which can lead to poor choices, confusion about missions, and many other pathologies.

In chapter 4, we explore some of the best practices to address these issues. We begin with reforms to the governance of these institutions that are long overdue. With structures that end up with dysfunctional oversight, it is almost impossible to expect that effective investment decisions can be made. We next turn to a seemingly mundane area: measurement. In many cases, institutions begin with broken yardsticks, and it is not surprising that the decisions that flow from there are troublesome. We also target the sensitive and messy issues associated with reward structures to investment team members. The tempting solution is to simply say, "Pay more!" But the truth is that compensation at public and quasi-public organizations is almost surely always going to be constrained. Instead, much of the challenge has to be how to design schemes that match tangible rewards with less costly (but often even more valuable) intrinsic ones, and making sure that the tasks people are being asked to do line up well with the skills the organization can plausibly attract. Finally, we emphasize the importance of investors effectively communicating about their strategy, both to potential financial partners and stakeholders.

In chapters 5 through 7, we turn to the perspectives of the fund pursuing long-term investing. We begin with a review of the evolution of these funds. We highlight the way in which the pursuit of long-run gains—long practiced informally—became institutionalized over the course of the twentieth century. We also trace how seemingly reasonable features became codified over time, and the way in which this introduced distortions into the industry.

In chapter 5, we turn to the dramatic changes that affected investing in the 1980s. A technical ruling by the US Department of Labor in 1978—little noticed at the time—opened the doors for pension funds to undertake alternative investment. This redefinition of the "prudent man rule" led to a flood of money into the industry, and profoundly reshaped many of the pioneering firms and opened the door to many others. By the end of the 1980s, the template for the current industry—with megagroups offering families of products and smaller specialists—was already taking shape. Each subsequent decade saw greater interest and an exacerbation of these trends.

We take a more comprehensive look at the issues afflicting long-run investment funds in chapter 6. We explore the inexorable lure of increasing fund size, and how it drives managers to make decisions that may boost their own personal bottom line but often not the performance of the fund, particularly when it comes to raising new funds. Finally, we look within the partnerships and highlight how in many cases problematic behavior seeps in here as well, as founders benefit themselves at the expense of the next generation and outside investors.

We spend a considerable amount of time on the changing structure of the industry in chapter 6, particularly the increasingly dominant role of publicly traded funds and the sale of minority interests to outside investment groups. While these steps can address some of the succession and alignment issues identified, they pose their own set of issues. We highlight some of the ways that these moves can intensify problems that have always been implicit in private capital funds.

Again, we turn to best practices in chapter 7. Looking across a wide spectrum of funds, we highlight an array of creative organizations—young and old—that are addressing the issues delineated above. We also explore why addressing these issues has been seemingly so difficult for the industry, and what mechanisms might encourage greater change.

We focus our discussion here on four categories of changes. The first of these involves changes to the nature of partnerships. In many senses, long-term partnerships are about funding change but are often extremely resistant to changing the approach that was enshrined in the early investment partnerships. The ten-year fixed-life partnership may have been appropriate for some investments but clearly does not fit others. Rethinking fund life, but also the way that funds are pushed to exit investments in set time frames more generally, is an important question. Our second suggestion is closely related: a rethinking of the way in which these partnerships are governed. While time and legal constraints limit what can be done there, a more active voice on the part of investors in these funds, typically called limited partners, or LPs, could be helpful.

Our third suggestion has to do with the way that fund performance is measured and reported. The current system, where each organization prepares their own numbers in an often inconsistent manner, is rife with issues: almost inevitably, groups present the numbers in the way that make them look best. Moreover, the common yardsticks used for these measures, such as internal rate of return, are themselves deeply flawed. Thus, there is a need for rethinking how long-term investments get measured, as well as who does the measuring: there is an urgent need for an independent certifying body to do these calculations.

Finally, we turn to incentives. When we look at the design of these reward schemes, it is clear that these features—originally established to ensure proper incentives to maximize value—became at some point "weaponized." Today they are a bargaining chip that swings back and forth, depending on whether investors or fund managers are in the driver's seat. Several reforms, having to do with the ways that investors are subsidized for costs incurred and the profits that are split over time, could help ensure better alignment.

In chapter 8, we look at the hybridization between investors and fund managers that has become commonplace in recent years. Institutional investors are increasingly attempting to do their own thing: to invest either alongside private capital groups or by themselves. We explore the very plausible rationales for such initiatives, as well as the substantial obstacles that they face. We conclude with some suggested best practices for groups seeking to invest directly.

In the chapter 9, we end by looking at the future of the industry. Given the spotty track record of financial economists in seeing the future—from

Irving Fisher's prediction in October 1929 that "stock prices have reached what looks like a permanently high plateau"[51] to the blindness of many of our colleagues to the imminent arrival of the Global Financial Crisis (not to mention the prognosticators, who, like Paul Samuelson's description of the stock market, "predicted nine of the last five recessions"[52])—we instead have hedged our bets by laying out four scenarios. We highlight a set of changes that we believe are necessary to reach the most optimistic outcome.

FINAL THOUGHTS

This chapter has introduced the complex, often mysterious territory that our book undertakes to explore: long-term investments. We seek to do so in a manner that is distinct from bewildering arrays of reports put out by organizations ranging from the World Economic Forum to the International Council of Sovereign Wealth Funds, which have previously explored these issues. These earlier works can almost universally be characterized as "inside baseball": written by industry professionals for industry professionals. Not only do they lack the texture and detail that an outsider would need to appreciate the issues at hand, they typically have all the excitement of a document produced by a committee of bankers and carefully vetted by a dozen lawyers.

We instead are writing a very different kind of book, one aimed at a general reader. As a result, we spend much more time seeking to lay out the critical issues, and illustrating through meaty examples how they manifest themselves in practice. The book does not presuppose technical knowledge of alternative investments, but instead seeks to walk readers through the key institutional features.

Just as the French statesman Georges Clemenceau argued that war was too important to be left to the generals, we believe that long-term investing is too important to be left to investment committees. The investment choices made by pensions, endowments, and other investors have profound implications for our future financial health and, more generally, the future of the world.

CHAPTER 2

The Most Important People in the Room

At any private capital gathering, the attention of those in attendance is immediately drawn to the men (for, alas, the senior echelons of private capital partnerships are still overwhelmingly a man's world) in Brioni suits speaking loudly about their latest deals. But these individuals, who run funds that invest in private equity, venture, and real estate projects, are managing money *on behalf* of large institutional and family investors. The investors they work for may be more shabbily dressed than those who manage the money, and certainly have fewer private jets, not to mention less spectacular birthday parties. But without the investors' capital, the world of patient capital would be a shadow of what it is today.

So too, any discussion of patient capital has to begin with the organizations who have the money. In this chapter, we introduce several main classes of institutional investors, who are undoubtedly the most important people in the room. We look, in turn, at endowments, families, and pension funds, which have been (and remain) key providers of patient capital.

This list is certainly not exhaustive: for instance, we don't spend much time in this chapter discussing banks, sovereign wealth funds, or insurance companies, which have been important capital providers as well. Even so, for each of our chosen classes of investors, the history of their interactions with private capital could fill a volume many times the size of this one. Instead, we focus on just a few critical junctures in the history of private capital. Thus, expect a few segues akin to the one in the movie *2001*, where the hominid's first club melds into a nuclear-armed spaceship. But despite these lacunae, we hope to convey a few insights about the critical characteristics of these investors and the evolution of interest more generally in long-term investment.

Structurally, all the investors discussed here share the ability to allocate large sums of money in long-term projects. As we argued in the introductory chapter, this ability is important not just to their own financial health but to all of us. But the path from theory to practice for many of these institutions has been daunting. The stories in this chapter hint at both the opportunities and the challenges of long-term investing.

ENDOWMENTS AND THE CENTRALITY OF EQUITY

> As time goes on, I get more and more convinced that the right method in investment is to put fairly large sums into enterprises which one thinks one knows something about.... There are seldom more than two or three enterprises at any given time in which I personally feel myself entitled to put full confidence.

The reader might be excused for guessing that this quote was taken from *The Essays of Warren Buffett*, but the quote belongs to John Maynard Keynes.[1] Keynes today is much more famous (and, in some circles, infamous) for his work on macroeconomic policy, which formed the foundation for the post–World War II economic world order and, more recently, for many governments' response to the Global Financial Crisis. But Keynes's multifaceted career had another dimension: shaping the strategy of the King's College endowment. His management of the endowment from 1921 until his death in 1946 included many then-radical practices that are well accepted today. As a result, his approaches have profoundly influenced the investment philosophies of modern long-horizon investors.

Founded in 1441 as one of the many colleges of the University of Cambridge, King's College traditionally had maintained the bulk of its portfolio in agricultural real estate located across England. (Interestingly, this strategy has come back in vogue among university endowments, but of course as only a small part of a diversified portfolio.) The college's investment strategy had long yielded attractive returns but suffered during the Agricultural Depression of the 1870s through 1890s, as declining transportation costs exposed British farmers to competition from the New World.

Keynes formulated a bold vision for his management of the endowment. In particular, he argued that its investment strategy should capitalize on the long investment horizon of the College. After all, it had been in existence for nearly five centuries and anticipated many more centuries of operation. One conclusion he drew was that the endowment could act as a contrarian investor during market downturns. Keynes successfully convinced his colleagues to allow him to create a "discretionary portfolio" within King's main endowment. This discretionary portfolio afforded Keynes unprecedented autonomy in choosing investments and freed him from any restrictions under the British government's Trustee Acts of 1893 and 1900, which restricted endowment investments to a narrow class of securities that notably did not include equities.

To implement this strategy, Keynes sold off one-third of the college's real estate portfolio by 1927 and channeled a portion of the proceeds into his new discretionary portfolio. Initially, the portfolio focused on short-term bets on macroeconomic conditions, sometimes with spectacular success and at other times less so. But in 1934, he departed from a market-timing strategy and instead undertook a new approach: buying and patiently holding specific equities, thus taking advantage of the endowment's long investment horizon. The equity turnover (the volume of purchases and sales divided by the value of stocks held) averaged 55% between 1922 and 1929, but decreased to 30% over the 1930s when Keynes transitioned to a buy-and-hold strategy. It dropped even further to 14% from 1940 until his death in 1946.

A second principle was extensive investment in equities, rather than real estate, cash, or bonds. The equity weighting of Keynes's discretionary portfolio was substantial, averaging 75% in the 1920s, 57% in the

1930s, and 73% in the 1940s until Keynes's death in 1946. By way of contrast, the traditional portfolio of the endowment averaged a 1% equity weighting under Keynes's management. During Keynes's tenure, none of the other Cambridge and Oxford college endowments shifted into equities, as he did. In fact, it was not until after World War II that St. Johns and Trinity, two of the largest Cambridge colleges, amended their rules in order to allow investments in equities. Similarly, the allocation to equities of Harvard's and Yale's endowments during the 1920s was just 16% and 24%, respectively.

Keynes's strategy also entailed focusing on a few holdings. In the 1940s, when the patient strategy was fully implemented, the portfolio consisted of about sixty stocks. These firms were characterized by a strong degree of international diversification, an idea well ahead of its time. Many of his holdings were of small companies and "value" stocks, or ones that yielded attractive dividends relative to their market prices. These categories subsequently have been shown by academics to generate attractive returns.

One quote attributed to Keynes (at least apocryphally) was that "ideas shape the course of history." In this setting, this quotation was certainly apt. Keynes clearly articulated a philosophy for the endowment: that it needed to focus on a long-term and patient investment strategy while taking an active approach to asset selection. He also established the centrality of equity, as opposed to seemingly safer investments, at the heart of a long-term portfolio. And this philosophy translated successfully into action. Over the twenty-five years of managing the King's College endowment, Keynes's discretionary portfolio generated a risk-adjusted return, or alpha, of approximately 7.7% annually.[2]

Keynes's lesson about the importance of equity in long-term investing has been ignored at investors' peril. One cautionary tale is the experience of another endowment, that of New York University, during the 1980s and 1990s.[3] If we are to grade endowments by the same criteria as President Trump seemingly evaluates cabinet members—that is, by their personal net worth—the team overseeing management of the NYU endowment over this period would be graded as an A+. The day-to-day management of the endowment was overseen by Larry Tisch, cofounder of the Loews Corporation, later CEO of CBS Television; and its investment committee consisted of a star-studded group of New York businessmen, including the then-president of Chase Manhattan, Thomas Labrecque, and the legendary Maurice "Ace" Greenberg of American International Group. But in an era when even the average mutual fund manager enjoyed double-digit growth, the NYU endowment under the leadership of these alums nonetheless gave up hundreds of millions of dollars. The reason was an overindulgence in the seeming safety of bonds.

To be fair, NYU's conservative management strategy has to be understood against the backdrop of its dire financial situation during the 1970s. Unable to make its payroll in 1973, NYU fired staff, closed its engineering school, and sold several of its assets (including its Bronx campus) to City University of New York.

Tisch entered the chairmanship of the NYU board of trustees at a time when NYU needed to recover from two brushes with insolvency, to grow its meager endowment, and to stop living primarily off of tuition revenue. Facing these challenges, understandably, Tisch sought to instill stability into the endowment. Unwilling to risk even a small operating deficit, the investment committee focused on investing in bonds. In so doing, they were influenced by the fact that bond yields were high at the time and a set amount from the endowment was needed each year to pay for university operations. Given this logic, NYU reduced its equity allocation from 33% to 7% between 1981 and 1982 while increasing the endowment's allocation to bonds from 62% to 90%.

By the mid-1980s, NYU's finances had stabilized and bond yields had fallen sharply as Federal Reserve board chair Paul Volcker tamed inflation. However, the investment committee maintained its conservative strategy, holding essentially a bond portfolio for several years. In a 1986 study published by the National Association of College and University Business Officers, NYU's performance ranked 254th out of 272 college endowments. After the stock market crash of 1987, the investment committee gave Tisch a standing ovation when he reported that NYU was the only endowment with over $3 million in the whole country that owned no stocks whatsoever in 1987. But the strategy warranted only brief celebration, as the S&P 500 ended the year 5.2% above its level at the beginning of the year. Although NYU's annual reports after 1985 stopped providing information about asset allocation, it seems that NYU's heavy allocation to bonds endured through the early 1990s.

How could NYU have left so much money on the table with this debt-heavy allocation, in spite of the disappointing returns year after year? The driver for these decisions seemed to be Tisch's own macroeconomic views. For instance, the CBS pension fund allocated approximately 1% of its portfolio to equities during Tisch's tenure as CEO. Later on, Tisch continued his bearish views at Loews Corporation: the firm reportedly lost approximately $2 billion of its capital between 1996 and 2000 through a series of large bets against the rising stock market. Back at NYU, George Heyman Jr., chairman of the school's investment committee in 1987 and advisory director at Shearson Lehman Brothers, noted, "No one stood up and said we should be in equities."[4]

Starting in 1996, the university's leadership belatedly took steps to improve the performance of NYU's endowment, which paled in comparison to those of its peers of similar size and academic stature. Rather than relying on the trustees and investment committee to steer the endowment exclusively, the school decided to bring new professional expertise to join the cause. In 1998, NYU established the new position of chief investment officer, hiring Maurice Maertens, former head of the Ford Motor Company pension fund. Under his leadership, NYU dramatically reshaped its allocation and also followed its peers into alternative asset classes.[5]

By 2007, NYU's portfolio had a diversified asset allocation similar to other endowments. Equities made up 45% of the portfolio, with large commitments to equity-focused hedge funds, while only 15% of the portfolio consisted of bonds. Private equity commitments amounted to 5% of the portfolio, with the remainder of the endowment invested in real assets and hedge funds that had low correlations with the stock market.

While NYU today is a terrific school, there is always a question of how much greater it could be. *Fortune* attempted to quantify NYU's missed opportunity: assuming average investment results, the magazine estimated that, had the NYU trustees instead invested in a standard portfolio consisting of 60% stocks and 40% bonds, NYU could have added another $200 million to the $500 million endowment between 1977, when NYU first adopted its bond-heavy strategy, and 1987.[6] Doubtless the shortfall in the subsequent decade would have been substantial as well. And had those lost funds been reinvested in the ensuing bull markets, it would have translated into a substantially larger endowment for NYU and more academic resources today.

FAMILIES AND THE EMBRACE OF ILLIQUID FUNDS

While Keynes established the centrality of equity in long-term investing, his was an overwhelmingly liquid portfolio. It took others to reach the second key insight: that long-term investing would thrive with illiquid investments, and that private capital funds were an ideal way to exploit long-term opportunities.

In some sense, a discussion of which twentieth-century investor discovered illiquid investing is like debating whether the inventor of the safety match or the Zippo lighter discovered fire. Investing in illiquid assets has always been with us. Indeed, many trace the history of such investments back to Section 46 of the Code of Hammurabi, written about 1750 BC, which explicitly codifies the practice of agricultural partnerships.[7]

But if we look at the first half of the twentieth century, which might be considered the dawn of the modern era of investing, investment portfolios were dominated by bonds and cash, with modest holdings of publicly traded stocks. To the extent that investors held illiquid investments, they were typically in the form of companies they controlled, individual real estate holdings (which the investors often hired managers to run), and angel investments in companies. Investments in private capital funds, which dominate the illiquid portion of many institutional investors' portfolios today, were virtually unheard of.

Today, of course, the picture is very different. And no class of institution was more important in this transition than the family office.

While several families could be highlighted as early pioneers in this style of investment, a natural choice is the Rockefellers.[8] We will pass over the story of how John D. Rockefeller turned a $4,000 investment in an oil refinery into a controlling stake in Standard Oil, which ultimately was broken up, only to blossom again into businesses that were the predecessors of Chevron, Exxon, and Mobil.

Our story really begins in 1934, when John D. Rockefeller Jr., John's only son, set up a complex series of trusts for his six children. At the time, the bulk of the family's investments was in the form of holdings in the family's business and real estate (to name a few, the oil companies, the Chase Manhattan Bank, and the Rockefeller Center in Manhattan) and, to a lesser extent, traditional public equities and bonds. Over time, however, the family's investment mix transformed into one where professionally managed funds played a substantially more important role.

Much of the credit for this transition goes to Laurance Rockefeller. As the fourth of the Rockefeller children, his visibility never rivaled that of several of his brothers, particularly politicians Nelson and Winthrop and banking magnate David. As the *Independent* noted in his obituary, Laurance was "for the most part neglected in the hundreds of books about America's most celebrated business dynasty [y]et . . . he may leave a more important legacy than his better-known siblings."[9] And one of the most important of these legacies was in the area of long-term investing.

Initially, many of Laurance's investment activities followed the template of wealthy individuals before him. His initial transactions were made based on personal relationships. Yet even here, he displayed a vision that surpassed most of his peers.

For instance, in 1938, he led what was essentially a carve-out of Eastern Air Lines from General Motors, which had bought an agglomeration of local airlines a few years earlier. Rockefeller's decision to pursue this transaction was driven by his friendship with race car driver and World War I fighter ace Eddie Rickenbacker. The war hero–turned-entrepreneur had persuaded the automaker to buy a series of airline companies, and then consolidated the new corporate holdings. But Rickenbacker grew frustrated with the automaker's management of these operations, and negotiated with Alfred P. Sloan, General Motors' legendary leader, for the right to buy out the subsidiary for $3.5 million. Rockefeller not only provided the bulk of the funding for this transaction, but served on the board for most of the next five decades.

Similarly, in 1939, he wrote a check for $10,000 to James McDonnell. The engineer had just set up a small business in St. Louis, which Rockefeller joined as a director, to explore the development of an advanced type of fighter plane using the newly invented jet aircraft engine. By the end of World War II, McDonnell Aircraft Corporation had five thousand employees. It would go on to become a major military and commercial aerospace manufacturer before ultimately being folded into Boeing. These two successes convinced Laurance of the proposition that "people who play it safe in the long run have very dull lives."

Laurance had two realizations during the course of his wartime service, where he was a liaison officer shuttling between the Navy's Bureau of Aeronautics and aircraft manufacturers on the West Coast. First, many of the technologies developed for the war, from navigation instrumentation to power systems, could have broad commercial applicability. Second, the innovations would require capital and management to make the transition to industrial and civilian applications. As a result, to be successful, his investing activities needed to become more systematized.

In January 1946, he began what at the time was called Rockefeller Brothers, Inc. (RBI) with capital of $1.5 million drawn from the family coffers. The fund had eight partners—Laurance and his five siblings as well as Harper Woodford, one of the top procurement officers during the war, and Ted Walkowicz, an MIT aeronautical engineer who had been a lieutenant colonel in the Air Force. Rather than having a set life, RBI was organized as an evergreen fund. Laurance anticipated that the investments would be held for a decade and then sold or taken public. Rather than being returned to investors (as in today's standard fund), the proceeds of the successful investments would flow back into the fund, ready to be used for subsequent investments.

Over the next twenty-three years, RBI made fifty-six investments. These included Piasecki Helicopter Corporation, which had a pioneering design for helicopter blades and was ultimately sold to Boeing, and Reaction Motors, which developed the liquid propellant engine (including for the Bell X-1, the first aircraft to exceed the speed of sound) and was acquired by Thiokol Chemical Corporation. RBI also funded a wide variety of companies developing other advanced technologies, such as Itek Corporation, which evolved from developing cameras for spy satellites to pioneering computer-aided design and optical disk technologies, and Thermo Electron Corporation, which developed an array of energy and instrumentation technologies.

During these first two decades, the Rockefeller family—especially Laurance—was intimately involved in the investment decision-making process. While the growing staff took on increasing roles over the years in evaluating and overseeing deals, the family had a critical voice. As Peter Crisp, who joined the firm in 1960 fresh from Harvard Business School and would go on to lead it for decades, related, "We didn't make any moves or take any action without the advice and consent of our partners."

In 1969, however, the firm reached a crossroads. The market for technology stocks was booming, creating extraordinary investment opportunities. Meanwhile, Laurance's own interests were moving toward conservation, including his efforts to expand numerous national parks and to pioneer the development of the ecotourism industry, and other, further-out areas, such as the UFO Disclosure Initiative. Meanwhile, he had already invested in a number of pioneering venture funds, such as Draper Gather & Anderson, as well as early real estate development efforts.

He decided to transform RBI into a new entity called Venrock (the new name was an amalgamation of "venture" and "Rockefeller"). The new group was much more institutionalized, having a formal fund of $7.5

million. Funding was provided not just by the Rockefellers but also by several nonprofit entities with long-standing connections to the family. But the crucial transformation was the movement from what was essentially a family office to an institutionalized entity, where investment professionals made the crucial decisions as to when to purchase and exit companies.

Under this new structure, Venrock would go on to make some spectacular investments within its first decade, including funding Apple and Intel. The venture group would continue to transform itself in the years to come—moving to a structure with decade-long funds and opening the doors to a broader array of limited partners—but the 1969 transition was a critical one.

The transition that the Rockefeller family investment strategy underwent, from individual to fund investing, was repeated elsewhere. Families increasingly realized both the opportunities that lay in long-term investments outside of the businesses that had made them rich, and their inability to manage the complexity of these investments alone. As Bill Elfers, who was raising capital for the initial fund of the venture firm Greylock about the time that Laurance was considering restructuring RBI, explained, one of the obstacles he faced was the desire for wealthy families like the Cornings to be the new fund's sole financial backer. As he related, he only overcame this challenge by pointing out the size of the potential opportunity and the likelihood that "a group of compatible limited partners . . . could bring more to Greylock in terms of advice and contacts" than a single family.[10]

Of course, this great transition to professionally managed private capital funds was not driven just by families. Life insurance companies were important pioneers in directly investing in companies, often providing risky debt (so-called mezzanine loans) or preferred stock to companies that needed capital to grow. In fact, they were so successful at this process that, as at numerous banks, many insurers ultimately spun off the private equity arms into independent entities. Ultimately, many moved a hybrid model, investing in both companies and funds. University endowments, led by Yale and Harvard (whose approaches and experiences we explore in depth in chapters 4 and 8), embraced investing in private funds in the 1970s and 1980s. A number of the chief investment officers there became intellectual leaders in formulating the case for long-term investments.

SCALING UP AND THE FOCUS ON FUNDS

The third key shift was the dramatic expansion of the institutional investors in private capital. The patient capital model, which began as a niche investment strategy practiced by a handful of family offices, insurers, and endowments, grew exponentially over the 1980s and ensuing decades.

Again, there were several transition points. One critical juncture was the clarification of an obscure rule in 1979 by the US Department of Labor. This administrative action changed what was known as the "prudent man rule," as stipulated by the Employment Retirement Income Security Act (ERISA) of 1974. For the first few years after the legislation's enactment, the rule had stated that private pension managers had to invest their funds' resources with the care of a "prudent man"; that is, carefully and conservatively. Consequently, many pension funds avoided investing in private capital entirely. It was just too close to the line.

In early 1979, the Department of Labor ruled that pension fund managers could take into account portfolio diversification in determining the prudence of an investment. Thus, the ruling implied that the Labor Department would not view allocation of a small fraction of a portfolio to illiquid funds as imprudent, even if a number of companies in the venture capitalist's portfolio or real estate projects in a developer's fund failed.

The policy shift was so little noticed that even the business journalists of the day did not cover it. But its consequences were dramatic. That clarification flung the door open for corporate pension funds to invest in private capital. While the allocations of these institutions to private capital in the 1980s were very modest, even a small allocation of such a large pool led to very rapid growth of the sector.

This transition was followed by the entry of public pensions into this space a decade later. Initially, neither private nor public pension funds invested in a dramatically different manner than the institutions and families that preceded them. But their impact was important because of their sheer size. According to the Federal Reserve's "Financial Accounts of the United States," as of the end of 2017, the assets of US private and public pension funds stood at nearly $20 trillion, split roughly evenly between government (federal and state) and private pension funds.[11] By comparison, the total financial assets of US life insurance companies were about a third of this staggering amount, and the total assets of 809 schools that participated in the 2017 National Association of College and University Business Officers was just over one-half trillion dollars. Although the allocations to private capital are often not as large as leading endowments and family offices, the sheer size of the pension fund assets mean that they dominate the charts of the world's biggest private equity and other alternative investors.

A third wave stemmed from the globalization of private capital investing. While private capital was originally a very US-centered game, the investor pool inexorably globalized. What was a trickle beginning in the 1980s turned into a flood in the 2000s. The pool of non-US investors changed as well, from a handful of British pensions, wealthy families, and sophisticated sovereign wealth funds to a much more diverse mix, including everything from the Chinese insurers to the Colombian pension funds.

But what is striking, as one looks at the scaling up of investing during the 1980s and 1990s, is how closely the investors adhered to the playbook first written by Laurance Rockefeller and his peers in leading family offices. Groups would allocate a percentage of their assets for private capital, evaluate funds, and then reap the proceeds, only to repeat the cycle. While the activity grew in scale and variety, the basic process remained the same.

One distinction from the approach of the early families was the increased focus on funds as the primary tool to access private markets. The Rockefeller family during the period from the 1930s through the 1960s held a variety of both partnership holdings and direct investments in companies and projects. This mixed approach was not untypical of families, insurers, and other long-run investors of the era. But over the ensuing decades, it became far more common for investors to focus on funds as the primary method of accessing illiquid, long-term investments: at least, those investors not motivated by explicitly "strategic" purposes.

To illustrate this point, we highlight the experience of Singapore, which created two government-backed funds, one with an explicit economic development mission (Temasek) and one geared toward long-run financial returns (GIC). Both of these funds were of a type that became far more visible near the end of the twentieth century: sovereign wealth funds (SWFs).

Assets managed by SWFs worldwide increased more than seven times from 2001 to 2016, rising to $7.4 trillion. Over the same period, the number of funds tripled, reaching seventy-eight in 2016.[12] Fueled by booming commodities prices, falling transportation costs, and globalization, exports for many nations rose at unprecedented rates for much of this period. For some of the countries, the newly obtained riches became so outsized that they could not be invested domestically without destabilizing the local economy.

As a case in point, take Norway's domestic fund, the Government Pension Fund Global (GPFG). With just $1 trillion in assets in the spring of 2018, it is the world's largest fund of its kind. The population of Norway, however, is only about five million people and the market cap of domestic companies is about $200 billion.[13]

These funds have been set up with differing motivations. In some cases, these are established to retain wealth for the current or future generations, particularly if the nation is dependent on exhaustible natural resources. A successful example can be seen in the experience of Kiribati, a collection of islands in the Pacific Ocean formerly known as the Gilbert Islands, with a population of under 100,000 residents.[14] For many decades, the dominant export from the country was guano, used for fertilizer. The island's leaders set up the Kiribati Revenue Equalization Reserve Fund in 1956 and imposed a tax on production by foreign firms. The last guano was extracted in 1979, but the fund remains a key economic contributor. At $700 million, it is ten times the size of the nation's gross domestic product, and the interest generated by the fund represents 30% of the nation's revenue.

In other cases, an SWF's mandate may explicitly or implicitly include strategic or political goals, such as securing a supply of vital commodities or specific industry development, that go beyond pure profit motives. For example, the Russian Direct Investment Fund has stated mandates to increase the inflow of foreign direct investment into Russia, to modernize the Russian economy, and to attract the best talent in technology to Russia from across the world among its objectives.[15] Abu Dhabi's Mubadala Fund was established as a "principal agent in diversification of Abu Dhabi's economy" and to "strengthen the Emirate's social infrastructure."[16]

Singapore's experience illustrates both the nature of these sovereign investors and an important change among long-run investors in general in the 1970s and 1980s.[17] Singapore had been born as an independent nation in 1965, after a brief and unsuccessful union with Malaysia. Having no natural resources to speak of and an undeveloped economy, under the visionary leadership of Prime Minister Lee Kuan Yew (in collaboration with Dr. Goh Keng Swee, who later served as deputy prime minister), the government intervened aggressively to set up a series of government-linked companies (GLCs) to promote industrialization and trade. In so doing, they were driven by necessity. Singapore at the time was desperately underdeveloped (with a per capita gross domestic product of $500), and relationships with its immediate neighbors were strained.

By 1974, this strategy was paying clear dividends, and the government moved to distance itself from the GLCs, so it could focus more cleanly on policy-making and regulatory roles. To do so, it created a new entity, Temasek, which received much of the equity in firms formerly held directly by the Ministry of Finance. Initially, Temasek's role was as an active shareholder in these firms. For instance, Temasek's board chairman during its first dozen years was simultaneously the chairman of Singapore Airlines. Beginning in 1985, however, Singapore began a privatization program, which entailed Temasek selling significant stakes in many of its holdings, such as telecommunications provider SingTel and Mitsubishi

Singapore Heavy Industries. As these transactions were completed over the ensuing decade, Temasek's coffers swelled.

In response, Temasek began making new investments. The agenda behind these transactions was formalized in its 2002 charter. It highlighted that the entity would make investments into "new businesses with regional and international potential in order to nurture new industrial clusters."[18] Thus, even in this new era, there was a strong emphasis on directly investing in companies—whether in Singapore or further afield—that would contribute to the nation's economic development. These transactions included many companies in advanced technologies, such as information technology and pharmaceuticals, infrastructure investments in power and transport, and wide swaths of companies in other Asian nations.

Meanwhile, a very different approach was taken by the Government of Singapore Investment Corporation (now known as GIC Private Ltd.). The origins of the GIC lay in the nation's concerns about its dwindling foreign reserves in the unstable global macroeconomic environment of the era and a sense that this investment activity was best pursued outside the central bank (where it had previously resided). Established as a stand-alone organization in 1981, GIC took a far less activist approach than Temasek.

The management of GIC first pushed the new fund to shift from holding government bonds to an emphasis on equities, with an allocation at the end of the 2016 fiscal year of 45% of its holdings in equity and 39% in debt.[19] It also expanded into private market investing, with 16% of its holdings in 2016 being allocated to real estate and private equity. In addition to eschewing the kind of economic development–driven model that Temasek employed, the fund in its first decades undertook investments through partnerships.[20]

This focus on funds—at least, for those institutions like GIC that had the goal of long-run wealth creation—was a dominant theme of long-run investors during the 1980s, 1990s, and much of the first decade of the 2000s. But the new century would see change, both for GIC and other investors. This brings us to the next example.

BACK TO THE FUTURE

As we have highlighted above, most financially motivated long-term investors during the final decades of the twentieth century focused their private market activities on funds. They typically invested alongside many of their peers as limited partners in funds.

The first decade of the twenty-first century, however, saw a sharp departure from this "business as usual" approach. Two major new strategies emerged: investors showed an increased willingness to go it alone, and to leverage their scale to extract concessions from their fund managers. We again highlight two funds that epitomized these trends.

Of all the investors based outside the United States who have become major players in the long-run investing arena in this millennium, certainly the most influential have been a handful within a couple of hours' drive of the northern border. A number of large Canadian pension funds, including the Ontario Teachers Pension Fund and the Caisse de Dépôt et Placement du Québec, developed an approach to private equity investing that incorporated the model developed by family offices and endowments, but they added a new twist: a major commitment to direct investing.

We focus here on the development of what arguably has been the most visible of these pioneers, the Canada Pension Plan Investment Board, or CPPIB.[21] The Canada Pension Plan (CPP) was established in 1966 as a layer of retirement savings sitting between the Old Age Security System (similar to Social Security in the US) and individual savings. It collected mandated contributions from employers and workers, and offered benefits that were a set percentage of wages, paid by the contributions of previous years and the returns from the Plan's investments.

For the first thirty years of the CPP's existence, expenses rose as benefits like inflation indexing were added. Funds were invested in nonnegotiable Canadian government fixed income bonds and also loaned to the provinces at submarket interest rates for projects such as building schools and roads. These projects may have benefited Canadian society but not surprisingly did little for the CPP's bottom line. Furthermore, population changes were working against the CPP. At the inception of the CPP, the coverage ratio, or the number of workers per retiree, was 6:1. In the early 1990s, with the demographic pressure of retiring baby boomers, the government realized that the coverage ratio was falling sharply. The CPP faced either drastic cuts in benefits or sharp increases in contribution rates. Between 1995 and 1997, the federal and provincial governments, which shared the responsibility for pensions and rarely agreed on anything, managed to craft a solution.

The CPP Investment Board was established in 1997 in response to these problems. It was given the mandate to contribute to the financial strength of the CPP and help sustain the pensions of eighteen million CPP contributors and beneficiaries by investing "with a view to achieving a maximum rate of return, without undue risk of loss, having regard to the factors that may affect the funding of the Canada Pension Plan."[22] As a first step to solvency, the mandated contribution was increased to 9.9% of wages.

The second step was an adjustment of the investment policy. From its inception until 2005, CPPIB generally pursued a passive investment strategy targeting a basket of 65% equities and 35% fixed income securities.[23] Moreover, it was compelled, like all Canadian pension plans, to keep at least 70% of its portfolio in domestic holdings.[24] Motivated by the need to generate satisfactory returns, CPPIB's new CEO, David Denison, shifted the fund's investment strategy, with help of Mark Wiseman, whom he recruited to head the new private investments group (and who subsequently succeeded him as the pension's head).

Part of CPPIB's new approach was quite similar to that employed by families, endowments, and pensions around the world. The CPPIB team searched for and invested in top private capital funds. While the group's investments had initially focused on large and mega buyout groups in North America and Europe, it moved steadily to more global and mid-market funds. The process of evaluating funds similarly followed a template familiar to sophisticated investors around the world. One difference from many investors was a more aggressive use of the secondary market—essentially, interests in funds that were already under way, in which the fund owners for some reason needed to sell.

Where the fund differed more dramatically from the traditional model was in its emphasis on what it termed *principal investing*. Initially, the group attempted to coinvest in transactions alongside private equity groups. In some cases, this approach led to spectacular results. For instance, the California-based private equity firm Silver Lake approached the team about possible participation in an acquisition of a well-known Internet phone service provider. Originally founded in 2003, Skype Technologies had been acquired by eBay in 2005, but eBay had later decided that Skype was not a good complement for its online auction business.[25] CPPIB had been an investor in several of Silver Lake's funds and had been actively exploring how to work together in other ways, so it was natural that the private equity group reached out when it had a large and complex transaction to undertake. In November of 2009, CPPIB invested US$300 million in Skype as part of a consortium led by Silver Lake that also included Index Ventures and Andreessen Horowitz. The group purchased a 65% stake of Skype from eBay for $1.9 billion in a deal that valued Skype at $2.75 billion overall and left eBay with a 35% equity stake.[26] Eighteen months later, in May of 2011, Microsoft purchased Skype for $8.5 billion, generating a return of $939 million for CPPIB from its direct investment (its investment in Silver Lake yielded another $50 million in gains).[27]

After honing its investment process coinvesting in deals, the group soon began cosponsoring deals. When cosponsoring deals, the team worked alongside the fund manager in due diligence and deal structuring, sharing information without duplicating efforts. In some cases, they would even go solo in transactions in Canada, where they had a deep understanding of the market. An example of such a cosponsored transaction was its purchase, along with the private equity fund Apax Partners and its Canadian pension peer the Public Sector Pension Investment Board, of San Antonio–based medical device maker Kinetic Concepts. The $6.1 billion deal was the second largest private equity transaction of 2011. The company, now known as Acelity, remains in the investors' portfolio, though they did sell off one of its three divisions for $2.9 billion in 2017.

CPPIB was also aggressive in championing new categories of private equity, where they typically led their own transactions. While they were not the first, they often invested in these at a speed and scale that relatively few other investors had done before. One of these categories was infrastructure. By investing in electric, water, and gas utilities, as well as transportation properties such as ports, airports, and toll roads, the investment board hoped to exploit their deep pockets and long time horizon. Another area was private debt, where they aggressively scanned the horizon for opportunities in private bonds, riskier mezzanine loans, and other forms of lending.

The second trend, as we hinted, was for investors to exploit what economists might term "economies of scale." Many public pensions, as the Alabama example in chapter 1 suggests, have faced challenges when they have tried to do too much in-house. Thus, many others have felt that they would do better to continue to rely on outside managers. But they have sought to translate the lure of their large pools of capital into better deals with fund managers.

This trend is most closely associated with Britt Harris, who for over ten years was the chief investment officer of the Teacher Retirement System of Texas (TRS). The pension fund, the eighteenth largest in the world and fifth largest in the US, invests on behalf of over 1.4 million active and retired educators in the state. Upon his arrival in Austin from the pension fund of GTE Corporation, Harris led TRS into alternative asset class investments. But he did so in a different way, reflecting the heft of the fund he managed.

Harris's big idea moment had come several years earlier while he was at GTE. He was inspired by a conversation with executives at Motorola, who urged him to think about his "product" and to determine who his "critical suppliers" were. These terms are commonly used in many industries but not in investment management. Harris explained: "No, they [outside asset managers] are not actually that critical. In fact, they are a kind of necessary evil. And every meeting that we have between them and us is basically a debate where they try to show us that they are a lot smarter than they really are, and we try to prove to them that they are not as smart as they think they are."[28]

Harris proceeded to examine GTE's portfolio management using the framework of a manufacturing company. And so the product was identified as "a customized investment return within certain risk parameters over a long period of time." Crucially, there was repetition: "Investing is a basic repeat process. It's not like producing screwdrivers, but there is a consistency there." Next on his list was to create a system to align incentives with GTE's suppliers (outside asset managers) through the formation of a few critical relationships.

Harris's work culminated in the establishment of a new strategic partnership program in which GTE allocated $1 billion to four large managers of public equities to invest using strategies customized for GTE. This strategic partnership program proved successful, resulting in top-quartile performance over the following decade. Having observed the benefits of maintaining close relationships with money managers while at GTE, Harris advocated establishing a similar program at TRS when he took his post as its CIO in 2006.

Harris began with his public market portfolio. After a nine-month vetting process, Harris and his team invited four firms to participate— BlackRock, Lehman Brothers, Morgan Stanley, and JP Morgan. Harris gave each firm $1 billion to manage on behalf of TRS. Despite a few issues, TRS's public equities strategic partnership network performed reasonably well. After Lehman's bankruptcy, Neuberger Investment Management acquired Lehman's TRS asset management accounts. The program was later expanded.

Harris then extended this logic to private capital. Here he was motivated by what he perceived as a one-sided deal between investors and fund managers. In particular, even when they underperformed, he felt the fund managers often received substantial economic windfalls. Thus, the interests between investors and their managers were not well aligned. He stated, "If you imagine a pendulum, with '100% pro limited partners' on one side and '100% pro private equity firms' on the other side, the pendulum only swings on one side, between the midpoint and the private equity firms."

In an attempt to address this issue, he offered multi-billion-dollar allocations to a select number of alternative asset management firms. The funds would have a flexible mandate to invest across different asset classes. In exchange, they would charge lower fees to TRS. The funds would also engage in "carry netting": if a fund's investment for TRS in private equity did well and its real estate deals did poorly, it would not be able to get its full profit share on the private equity deals. Apollo and KKR, which were selected in a competitive process, have each received $3 billion to manage as of mid-2018.

The jury is still out on both of these innovations, with important questions being raised about their viability. (Harris himself has moved on to a role as chief investment officer of the University of Texas Investment Management Company, which managed $43 billion at the end of 2017.) For instance, can investors build and retain top-tier internal investment teams? And will the investors be able to convince the very best fund managers to accept a large allocation of funds in exchange for lower compensation? We explore these and other issues in depth in subsequent chapters.

But what is clear is that the past decade has seen a rethinking of the traditional relationship between investor and fund manager. The innovations closely associated with Denison, Harris, and Wiseman have been widely emulated across pensions and sovereign wealth funds around the world.

FINAL THOUGHTS

These accounts have sketched the broad arc of how the thinking of investors about patient capital has shifted over time. Nonetheless, we hope a few clear messages have come through:

- A systematic approach to long-term investing is a relatively recent phenomenon.

- Institutional investors have gradually developed a variety of approaches to overcoming the main challenges to long-term investing.
- There is no one right answer here, but a variety of alternative approaches.

In chapter 3, we helicopter up to consider the broader challenges that await would-be long-term investors.

CHAPTER 3

The Long-Term Conundrum

The need for or the dream of attractive returns has lured many investors to patient capital, whether families, insurers, endowments, pensions, or sovereign wealth funds. With deep pockets and extended horizons, these investors are increasingly hopeful that long-term investments will yield outsized returns. And indeed, there are any number of such long-term investments that have yielded tremendously attractive returns. In chapter 2, we saw several case studies, where institutions—sometimes through trial and error—figured out novel and apparently successful approaches to providing patient capital.

This all sounds terrific! The problem is that, in many cases, well-intentioned strategies to pursue long-term investments have *not* garnered happy outcomes. Rather, they have turned into the financial equivalent of black holes. In part, this has reflected poor decisions made by investment committees and staff at the individual groups. But there are also common denominators; more fundamental problems that make long-term investing difficult. The stories of the Alabama and Kentucky pensions that we recounted in chapter 1 are more common than might be hoped.

These types of difficulties are the focus of this chapter. Here we helicopter up to look at the broad sweep of the landscape, and highlight two fundamental challenges that lie at the heart of the problems that many investors have faced in this arena. First, it is hard to understand what realistic returns can be expected. Second, and following from the first issue, selecting managers that can deliver such returns is very challenging.

APPEARANCE VERSUS REALITY

The first challenge is, despite claims to the contrary, that returns in this arena simply have not been that good in recent years. Essentially, long-term investors may be fishing for a large bass in a pond where bluegills and guppies predominate.

This claim may appear puzzling. In virtually any forum where the managers of private capital funds (frequently termed general partners, or GPs) assemble—from star-studded confabs such as the World Economic Forum gathering at Davos to the humblest annual meeting—claims that they are wonderful investors invariably follow. In this respect, long-term investing has its similarities to Garrison Keillor's Lake Wobegon, where "all the children are above average."

In part, this reflects the imprecision with which performance is often measured and the lack of clear guidelines as to how to calculate returns. The consequence of this "fuzzy math" has been readily apparent in private equity. For instance, Bob Harris and Ruedi Stucke, using three popular data sources, found that even modest variations in methodology can result in half of all funds being able to claim "top quartile" results.[1]

By far the favorite tools that private investors use to present their performance are two warhorses. The multiple of funds invested is the ratio of money out to money in, while the internal rate of return (or IRR) captures the annual yield of these investments. These two measures are remarkable for both their limitations as metrics and the inconsistency with which they are applied. As pioneering venture capitalist Bill Elfers once observed, "If the devil can quote Scripture, in his spare time he may be working on [private capital] return methodology."[2]

Consider, for instance, the multiple of invested capital. Knowing how many times your money you have made is nice but not sufficient information. Your happiness upon doubling your money is likely to be tempered, if instead of doing so over a year and a half (an annualized return of 58%), the doubling took fifteen years to accomplish (a yearly return of 5%).

The IRR is an even uglier nag. Essentially, it measures how quickly a manager grows investors' money, no matter how small an amount is grown. An investment that turns one penny into two pennies in a day would generate an IRR roughly equal to 8 with 109 zeros afterward, but you would still only be one cent richer! Not surprisingly, this performance metric rewards groups that have a few quick hits over a short span of time—whether a real estate project that is quickly flipped to another developer or a start-up that is sold off to a large corporation—over those who patiently build capital over longer periods. Thus, during periods where the markets are frothy, the IRR definitely favors the hare over the tortoise.

It might be asked, "Isn't it in the best interests of the investors to have high returns?" Of course, high IRRs are good news in the short run. The problem is what is often termed *reinvestment risk*. Even if someone has backed a fabulous fast rabbit for a 100-yard dash, there is no guarantee that there will be another hare ready and waiting for an investment when the first one finishes its sprint. And if there is no next fast rabbit, the alternative may be much slower: a lazy bunny, lollygagging in a clover patch. As a result, the overall performance is likely to be far lower than the IRR of the initial rabbit suggested. Because it is risky and costly for long-run investors to fund, evaluate, and oversee funds, it is likely in their best interest to opt for groups that can generate less stratospheric returns over longer periods. Yet the ubiquitous IRR measure may point them in exactly the wrong direction.

Moreover, the IRR measure is relatively easy to manipulate to generate higher returns. Groups use a magician's bag of tricks to "juice" their IRRs. For instance, a popular variant is called the "time zero" method. This approach assumes that all the investments made by the fund occur on the first day of the fund. Sometimes this methodology generates a lower IRR than placing all the investments on the actual days when they occurred; at other times, it generates a higher return. Needless to say, groups prefer to use this methodology in the latter case!

A more pernicious form of gaming is the recent craze for subscription credit lines. Essentially, the process works as follows. In the traditional world, investment funds drew down capital as they needed it from their investors, typically just before they deployed it in investments (often alongside debt from banks and other sources). In recent years, however, the funds have been employing a new strategy: borrowing from a bank against the promised (but undrawn) commitments. Ultimately, they call down the funds, repaying the credit line (and the associated interest) with the money from the investors. Because the investment period in which the investors' money was tied up in the firm is so much shorter, but the entry and exit amounts similar (less the interest paid to the bank), the IRR will in all likelihood be much higher.

This practice is troublesome in two ways. First, it makes the IRR a less meaningful measure of performance (like the time zero method described above). In the extreme, an investment fund could call down its funds a day before it exited a transaction and end up with a nearly infinite IRR! Even more worrisome, as the founder of Oaktree Capital, Howard Marks, notes, is the way in which this borrowing may magnify the impact of a crisis in the notoriously cyclical private markets.[3] In particular, if these lines are withdrawn by banks during a financial crisis, then investors are likely to receive a wave of demands for capital during precisely those periods when liquidity is tightest. These capital drawdowns would be not to fund new investments, but rather to replace bank debt in deals made quarters or years before—many of which are likely to be underwater. In this scenario, many investors may be unable or unwilling to fund their capital commitments, leading to massive defaults.

This discussion might lead you to ask whether there are better yardsticks for performance, where such measurement and gaming problems are less prevalent. The answer is undoubtedly yes—to a point. Finance researchers—and a small set of thoughtful practitioners—have gravitated to an alternative known as the *public market equivalent* (PME). This measure computes the ratio of the return of a private market fund (or a basket of funds) to the equivalent returns that would have been garnered in the public markets, had one bought and sold stock at exactly the same time. If the PME is greater than one, the private fund (or funds) has done better than the public market; if less than one, the private fund has underperformed.

This methodology can best be illustrated with a couple of examples.[4] Consider a case where a buyout fund draws down $100 million in June 2004 and returns a distribution of $200 million in April 2007. An investor could have alternatively invested in the public market, but the same investment in June 2004 in the S&P 500 would have yielded only $139.52 million if sold in April 2007. The PME of 1.43 (or 200/139.52) in this case indicates that the private equity investment was superior. On the other hand, a $10 million investment in a venture fund in January 1993 that was liquidated in December 1999 for $40 million looks pretty spectacular. But since an investment at the same time in the S&P 500 would have yielded $39.16 million in December 1999, the PME is a disappointing 1.03 (40/39.16)—indicating that the investment yielded barely more than the public market securities that would not have tied up the investor's money in an illiquid vehicle.

As is often the case, there are today a variety of variants of the PME. For instance, while initial versions used the S&P 500 or another broad market benchmark as the measure of public market activity; today's tailored PMEs use benchmarks of firms with similar size, risk characteristics, and/or industry composition.

PMEs have many virtues. They give a clear sense of private market fund performance, not just on a stand-alone basis but relative to the most important benchmark of all, the public markets. PMEs avoid some of the strange features of IRRs, whose weirdness we have not even begun to do justice to.

At the same time, they are not a panacea. For instance, a PME calculation would have problems grappling with assessing a group that made aggressive use of subscription credit lines. Similarly, there are reports of funds that "shop for an index" that purportedly best reflects their strategy, but in practice simply makes their performance look better. One solution might be to insist that everyone benchmark their performance to the S&P 500. But this would be throwing out the baby with the bathwater.

After all, even the newest pension trustee is likely to appreciate that it is more exciting to earn a 15% annual return from a less risky fund: from a credit fund than from an equity fund, from a large-capitalization stock than from a small-cap one, and from a deal in the US than from one in Turkey.

In any case, once we look behind the seemingly shimmering curtain of gaudy claims by individual private capital managers, the picture is very different. Consider private equity, whose performance has been the best documented. The industry leaders are not bashful in proclaiming their outperformance: the 2017 Milken Institute panels, for instance, were full of industry titans proclaiming the superiority of the asset class. But the evidence increasingly shows exactly the opposite: in aggregate, private equity performance has deteriorated to the point of mediocrity.

Consider, for example, a provocative recent analysis by Bob Harris, Tim Jenkinson, and Steve Kaplan.[5] The researchers looked at the performance of private equity funds using information from Burgiss, which compiles data from pensions and other investors. At first glance, the returns of different crops of funds in figure 3.1 seem reasonable. (The data are divided by the year in which the fund forms, or the vintage year. The most recent vintage years are not included because these investments require several years to mature sufficiently to have meaningful performance numbers.)

But when the authors compute the PMEs of the various vintages, presented in figure 3.2, a much starker picture emerges. Private equity funds, after an extended period of performing better than the public markets, have done no better than the public markets over the past decade. The thought comes to mind that this might be an artifact of some peculiarity in the Burgiss data. But a similar analysis of data compiled by State Street Bank in their role as custodian for many large institutional investors shows a very similar pattern (also depicted in the figure).[6]

Of course, our interpretation of this finding must be cautious for several reasons:

- First, these analyses include funds that are yet to be liquidated. A number of studies suggest interim valuations by private equity

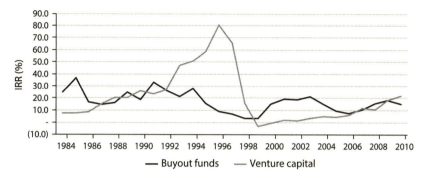

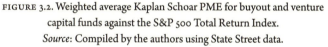

FIGURE 3.1. Weighted average IRR for buyout and venture capital funds.
Source: Compiled by the authors from Harris, Jenkinson, and Kaplan (see note 5).

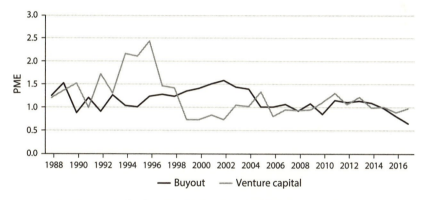

FIGURE 3.2. Weighted average Kaplan Schoar PME for buyout and venture
capital funds against the S&P 500 Total Return Index.
Source: Compiled by the authors using State Street data.

groups are frequently conservative, so performance for more recent
years may increase for these funds over time.[7]

- Second, virtually all performance papers are limited to the US
  market, which is understandable in light of the availability of data.
  While the time series for Europe is considerably shorter, it seems
  that PMEs are significantly higher (against European stock indices)
  and do not necessarily show the same downward trend as in the US.
- Third, as we will revisit in chapter 9, the decline in performance
  could be a permanent shift in a maturing industry, or it could also

have to do with the highly abnormal investment environment in the postcrisis period.

- Finally, these results say nothing about the ability of private equity groups to generate attractive gross returns. It simply says that after fees, the returns that investors have received have declined. This is a theme we return to in chapter 6.

The lack of outperformance is worrisome because of the nature of private capital investing. One key feature of these funds, as we have repeatedly emphasized, is their illiquidity. As a limited partner, this entails making a commitment of a decade or longer to a fund. While investors can sell their partnership interests on what is termed the secondary market, it is an inefficient one in general. Just like the foreign exchange operators dealing in dollars and euros at the airport, the gap between the price at which someone can buy and sell partnership interests is frequently substantial. This is particularly true if an investor is seeking to sell interests not in a Blackstone or Carlyle fund but rather in a smaller, less well-known group.

Normally, investors expect to be compensated for holding illiquid securities by receiving higher returns. In one influential paper, Lubos Pastor and Rob Stambaugh suggest that over recent decades, the holders of the least liquid 10% of US stocks enjoy an annual return 7.5% higher than those holding the most liquid decile of stocks.[8] These authors, and many who have followed, have interpreted this liquidity premium as not some anomalous bonus, but rather as compensation for assuming the risks of illiquidity: holding a liquid security is valuable, as the holder can generate cash when it is really needed.

To cite one famous example of the dangers of illiquidity, the hedge fund Long-Term Capital Management specialized in buying less liquid securities, while selling short (i.e., betting against) more liquid ones.[9] A typical trade that they undertook might have involved the purchase of Treasury bonds that had twenty-nine years maturity remaining (termed "off the run" in trader argot) while selling short the thirty-year ones ("on the run"), which had a much more robust market. The firm thrived for a number of years, harvesting the premium for holding illiquid assets. But when the markets seized up after the 1998 Russian debt crisis, Long-Term Capital faced a different kind of "run." Investors began demanding their money back and the banks—which had been all too willing to allow the hedge fund gurus to become extraordinarily leveraged—began calling in their loans. As a result, the hedge fund was forced to liquidate its illiquid securities in a fire sale. Needless to say, many of these trades were executed at huge losses, and the ensuing collapse of Long-Term Capital almost brought down Wall Street with it.

A second reason why the disappearance of outperformance is worrisome has to do with the risk of private equity funds relative to the public market. One of the guiding principles of financial economics since the pioneering work of John Lintner, William F. Sharpe, and Jack Treynor—which built in turn on the revolutionary insights of Harry Markowitz—is that investors in riskier equities should be compensated with higher returns. Moreover, one of the key drivers of riskiness of equity is how indebted the firm is. These insights, while derived from elegant mathematical modeling, are also intuitive: a highly indebted firm is more likely to go bankrupt, wiping out the equity holders. But if the firm prospers, the equity holders in a highly leveraged firm will garner a greater return on (considerably smaller) investments.

And of course private equity firms are typically more leveraged than the standard firm in the S&P 500. While the typical nonfinancial company on the index in 2016 had a debt-to-EBITDA ratio of 2.3—that is to say, their debts could be repaid by a little more than two years of pretax operating earnings—the ratio for large private equity transactions closed the same year was 5.5.[10] Thus, it would not be surprising if private equity portfolios were riskier than the S&P 500, a risk that investors should be compensated for. Indeed, there is a substantial (though somewhat daunting to read) academic literature that seeks to determine the beta of private equity transactions. While a thorough review of this literature is beyond the scope of this book (especially since we hope our readers will stick with us for a few more chapters!), there is consensus that the beta is well above 1 (a beta of 1 implies the same risk as the market as a whole). The high leverage of private equity–backed firms makes the equity quite risky.

Thus, the apparent lack of outperformance of private equity in recent years can better be characterized as true underperformance, once the expected rewards for lack of liquidity and greater risk are taken into account. Moreover, when we look at the performance of other forms of private capital, many of the recent report cards are also disappointing. For instance, Preqin reports that the annualized returns of real estate private equity for the ten years ending in June 2016 are 5.0%, which lags what you would have earned had you held a basket of equities or long-term bonds over the same period (7.4% and 9.5%, respectively).[11]

The crucial final question is how to interpret the data of poor returns. One possibility is that this is an anomaly. Figure 3.2 suggests that the Reagan years—another period of rapid growth in private equity investing—saw poor returns as well. Once the market corrected after the 1987 market crash and the ensuing junk bond collapse, and many investors exited the industry, the PMEs of the survivors climbed steadily higher. In the same way, the most recent decade may be an anomalous period in terms of private investing, with too much fund-raising, overly high valuations, and, consequentially, poor returns.

Alternatively, it may be that the experiences of the 1990s and 2000s have been the anomaly. In this scenario, private capital may be increasingly resembling the hedge fund world, where it appears the large number of players competing in a highly efficient market have been unable to earn returns (at least after their substantial fees and incentive payments) that adequately compensate investors for the risks they are taking on. It may be that the combination of highly competitive markets and substantial fee structures preclude attractive returns in private capital as well. We return to these questions in chapter 9.

THE GREAT GAZELLE HUNT

If returns in private capital as a whole have been unexceptional, then the route to success has to be through the selection of particularly good managers. But finding these fleet gazelles can be a daunting task in its own right. Moreover, the difficulty of selecting top-tier managers seems to have increased substantially in recent years, for reasons that we now discuss.

To be sure, illiquid markets populated by long-term investors are characterized by broad disparities in performance. This divergence is highlighted in figure 3.3, which shows the difference between the long-term performance of a manager whose performance beats three-quarters of the other managers and one who only achieves the median, that is, the midpoint of performance.[12] Essentially, the calculation asks what the difference would be in yearly returns if capital were committed for a decade (ending in December 2016) to a top-tier manager versus a typical manager. Among bond managers, the divergence is very small: less than four-tenths of one percentage point annually. This lack of divergence reflects the fact that the market for US Treasury bonds is huge and very efficient. Unless a fund manager is willing to gamble on the direction of interest rate movements, the gains to be had here are very modest indeed.

Turning to managers who hold equities, it is not surprising that we find that the dispersion of returns is larger than for bond managers. These securities are far less likely to move in lockstep, and there should be more rewards for superior investment insights. Nor is it remarkable that those who invest in emerging market securities have a larger dispersion than those who hold US large-capitalization stocks.

But what is less expected is how modest the dispersion is (0.9% and 1.3%, respectively). The small magnitude of these gaps reflects the fact that we are looking at decade-long returns. Thus, while in 2015 an investor specializing in Chinese securities may have done well, and a Brazilian specialist undoubtedly prospered in 2016, over the long term, these differences are much less pronounced. And similarly for investors in technology versus financial stocks, growth versus value securities, and so forth. The kind of gains that an individual manager is likely to make are thus quite limited. This bunching of performance explains why, in many compilations of the best fund managers over the long term, groups that specialize in index funds (such as BlackRock and Vanguard) crowd the top of the list. The indexing approach of these groups allows them to

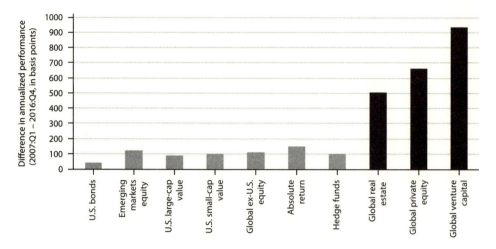

FIGURE 3.3. Difference in annual return (1st quartile vs. median).
Source: Compiled by the authors using Cambridge Associates data.

charge dramatically lower fees, which often trumps the added performance that all but the very best active managers can achieve.[13]

As we move across the spectrum to investors in private securities, however, we see a different pattern. The interquartile ranges are dramatically higher, with leveraged buyouts of real estate at 5.1%, private equity at 6.7%, and venture capital at 9.4%. Why might the performance differ so dramatically across managers in these markets? There are at least three answers:

- First, it is simply harder to evaluate private managers in advance, which implies that some managers who are of lower quality will get funding. A real estate group may have a good track record because the team is smart and competent, or it may have simply gotten lucky with a large transaction. A departing executive may have been an underperformer (as the partners he is deserting may claim) or the key architect for the fund's success. As a senior partner at one of the largest private equity firms told the MBA students whose class he was visiting, "The secret of this [private equity] profession is that those of you who will make it to partner will do so without any sensible record of performance." More formally, Arthur Korteweg and Morten Søorensen have shown that to really distinguish between whether a private capital group is actually better than its peers or just lucky, analysts must assess the performance of as many as twenty-five funds![14] Because of the long-term nature of these investments, it takes a lifelong career to build a track record that shows consistency. While potential investors try to answer these questions during their "due diligence" process, definitive answers are hard to come by. Thus, almost inevitably, substandard groups will glean capital from even the most sophisticated investors.

- Second, it is far harder to duplicate the success of funds. By carefully observing the trades of a mutual fund or even a hedge fund, someone might be able to "reverse engineer" its decision-making process. But replicating the approach of a top-tier private investor is much more challenging. Senior venture capital investors are likely to have a rich network of contacts with entrepreneurs, investment bankers, and senior corporate executives, which allows them to help portfolio companies extensively. Moreover, such a senior investor is likely to be a proven "brand name," whom entrepreneurs seek to involve with their company as a signal of their quality. These skills are hard for an outsider to replicate, no matter how keen their insights about market evolution.

- Finally, Lady Luck deals capricious hands in the private investment business. Many groups have gone from being highly sought after by investors and admired by their peers to a much less happy place in a few bad years, whether due to mistaken insights about a sector or an entrepreneur or overoptimism about their ability to grow. An example is Bain Capital, which, after a series of spectacular funds in the 1980s, 1990s, and early 2000s, had a third-quartile result with its 2006 fund and a bottom quartile finish with its 2008 fund. (Perhaps not coincidentally, these were the two largest funds the group ever raised.) After righting the ship, the firm raised an eleventh fund in 2013, which again sits comfortably in the top quartile.[15]

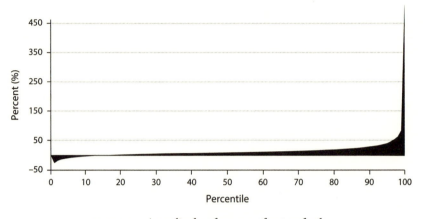

FIGURE 3.4. Annualized performance of mature funds.
Source: Compiled by the authors using Preqin data.

These differences are even more dramatic as we approach the extreme ends of the performance spectrum. Figure 3.4 plots the annualized performance from inception to closing (or until the end of 2016) of all mature funds with performance data in Thomson Reuters, based on our own analysis. It highlights that, while the range between the median and the seventy-fifth percentile may be large, it is dwarfed by the performance differential between the median and the ninetieth, ninety-fifth, and ninety-ninth percentiles (20%, 31%, and 75%, respectively). Thus, if an investor chooses the right managers, decent returns can result, even during the years when private capital as a whole performs dismally. There is just such a gap between the "contenders" and the "pretenders."

The second defining characteristic of private markets is the stickiness of performance. Groups that have performed well in one fund have tended to do so in the next fund, and the fund after. The left-hand panel of table 3.1 shows the historical pattern for private equity funds, as identified by Bob Harris, Tim Jenkinson, Steve Kaplan, and Ruedi Stucke.[16] The table illustrates the probabilities of transitioning among different performance quartiles for two subsequent funds raised by the same private equity firm. The columns assign any given fund to a performance

TABLE 3.1. Buyout Fund Performance by Performance Quartile

Pre-2001						Post-2000					
		Subsequent fund quartile						Subsequent fund quartile			
		1	2	3	4			1	2	3	4
Previous	1	37.5%	25.0%	18.8%	18.8%	Previous	1	22.0%	28.8%	30.5%	18.6%
fund	2	30.4%	21.7%	30.4%	17.4%	fund	2	24.5%	22.6%	32.1%	20.8%
quartile	3	21.4%	25.0%	32.1%	21.4%	quartile	3	15.4%	28.2%	38.5%	17.9%
	4	17.4%	26.1%	30.4%	26.1%		4	21.4%	14.3%	32.1%	32.1%

Source: Compiled by the authors from Harris, Jenkinson, Kaplan, and Stucke, "Has Persistence Persisted in Private Equity?"

quartile, "1" being the top performers. The rows show the same division, focusing on the next fund raised by the group. The left panel only includes funds raised in 2000 or before. If there were no persistence of performance—that is, if top performers would be no more likely to out-perform than underperform in the next fund—the number in each cell would be 25% (since there are four possible outcomes and they are all equally likely). But in reality, the prior winners are far more likely to be in the top quartile: 37.5% will repeat. And similarly, funds in the bottom quartile are more likely to again be losers.

This pattern is striking because of the difference with public markets. A substantial literature has examined the persistence of performance in mutual funds—or lack of it. Although financial economists initially be-lieved that mutual fund managers had "hot hands"—that is, groups that did well in one year were likely to continue to do so in the following years—more sophisticated analytical techniques revealed these as sta-tistical flukes.[17] Even among hedge funds, which rely on the development of proprietary analytical tools, financial researchers have been able to find little evidence of long-run persistence.[18] There has been some evidence of persistence on a quarterly basis: that is, a hedge fund with superior performance in a given quarter may continue for a second quarter. But academics have been unable to find any sign of higher performance a half year (two quarters) or year later. (Indeed, hedgies have a phrase, "alpha extinction," to capture this phenomenon.)

The wide disparity of returns, and the persistence of the winners, has meant that the returns to successful manager-picking in private equity have been high. Essentially, private capital has been a racetrack where, if someone can select a winning horse in a race, it is the odds-on favorite to win the next race and the race after. Moreover, private capital has traditionally featured *grandfather rights*: the tendency of groups to traditionally first turn to their existing investors before engaging in discussions with new ones. Thus, the successful bettors get to go back to the betting window first when the horse runs again, leading to many would-be punters deprived of a chance to make a wager. This description suggests that private capital may have been a very unfair game, but also a quite lucrative one for those with a deep understanding of the industry.

Traditionally, it has been one class of investors who have very much benefited from this "inside game": endowments and foundations, particularly at elite schools. Historically, there have been dramatic differences in returns across classes of limited partners. In an examination of private equity investments from the 1980s and 1990s by Josh Lerner, Antoinette Schoar, and Wan Wongsunwai, the average annual returns of the private equity funds that endowments invested in were nearly 21% greater than those of the average limited partner in the sample.[19] These differences in performance held even when controlled for observable characteristics, such as the year the fund was formed and the type of fund, which are important determinants of success.

It is natural to wonder whether this reflects greater sophistication in picking funds on the part of endowments or just the vision of having been early to the asset class. This alternative explanation is not implausible: endowments recognized the potential of private capital long before most pension funds did. After all, Harvard's endowment was the first institutional investor in Kleiner Perkins, and consequentially had a seat at the table when thousands of investors were clamoring to get into the venture group's subsequent funds.

The analysis by Lerner, Schoar, and Wongsunwai seeks to unscramble this puzzle in a variety of ways. For instance, it focuses on reinvestment decisions where, as mentioned above, getting access should be

much less of a problem. Follow-on funds in which endowments decide to reinvest have much better performance than those funds in which
they do not reinvest, suggesting that these investors are good at forecast-
ing the performance of follow-on funds. Other classes of investors do
not demonstrate these performance patterns. In fact, for corporate pensions, the funds in which they turn down reinvestment opportunities
actually outperform the ones they green-light: these groups would
have been better off using a Magic 8-Ball to make their reinvestment
decisions. These findings suggest that endowments proactively use the
information they gain as early investors to improve their investment decisions, while other limited partners seem less willing or able to use this
information.

Similarly, the analysis looks at investments in young private equity
groups and those that raised less than they originally sought. If performance differences are driven mainly by the superior access of endowments to top-tier, established groups, then the performance difference
should disappear in this setting. These struggling groups are typically
desperate to raise money anywhere they can. Again, the endowments do
better than their peers. Nor do the funds selected by the endowments
appear to be riskier than those chosen by the others, which might be
another explanation for the differences.

It is important to note that this is simply a general pattern, not a universal result. And the effects documented in this study were concentrated
in the larger endowments, typically at larger schools that were more selective in their admissions.[20] And to be sure, these same years saw poor
decisions on the part of certain endowment managers, some worthy of
the Kentucky pension managers that we met in chapter 1. For instance,
the University of Rochester fell from having the third largest endowment
in the country during the early 1970s to the twenty-fifth largest by 1995.
The root cause was the endowment managers' decision to make heavy
allocations to local companies, apparently out of some misplaced spirit
of civic pride.[21] This strategy went awry when many of these firms proved
to be spectacularly inept in adapting to technological change, especially
Kodak and Xerox.

Why have other investors not duplicated the secret sauce of the endowments? In part, this may reflect the limits that these institutions face. Many public pension funds and sovereign wealth funds are extremely large, with hundreds of billions of dollars in assets. They often feel constrained to have a relatively modest number of relationships with outside managers, so their staff can really understand how each of their fund managers is doing. Thus, the minimum check size that these groups can write is often very large. (It might be worth wondering why these groups don't hire more investment staff, or even an outside manager, so they can write smaller checks. We return to this question below and in chapter 4.)

For instance, one Canadian fund indicated that, because of reasoning similar to that above, it would undertake no investment smaller than $250 million. Furthermore, out of a desire to avoid being seen as having a disproportionate influence on any fund, it sought to limit its investment to no more than 10% of any fund. These rules meant that there were numerous promising classes of investments where it could not invest: for instance, in venture capital, only a handful of funds have reached a size of $2.5 billion or above.

Even if the institutions are able to undertake these smaller transactions, they often lack the resources and incentives to carefully assess, for instance, the fifteen Scandinavian buyout funds in the market, to figure out which has the most promising strategy. Instead, writing a large check to a well-known group is often the preferred answer. The phrase, sometimes attributed to Gene Amdahl (who left IBM in 1970 to start his own competing firm), "no one ever got fired for buying IBM" lives on in the investment world!

And alas, in many investment classes, big is not necessarily beautiful. Figure 3.5 presents what we believe to be the most careful look to date at the relationship between transaction size and returns. The figure depicts the gross returns (i.e., returns before fees) calculated in a variety of ways, for mega- versus middle-market transactions in the United States and Europe. The superior performance of the middle-market transactions are apparent, with returns several percentage points higher using each metric. This disparity is not surprising: the largest transactions are almost

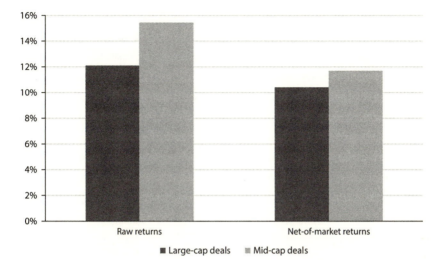

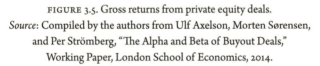

FIGURE 3.5. Gross returns from private equity deals.
Source: Compiled by the authors from Ulf Axelson, Morten Sørensen,
and Per Strömberg, "The Alpha and Beta of Buyout Deals,"
Working Paper, London School of Economics, 2014.

surely well shopped across sophisticated investment groups. Consequently, the dimensions of each transaction are carefully analyzed by
many parties and the chances of a bargain limited. Moving down into
middle-market transactions, the ability of groups to snag a diamond in
the rough is considerably greater. On a similar note, researchers have highlighted that first-time funds—frequently, smaller funds that are shunned
by investors as too risky—actually perform well above the median fund.[22]

Resource constraints are also a real issue. Despite the huge amount
of capital that these institutions control, they are often starved for funds
internally. One sovereign fund manager of our acquaintance has noted
while he could buy the General Motors Building on Fifth Avenue in Manhattan if he wished, it is impossible to buy a new chair for his office. The
picture within many US public pension funds is even grimmer. We have
seen groups who deploy billions of dollars of private capital per year yet
are unable to obtain permission to spend $20,000 for a subscription to
a basic data set such as Preqin or to undertake more than one overseas
trip per year. Needless to say, if the data purchases or travel allowed the

investment team to make decisions that boosted the pension's returns by even a tiny amount—say, 0.001%—the expenditure would have paid for itself many times over! When considering these groups, it is hard not to think of the Air India pilots, whom the *New York Times* memorably depicted as preferring to fly with newspaper-covered windows.[23] Perhaps they will avoid disaster for quite a while, but it is hard to feel that "flying blind" is a wise policy.

This penny-wise and pound-foolish mentality also manifests itself in compensation policy. In many public pensions, investment officers individually handing out hundreds of millions of dollars a year are earning under $100,000. In extreme cases, this can lead to outright bribery of investment professionals, as happened in the notorious scandal at the California Public Employees' Retirement System. In this case, senior officials at CalPERS were provided with private jet trips, luxury hotel suites, gifts, and even a paid wedding from a prominent placement agent, Alfred Villalobos, who in turn charged tens of millions of dollars in fees to the groups he represented (such as Apollo, Ares, Aurora Capital, CIM, and Relational).[24]

But these kinds of egregious scandals obscure the more pervasive distortions that low compensation can engender. Organizations seeking to offer even modest bonus schemes to their employees can come under scrutiny, as Britt Harris at the Teachers' Retirement System of Texas (whom we introduced in the last chapter) found out when it was revealed that he had paid out bonuses to his investment managers to make up for stagnating compensation that the fiscally conservative state legislature refused to raise.[25] By way of context, in the 2010 fiscal year, TRS was the top-performing large public investment fund in the nation. The incentives were based on specific criteria and paid out $9 million in bonuses to fifty-four staff members whose performance had surpassed previously stipulated benchmarks. Represented as an annualized share of assets under management, this sum was tiny: about 0.002%. (Contrast that with the 1.5% or 2% annual fee that TRS was paying many of its fund managers, not to mention profit shares.)

These payouts nonetheless triggered an investigative piece by the *Dallas Morning News*, entitled "Texas Teacher Pension Fund Gave More in Bonuses Than All Other State Agencies Combined, Analysis Shows."[26] The story noted that Texas was giving millions of dollars in bonuses even while slashing budgets for education and health care. The article and follow-ons highlighted that the $9 million in payouts between 2007 and 2011 represented the lion's share of the $13 million in bonuses paid to Texas state employees over these years.

Stakeholders were quick to weigh in. Tim Lee, executive director of the Texas Retired Teachers Association, said the bonuses left him with a feeling of "almost, maybe disgust."[27] And Texas politicians were united in a rare display of bipartisan agreement. For instance, Representative Sylvester Turner, a Houston Democrat, noted: "I don't care how well things have performed in their investment portfolio. Anyone would be hard-pressed to justify those types of bonuses, at this particular time, in this particular state."[28]

The result of these constraints is frequently a revolving door, where young people come to a pension, build experience and networks for a few years, and then depart. In theory, such a revolving door may not be a bad idea. Such a policy may allow a public institution to hire high-quality personnel that they might not attract otherwise. For instance, US Attorney's offices have traditionally hired bright law school graduates, knowing that the vast majority will head off to private practice after a few years of honing their litigation skills.

But frequent rotations can be more worrisome if they affect investment decisions. And indeed, in many cases, individuals departing large pensions head to investor relations positions at large investment groups (which have large internal teams) or to intermediaries who primarily work with (and for) large firms. In such a setting, it is likely that there are great incentives not to "rock the boat" and to view investment requests from large groups favorably. More generally, given how long it takes for a fund to reveal itself as successful or not, a fund manager may be strongly tempted to recommend a "name brand" fund rather than a more adventurous pick of a first-time fund. By the time the new fund proves itself a success, the investment officer will be long gone, and someone else will claim all the credit. Meanwhile, if the new group runs into early difficulties, the investment professional who went out on a limb to recommend it may be blamed.

And it is worth noting that in recent years even endowments are finding the private investment process increasingly tough going. A recent update of the study of performance across limited partners by Berk Sensoy, Yingdi Wang, and Mike Weisbach found that funds chosen during the first few years of the new century displayed a different pattern. In investments made during the 1999–2006 period, endowments no longer seemed to have a differential advantage in private capital investing. Not only did they no longer seem to have superior access to funds that were likely to restrict admission, but they did not make better investment selections than other types of institutional investors.[29]

It is natural to wonder what might be behind this weakening of the endowment advantage. In large part, the deterioration of the circumstances that were conducive to successful long-run investment returns in this area seem to be at fault. First, as figure 3.6 depicts, the dispersion of returns seems to be getting smaller in more recent vintages of funds: the funds that are at the seventy-fifth and twenty-fifth percentiles differ less than in earlier years. Thus, the returns from being a good selector of investment managers are lower than in the past.

Second, as the right side of table 3.1 depicts, it seems the private capital performance has become less persistent, at least in private equity.[30] Only 50.8% of funds that follow an above-the-median fund are above the median themselves, just as we would expect if there were no persistence and performance was being driven by chance. These results are not uncontroversial. Other scholars, using differing data sets, have concluded the decline of persistence is actually modest in buyouts but striking in venture capital. But the results do suggest that even for the most seasoned private capital investors, the selection of good groups can increasingly be a struggle.

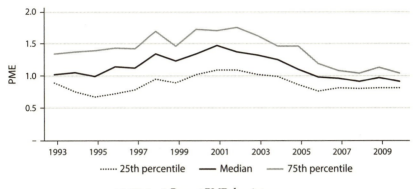

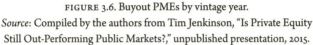

FIGURE 3.6. Buyout PMEs by vintage year.
Source: Compiled by the authors from Tim Jenkinson, "Is Private Equity
Still Out-Performing Public Markets?," unpublished presentation, 2015.

In part, this pattern may be due to the transparency of today's investments and the consequent speed of imitation. In the past, there was often a substantial lag between the time endowments first began investing in an asset class and other institutions followed. For instance, many of the Ivy League schools and their peers began investing in venture capital in the early 1970s. Most corporate and public pensions did not follow until the 1980s and 1990s, respectively. But today the lags are much shorter. Within a couple of years of Harvard's initiating a program to invest in forestland, for instance, many other institutions had adopted similar initiatives. The same dynamics also play themselves out at the individual fund level: an investment by an elite endowment into a fund can trigger a rush of capital seeking to gain access to the same fund. It is ironic that on the campuses of a number of elite universities, student activists are demanding greater disclosure of their endowment's holdings. Such steps would be likely to intensify the problem of imitative investment, leading to lower returns and fewer resources for future generations of students.

We dig deeper into what may be behind this seeming decline in persistence in chapter 6, when we explore the challenges that managers of investment partnerships face.

FINAL THOUGHTS

This chapter has highlighted the fundamental challenges that long-term investors face as they seek to implement these programs. It may have been a little depressing as a result, but these problems are important to understand.

Chapter 4 is far cheerier, as we highlight approaches through which institutions and families around the world have overcome these difficulties.

CHAPTER 4

Investing as If the Long Term Mattered

As we noted in the previous chapter, it is much easier to diagnose problems than to offer solutions to them. Many shelves full of articles, reports, and books seek to offer analyses and remedies to the alleged failures of investors and the managers to whom they provide capital.

Looking back at the granddaddies of this literature—pieces with titles like "Managing Our Way to Economic Decline" (published in 1980)[1] and *The American Disease* (1984)[2]—it is hard not to get the feeling that the same diagnoses and same cures have been offered for a long, long time. Certain aspects of this literature have changed over time: for instance, the enthusiasm for exhorting Americans to follow the templates of Japanese investors and European managers as role models has markedly dimmed. But many of the same themes have been sounded again and again.

Making this task particularly challenging is that the precision with which we can assess solutions is limited at best. Normally, economists and other social scientists try to assess new ideas—whether the efficacy of new classroom strategies or medical reimbursement schemes—by running experiments. A randomly selected group encounters a changed policy while otherwise similar controls remain unchanged. Unfortunately, we have not found a large number of pensions and sovereign funds willing to let us experiment with the governance and compensation schemes! Thus, we proceed here not with the 95% certainty that journal publications demand but rather much closer to 60% or 70% confidence. As a result, we are almost certain that some of our prescriptions will not stand the test of time. Nonetheless, it is our hope that these insights, derived from case studies, conversations with practitioners, and academic frameworks, will nonetheless be helpful.

Many of the critiques of institutional investors in the earlier literature have been at the thirty-thousand-foot level, with broad admonitions to "think like an owner!" As inspiring as these broad exhortations might be, we focus our advice on a more granular level. We highlight here four specific areas where we feel there are important opportunities for investors to improve: *governance, measurement, incentives,* and *communication.* In each of these areas, we argue, investors have a long way to go in addressing the limitations of the traditional approaches. But before we plunge into the weeds, we highlight two examples of investors who are taking creative approaches to long-term investing.

Writing about great long-term investors can be boring because there is just too much agreement as to whom to put at the top of the list! A sports talk host arguing that Usain Bolt is at the top of the list of great sprinters or Serena Williams is the best female tennis player is unlikely to light up the studio lines with angry and excited callers. In the same way, putting Yale's endowment on a list of top long-term investors is unremarkable.

This lack of controversy reflects, of course, how well Yale has done over the past three decades. Under the leadership of David Swensen and Dean Takahashi, the endowment has increased tenfold in inflation-adjusted value since 1985.[3] Looking over the twenty years from July 1996 to June 2016, the endowment experienced extraordinary success in a wide variety of asset classes, from venture capital (an annualized return of 77%) to natural resources (16.2%) to foreign public equities (14%). Even in the last decade, a difficult period for many endowments, Yale has beaten its active benchmarks in every asset class. Had it performed instead only as well as its benchmarks over this period, the school would have been $6 billion poorer.

Yale's success might be likened by a cynic to the infinite monkey theorem postulated by mathematician Émile Borel, who envisioned a massive room of typing primates eventually replicating with near certainty the sonnets of William Shakespeare. With all the institutions seeking to beat the market in a myriad of ways, surely it is inevitable that a handful will.

Perhaps alleviating this concern is that Yale's success did not appear to be the consequence of random choices but rather was grounded in a clear philosophy:[4]

- An emphasis on equities, whether publicly traded or private. The endowment team argued that equities have two advantages. First, stocks have historically performed far better than bonds. Second, unlike debt instruments, which typically fall in value during periods of inflation, equities should fare better during these times, which place substantial pressure on endowments.
- A second principle was diversification. In general, Yale believed that risk could be more effectively reduced by limiting aggregate exposure to any single asset class, rather than by attempting to time markets. Underlying this approach was a skepticism that the team was better than the market in anticipating economic fluctuations.
- Third, Swensen believed strongly in using outside managers for all but the most routine or indexed investments. These external investment advisers were given considerable autonomy to implement their strategies as they saw fit, with relatively little interference from Yale. The managers were chosen carefully after a lengthy and probing analysis of their abilities, comparative advantages, performance records, and reputations.
- A fourth principle was to seek opportunities in less efficient markets. Because the differences in returns between managers have historically been so much greater in inefficient asset classes, as we discussed in chapter 3, the returns from selecting better managers were greater here. As a result, less than a quarter of Yale's endowment was in public stocks, bonds, and cash at the end of the 2017 fiscal year.

- Finally, the Yale philosophy focused critically on the explicit and implicit incentives facing outside managers. In Swensen's view, most of the asset management business had poorly aligned incentives built into typical client-manager relationships. For instance, managers typically prospered if their assets under management grew large, not necessarily if they performed well for their clients. The Investments Office tried to structure innovative relationships and fee structures with their external managers to align the managers' interests as closely as possible with those of Yale.

Now the phone lines *are* lighting up! Yale's success has nonetheless attracted depreciators. One critique, voiced by grandees as diverse as Malcolm Gladwell and Warren Buffett,[5] is that this strategy has entailed the payment of too many fees. For instance, Buffett has pointed out that the amount paid to investment managers would have been far less had Yale adopted an allocation to equity and bond index funds. While this particular claim of the "sage of Omaha" is undoubtedly true, it obscures the fact that Yale's performance is far better than what a passive approach would have yielded. In fact, the endowment estimates that had it adopted a passive approach (for instance, 60% indexed equity and 40% debt) between 1986 and 2016, Yale would have ended up more than $25 billion poorer![6] While this lesson is one that many investment committee members have struggled to absorb, higher fees do not necessarily equal lower returns. In fact, David Robinson and Berk Sensoy have found no consistent relationship between fees and returns across over 800 private equity and venture capital funds. Managers with higher fees delivered sufficiently higher performance to offset the drag of the compensation.[7]

A second line of attack has been to compare the endowment to other investors that have had spectacular success. Typically, the critics select a small endowment holding a highly undiversified portfolio, and highlight that institution's success. For instance, *New York Times* columnist James Stewart compared Yale's performance in the 2015 fiscal year unfavorably to Southern Virginia University (SVU), a small Mormon college, which at the time had an endowment of about $1 million. The endowment head there had focused on a handful of US stocks and had chosen Apple and a hot biotechnology company. Stewart concluded that "maybe one day we'll be reading about the Southern Virginia model."[8] Of course, the thrust of this argument was dented somewhat when the value of SVU's endowment fell by 4.8% in fiscal year 2016, placing it well in the bottom quartile of very small university endowments (those with under $20 million at the end of 2016).[9] Meanwhile, of the eight largest endowments (those with over $10 billion in assets), only one school had a worse performance than Southern Virginia in 2016. Dare we utter the words "fake news"?

A harder-to-rebut critique is that, viewed as a whole, the past thirty years have been a benign environment for Yale's strategy. With Yale's current target asset allocation, over 90% of the endowment's assets were expected to produce equity-like returns. The past three decades have been fabulous for equity. An original $1 investment at the beginning of 1986 in large-company US stocks would be worth almost $17 by the end of 2016, and one in small-company stocks nearly $27; meanwhile, a comparable investment in US Treasury bills would have yielded under $3.[10] At the same time, alternatives have prospered. On the venture capital side, there has been extensive innovation and (until 2000) a robust market for new issues. Buyouts and hedge funds have benefited, at least until recently, from the plethora of "value" investment opportunities and the ready availability of debt on favorable terms. Whether these conditions continue to hold in the decade to come remains to be seen.

But it would be misleading to think that innovation in long-term investing has begun and ended with Yale's endowment. For over the past decade, we have seen around the globe a rich and creative variety of approaches emerge across the full range of the institutional spectrum. A thoughtful strategy that originated from a very different place is PensionDanmark's initiative regarding infrastructure investing.[11] While this program is much newer, and thus our evaluation of its success must be much more tentative, its design and execution seem highly promising.

Denmark is a small, pleasant place known to most—at least since the Viking era—for LEGO, Hans Christian Andersen, and remarkable taste for information transparency. Another of its claims to fame, however, is its pension system, frequently ranked as the best in the world in compilations such as the Australian Centre for Financial Studies' Melbourne Mercer Global Pension Index. As they note, a "first class and robust retirement income system that delivers good benefits, is sustainable and has a high level of integrity."[12]

PensionDanmark is the largest of the nation's occupational pension schemes and the fourth-largest pension provider in Denmark overall. It offers pensions and insurance products to more than 660,000 members working in 27,500 companies, managing roughly $25 billion. As part of a portfolio overhaul in 2010, PensionDanmark allocated 20% of its investment portfolio to "stable alternatives," a portfolio of real estate and direct infrastructure investments. We highlight here its direct infrastructure investing program.

As we noted in the book's introduction (chapter 1), despite the tremendous need for infrastructure investment in the developed and developing markets, infrastructure assets still make up a minor part of most institutional investors' portfolios.[13] One reason is that the track record of these investments has been poor, due to a wide variety of issues ranging from political interference in projects, to the problematic incentive structure of many funds, to the incompatibility of the long project lives with frequently limited fund durations.[14] While some pensions and sovereign funds have set up groups to invest directly, only the largest groups have generally played in this arena. Moreover, institutions have struggled with the more general challenges associated with direct investing, which we highlight in chapter 8.

Following the 2010 review, PensionDanmark decided to allocate 10% of its assets to infrastructure investments. Conscious of the potential pitfalls of these funds, PensionDanmark decided that its infrastructure portfolio should consist primarily of direct investments; specifically, that it would focus on direct equity investments in unlisted infrastructure projects. The rationale for this strategy was the sense that there were opportunities in the newer and less crowded segments of the infrastructure market.

The team then established a number of criteria for choosing investments:

- First, they sought assets that were characterized by low demand and price risks. Thus, they sought projects where the demand was not strongly correlated with the business cycle, or where the prices could be locked for extended periods. Examples included power distribution networks and regulated utilities with fixed price agreements.
- Second, the team looked for investments that they believed had low regulatory or political risk. Thus, they limited themselves to investing in the European and North American markets, where the regulatory framework for private infrastructure investments was stronger and better understood. This approach, while avoiding the "surprises" that investors in China and Russia have encountered, was not foolproof. For example, under the pressure of the financial crisis, between 2008 and 2013 Spain retroactively rolled back various subsidies and imposed tax hikes on the solar power sector, which previously it had been energetically encouraging.[15] Many investors, including PensionDanmark, were financially hurt by this decision.
- Third, their small size (at least relative to many of their sovereign fund competitors) allowed them to be more nimble and pursue smaller opportunities that were "below the radar" of their peers. They were willing to invest in earlier-stage opportunities that many infrastructure investors avoided, such as greenfield infrastructure projects where the asset was still being constructed.
- Finally, by law, the maximum equity stake that PensionDanmark could take in a direct investment was 50%. Thus, the direct infrastructure investments had to be carried out in partnerships. The fund focused on experienced industrial firms with deep technical expertise and similar risk appetite, such as DONG Energy, E.ON, and GDF Suez. Furthermore, because partners were in charge of managing the asset, it was especially important that interests remained well aligned over the life span of the investment. To this

end, the team aimed for deal structures where its joint venture partners held significant financial stakes in the projects, so that the partners would have "skin in the game" and be invested in the success or failure of the projects.

The seven-member team took an incremental approach to investing, seeking to build out their capabilities and the comfort of the investment committee. Consider its experience with wind power. In 2010, the team began with a straightforward investment in a brownfield (already-built) Danish offshore wind farm, Nysted. In 2011, they moved on to a significantly larger investment in the Anholt offshore wind farm, the largest offshore wind farm in Denmark and the third-largest in the world. In this transaction, they deployed five times as much capital as before. While this investment was made before construction began, PensionDanmark limited its risk: the turbine manufacturer, Siemens, agreed to guarantee the output of the wind turbines for five years. The contract also dictated that once Anholt was operational, the power generated was to be sold for a rate guaranteed by the Danish government for twelve years. In 2012, they invested in three US onshore wind farms operated by E.ON, where 90% of the power generated was to be sold under a fifteen-year, fixed-price purchase agreement.

The firm has also sought to address the perceived limitations of existing infrastructure funds in an entrepreneurial way. PensionDanmark seeded Copenhagen Infrastructure Partners (CIP), an infrastructure fund management company founded by five successful investors at DONG Energy. In 2012, PensionDanmark became the sole investor in CIP's first fund, committing €800m (at the time, just about $1 billion) to the newly established fund manager over a 20-year investment time horizon. Being the seed investor gave PensionDanmark privileged access to CIP's ideas and future investment funds. The partnership also charged significantly lower management fees than the market norms.

Working closely with an aligned counterparty like CIP allowed PensionDanmark to benefit from the expertise of a third-party manager while avoiding many of its typical downsides. It also enabled the pension to significantly increase the pace of investment into infrastructure projects, and to invest in projects whose complexity was beyond the capability of its internal team and not of interest to its corporate partners. Of course, the relationship was mutually beneficial. CIP found a long-term, committed partner to back its inaugural fund. In 2015, PensionDanmark committed another €500m (about $555 million) to CIP's second fund.

While the ultimate success of the program will not really be knowable for a while—say, until 2030—PensionDanmark presents an interesting case. Its experience illustrates how a medium-sized fund without the pedigree or track record of a Yale can identify a relatively neglected market niche, proceed in an incremental manner, and garner the partners it needs. By gradually building up a team with a clear vision and mandate, targeting well-differentiated markets, and carefully structuring deals, PensionDanmark is a counterpoint to the kind of impulsiveness and trend-following that we have seen in much of the investment world.[16]

GOVERNANCE

We now turn to the hallmarks of what we regard as keys to successful long-run investing programs.[17] While each of the four aspects we explore here are essential, none is more critical than effective governance. Long-term commitments, as we have highlighted, are hard to assess for a considerable time, leading naturally to questions about the quality of investment decisions. Good governance is the first line of defense to ensure that good judgment is exercised, and patience prevails.

An active and professional board or investment committee can make an enormous difference in the design and implementation of a long-term investment strategy. The most effective of these bodies in our observation see their role not as micromanaging the decisions of the investment staff, but in setting broad policy directions and serving as an informed sounding board as the staff grapples with challenges. A board with a solid long-term orientation can ignore the noise of short-term market movements and focus on the predictors of long-term growth and opportunity. The governance of the investment effort can contribute to creating an environment that nurtures talent and encourages a long-term perspective.

So how does an organization construct such a visionary governance body? Even if the fund is investing on behalf of its employees, having them dominate the investment committee—as is so often the case— makes little sense, whether they are schoolteachers or generals. Our prescription may sound dangerously close to advocating that long-run investing be entrusted not to the people but rather to the elites. We realize that this has been an unpopular position in the United States at least since William F. Buckley declared in 1963 that "I should sooner live in a society governed by the first two thousand names in the Boston telephone directory than in a society governed by the two thousand faculty members of Harvard University."[18] Certainly, the bus drivers, nurses, and teachers that we have met at investment committee meetings have been incredibly dedicated people, frequently discharging their board duties in addition to their taxing and modestly compensated day jobs.

Moreover, having "elite" investment committee members is no cureall. To quote sports data guru Paul DePodesta, "Your goal shouldn't be to buy players. Your goal should be to buy wins."[19] Some of the examples we gave earlier highlight the pathologies that elite board members may introduce, from the politician pushing for an investment in a fund of a major donor, to the wheeler-dealer entrepreneur who encourages reckless market timing, to the private capital investor who pressures an endowment to invest in his funds.

There are also more subtle failures of elite board members. Even in the world of private university endowments where the constraints that public pensions face are less likely to rear their heads, episodes abound where schools have pursued strategies that ultimately would have been successful. But despite these good directions, the investment committees abandoned them in the face of initial losses, which triggered media scrutiny and alumni complaints.

To cite one vivid example, the Ford Foundation had encouraged universities to invest more into small-capitalization stocks in the late 1960s. A task force consisting of McGeorge Bundy, the foundation's president (who had previously been the national security adviser to Presidents Kennedy and Johnson), and a number of distinguished academic leaders reviewed the historical returns data. They concluded that "past thinking by many endowment managers has been overly influenced by fear of another major crash. Although nobody can ever be certain what the future may bring, we do not think that a long-term policy founded on such fear can survive dispassionate analysis."[20] Rather, they recommended an equity-heavy investment strategy, with a particular emphasis on small-capitalization stocks.

This recommendation, if followed by the endowments for the next several decades, would ultimately have yielded very attractive returns. But in practice, it was almost as much of a disaster as Bundy's earlier advocacy of aggressive US military intervention in Vietnam. Having increased their allocation to small-capitalization stocks at the peak of the 1960s bull market, the schools' endowment staffs were bitterly criticized by the media, alumni, and their investment committees for their poor timing: returns for stocks in general, and small-capitalization stocks in particular, were poor for most of the 1970s. In the face of unrelenting criticism, the investment committees at many of these schools abandoned these strategies at exactly the wrong time.

Another example along the same lines are the endowment managers who attempted to hedge out their exposure to venture capital in the late 1990s. A number of these managers were forced by their investment committees (often dominated by venture investors!) to abandon their positions right before the 2000 technology market collapse after experiencing several quarters where the hedges lost money. They then experienced huge losses during the dot-com crash that followed, with no hedges in place.

So what are the governance qualities that allow some investors to pursue successful, frequently unconventional investment strategies while many others do not? Research touts the benefit of a board with financial expertise, long terms of service with appropriate term limits, substantial disclosure, and relatively few meetings.[21] As one practitioner prescribed: "Board members should be collegial, helpful, humble, and open-minded individuals with relevant experience and a deep dedication to the organization's mission."[22]

Yet despite these seemingly obvious qualifications, studies have found that many board members may not be particularly well prepared for their responsibilities. One study of UK pension boards found not only that "many trustees are not especially expert in investment," but more worrisomely, they did not avail themselves of opportunities that the institution provided to increase their knowledge. Nor, it appeared, did many prepare for meetings.[23] Observing that board members were supposed to represent the beneficiaries of the fund, a later study had a gentler appraisal, saying, "It is not a question of whether Board members should become experts in this area [investment], as that is not a realistic expectation. That said, board members must be capable of strategic thinking."[24] In November 2009, the UK's Pensions Act established a code of "Trustee Knowledge and Understanding" to help ensure that trustees had "appropriate knowledge and understanding of the law relating to pensions and trusts . . . and the investment of the assets of such schemes."[25]

Assembling an expert board can be particularly difficult for public pension funds because they serve a number of constituencies.[26] Many have to balance the demands of politicians, for instance, when the governor appoints a few members, with the need to provide wide representation of their contributors, and the ex-officio membership of certain officeholders. For example, CalPERS has a thirteen-member board that includes six directors elected by the membership for four-year (renewable) terms, three political appointees (two by the governor and one by the senate), and four members who serve ex-officio, such as the state treasurer. The board meets monthly and its presidency is decided annually.[27] Among other issues, a significant potential exists for shifting membership, which can hamper the creation of an effective team dynamic.

High-performing pension boards, we would argue, should include appointees chosen for their financial acumen. A fraught question relates to the selection of members elected or otherwise chosen by the beneficiaries. According to one intriguing analysis based on a small sample of US funds, too few or too many beneficiaries reduce performance.[28] "Just enough," the author argues, may help to ensure responsibility to their electorate and to disseminate information more broadly throughout the membership. But excessive representation, especially of retirees, has been found to create short-termism, risk aversion, and herding behavior.[29] A starker conclusion emerges from recent, more rigorous work by Aleksandar Andonov, Yael Hochberg, and Josh Rauh, who show that direct or indirect representation on pension fund boards by state officials is negatively related to the performance of private equity investments made by the fund. More generally, they find that a lack of financial experience among the board members also contributes to underperformance.[30]

To address the issue of underperformance stemming from the composition of a fund's board, some have noted the need for controls to mitigate conflicts of interest.[31] One common manifestation of these conflicts are political distortions at public funds of all kinds. As we discussed in chapter 2, the Canadian Pension Plan struggled in its first decades with pressures to undertake politically favored investments. One crucial part of the reforms adopted by the Canadian government when the pension was placed under the oversight of its new investment board was a dramatic restructuring of its governance.[32] It adopted a structure that former CEO Mark Wiseman referred to as "turducken," except instead of a series of stuffed poultry, it featured "a partnership model inside a Crown corporation inside a pension plan."[33] In order to limit political influence, the CPPIB governance was set up as a twelve-member board notionally appointed by the federal and provincial governments, with appointments based entirely on business acumen, not political connections. The board of directors in turn appointed the CEO, with no right of veto from any government. The organization's mandate was set as to invest "solely for the benefit of CPP members" to achieve the best long-term risk-weighted returns for the plan's beneficiaries, regardless of government policy objectives. To further insulate CPPIB from political influence, any changes to its charter required approval by an amending process more stringent than that of the Canadian constitution itself.

It is interesting to note the impact of two aspects of board life— meeting frequency and tenure—on the performance of boards overseeing long-term investment programs. Frequent meetings can be difficult to integrate with a long-term strategy.[34] They provide the opportunity for nearly constant feedback, conveying overly precise information on short-term changes in the portfolio's value. This can lead to more frequent assessments of the portfolio's performance. The sense that the board needs to *do something* can lead to micromanagement of the investment strategy, which at its worst can lead to rapid changes in strategy rather than long-term commitments.

It is often difficult for inexperienced board members to see the big picture of an entire investment portfolio and strategy. Rather than assess the level of risk in the portfolio overall, for instance, it can be easier, especially for individuals new to investing, to focus on a particular fund or deal. Such micromanagement distorts the goals of long-term investment and distracts the investment staff from exploring strategies, evaluating managers, and developing long-term relationships with the best funds and trust with the market.

Even without going to that extreme, if the staff knows it must defend its strategy to the board on a monthly basis, it may tend toward more conventional approaches that are likely to perform as well as the market, rather than a long-term strategy that might deviate from short-term benchmarks and require extensive explanation. This can create "closet indexers," the phenomenon of ostensibly long-term investors pursuing a strategy that closely follows shorter-term indexes.[35]

Tenure also appears to play a role in board performance. While the boards of many university endowments are known for their many years of service, other boards—particularly those of public pension funds—have shorter appointments, sometimes legally mandated terms of two to four years. A tension immediately arises: individuals with a two- or four-year term are overseeing an investment program that ought to have a time horizon many times that. This difference can set up a tension between the director's desire to make an impact in a relatively short period and the timeline over which a long-term strategy shows results, especially if a new strategy might incur losses in the short term.

Such institutional risk aversion could increase, with an inevitable focus on short-term results, if the pension plan's chief investment officer or other staff members have a short time horizon as well. A CEO/CIO seeking to be well-positioned for the next move and a board member with a short legally mandated tenure may both be inspired to focus on good performance in the short term rather than the long term, given the time lag between implementation and fruition.[36] Meanwhile, a leadership and staff with considerable experience who have worked together for many years can be a powerful advantage. Long-run investing is by its nature a highly subjective process. Shared experiences provide a common background that helps them undertake complex investment decisions with seemingly no right answer.

MEASUREMENT

While both the origins and generality of the phrase "if you can't measure it, you can't manage it" have been debated, its applicability to long-term investing is undeniable. In a world with a real need for returns and very ambiguous routes to reaching them, investment committees gravitate toward metrics like an overboard man in a cold sea to a life buoy. And as we described in chapter 3, the common metrics used to track performance of long-term investments have clear benefits but also possess substantial drawbacks. In an effort to measure performance, investment committees frequently choose inadequate metrics. Moreover, they typically look at them far too frequently. How the organization articulates its performance profoundly shapes its ability to successfully commit to a long-term strategy. It is important, then, that an organization takes these biases into account and thinks carefully about how to place each of the measurements into a long-term context.

The desire for measurement undoubtedly leads to unproductive decision-making. Noted one practitioner, "In private equity, people want to pull out their cards to see if they were right in making a given investment. The most objective measure of performance is an exit. So the investors encourage the fund managers—or sometimes it's the managers themselves—to create realization events to validate their strategies."[37] In many cases, a later exit would allow the company to accrete more value, but fund management requires an earlier exit. Indeed, our colleague Paul Gompers has shown how the pressure to generate exits to raise follow-on funds leads young venture capitalists to leave substantial "money on the table," by rushing companies to market too early.[38] Of course, these pressures are augmented by the compensation scheme that private capital funds employ. As one investor stated, "We invest in assets that should be held for more than five to seven years. Yet the GPs want to realize carry for the end of a 7–10 year fund, so we end up with short-term exits on a long-term asset."[39]

These observations bring us face-to-face with a complex dilemma. A major focus of accounting policymakers over the past decade has been ensuring that financial statements more readily reflect what is really going on. This desire first manifested itself in the US when the Financial Accounting Standards Board issued Standard 157 in 2006. This rule defined what it termed *fair value*: "the price that would be received to sell an asset or paid to transfer a liability in an orderly transaction between market participants at the measurement date." Similar measures had been adopted by the International Accounting Standards Board several years before and in Europe in 2004.

On the one hand, transparency sounds like an indisputably good thing. If private capital groups valued their companies fairly, and everyone believed these valuations, the kind of distortions that we alluded to before would go away. For instance, private capital groups would feel no compunction to rush their firms to market because the companies could plausibly get as high a valuation as private entities. There would be fewer surprises as a company valued at cost suddenly soared in value after an IPO or acquisition. Valuations would more closely approximate reality and make it easier for the institutional investors to plan their budgets, make investment allocations, and assess their future liquidity needs. Moreover, investors would better understand the amount of risk in each asset class because they would receive more frequent information on price changes.

On the other hand, a dozen years in, mark-to-market just does not seem to be working too well in private capital. The kind of ideal world where financial statements are highly transparent has not arrived, despite the adoption of this standard by the high gods of accounting. In part, this reflects the fact that valuing most risky entrepreneurial ventures is a complex exercise, with a large number of unknowns. Groups can very plausibly take different approaches to valuing firms. But it also reflects the fact these funds are run by human beings! For instance, Greg Brown, Oleg Gredil, and Steve Kaplan have found that leading groups tend to be more conservative in valuing unexited investments.[40]

An interesting illustration of this observation came in response to a *Wall Street Journal* exposé highlighting the seemingly lagging returns of Andreessen Horowitz.[41] In response, the venture group put out a memo—with the discerning title "When Is a 'Mark' Not a Mark?"—highlighting how their mark-to-market methodology differed from many peers.[42] In particular, they pointed out that many other venture firms were quite aggressive in their valuations.

Consider a case where a hot "unicorn" like Slack sold a 10% stake in itself for $400 million to a group. In this instance, many of their peers would value the firm at $4 billion and value their equity stake accordingly. This approach would be correct had the new investors bought common stock. But in actuality, in most cases, this type of financing is done using preferred stock, with all sorts of special rights and privileges, such as the right to get paid first if the firm is wound down. Thus, even though the shares the new investor bought were convertible into 10% of the common stock, they were actually getting considerably more of the likely payouts. Andreessen Horowitz noted that reflecting this fact, they (correctly, we may add) valued Slack more conservatively, and this contributed to their seemingly lower returns.[43]

But there is a second issue as well. More frequent pricing may work against long-term investment by explicitly reporting interim variations that have little if any impact on the investment's eventual realized value. This can introduce deleterious consequences even when the fund has performed better than the market as a whole.

At least in private, chief investment officers often argue that frequent valuation information about long-term investments may actually be counterproductive. Excessively frequent measurement, they feel, introduces a short-term orientation that may distort long-term investments. For instance, a wholesale drop in the public markets will undoubtedly reduce the value of a portfolio that is marked-to-market. But what if the investor plans to hold the assets for decades? The investor might well wish to buy into the depressed market. But a combination of regulatory pressures and human psychology may lead to pressures on the organization to do the opposite. Such behavior ends up defeating the entire purpose of long-term investments: making and holding investments over an indefinite amount of time by an organization with the capability of doing so. Especially for a high-profile fund, such as a public pension, an announcement of quarterly portfolio losses is usually followed by intense media and political criticism. Requiring long-term investors to adopt short-term measurements introduces a short-term orientation. Such short-termism robs society of the important benefits that long-term investment provides.

So how, then, can investors effectively keep a scorecard of their performance? We highlight four approaches:

- *Commit to the use of long-term measurements.* Accepting and defining a long-term perspective can set expectations. An example is the decision by the Future Fund, Australia's sovereign wealth fund, to measure performance over a rolling ten-year period (although the fund's managers would report these results on a quarterly basis).[44] The longer time horizon, along with a strategy to invest across six broadly defined asset classes, provided the fund with greater flexibility. As of March 31, 2017, it reported that the fund has returned 7.7% annually since its inception, exceeding the benchmark return target of 6.9%.[45] While the firm also actually reports its quarterly performance, it does so at the bottom of a table at the end of the report. A number of chief investment officers have used similar framing to get their committees to focus on long-run performance measures.

- *Focus on a limited—but diverse—set of metrics.* In our interviews, a number of experts mentioned that they focused on a limited number of metrics. All were slightly different, so it is difficult to create a definitive list of key performance measures. The critical aspect, however, is that in each situation the investor determined the metrics that provided the information deemed necessary to make decisions. Reams of data that cannot be acted upon are not information but inconveniences. As one expert noted, paraphrasing Einstein, "[Risk metrics] should be as simple as possible, but not too simple."[46]

- *Be directionally correct.* Being "precisely wrong" rather than "roughly right" is a dangerous waste of energy. For instance, although risk measurements are difficult to calculate, risk is ignored at our peril, as many investors discovered in 2008 and 2009. Being consistent and transparent about an approximate value is preferable to either ignoring it or spending excessive energy on precise but short-lived quantifications.

- *Pause periodically to take a holistic view.* A last observation would be the importance of a critical, almost academic, perspective. Many of the most successful long-run investors and their leadership indulge periodically in a process of self-evaluation, pausing to consider the circumstances that led them to make investments that proved to be particularly successful or problematic. For instance, this exercise might consist of a review of the five best investments that were turned down, or the rationales behind the original decisions to invest in what proved to be the lowest-performing funds they selected. Thus, moving away from the traditional metrics of success, the investors can get a perspective on their activities.

INCENTIVES

If boards and staff are to work well together in an environment marked by long time frames and uncertain metrics, they must establish a significant level of trust. A key concern in turn is longevity among the staff. In long-term investing, much intellectual capital accumulates over time. Fund staff and their investment managers who develop relationships and understanding can generate ideas and share information. If a group does not have a stable team, or lacks the experience to make credible judgments, it is unlikely to be regarded as a credible investor. Meanwhile, their shared experiences provide a common background that helps them undertake complex and subjective investment decisions.

This argument is easy in theory but much harder in practice. The "revolving doors" in recent years at many high-profile endowments and pensions underscore that the demand for investment talent is probably greater than it has ever been. The increased interest in alternative investments, and the demand for talent to lead the growing number of investment funds pursuing sophisticated strategies worldwide, are likely to increase the temptation for managers to pursue their activities elsewhere.

This brings us to the topic of compensation. Getting the incentives right for long-term investing is very hard. First, many of these institutions are governments or nonprofits, where even the hint of market-level compensation can spur outrage, whether justified or not.

But even if we lived in a world without media and its spectacle-hungry audience, designing an ideal pay scheme would still be challenging. For ultimately, as behavioral finance researchers have documented, humans are a peculiar kind of animal: we like the short term. An average person is highly averse to short-term losses and to avoid them would be willing to forego substantial payoffs later.[47] Thus, the challenge for any long-term investor is tailoring an evaluation scheme that balances short-term rewards with the organization's long-term goals.

Complicating things further, often well-intentioned incentives may lead managers to behave in ways that are quite different from those intended by the owners (for instance, sovereign entities or pension fund contributors). The classic "principal-agent" problem manifests itself when individual managers (whether internal staff or hired consultants such as gatekeepers) pursue activities that reward them the most, even if they run contrary to the best interests of the principal or owner. These distortions can occur, for instance, when an endowment's staff is compensated based on year-over-year performance, encouraging the adoption of short-term high-growth strategies, although the owner wants long-term outperformance. In part, this issue can be overcome with a carefully chosen and thoughtfully applied incentive scheme. While there is no magic bullet, there is a large body of thoughtful research to guide us through issues related to compensation.

In short, in addition to the level of compensation, we have to reexamine the *structure* of rewards that has been used by many investors and has proved problematic. The favored tool has been a salary and bonus, which almost invariably leads to a focus on current performance that is counterproductive. Instead, in many conversations across all investor types, there appears to be a consensus that the compensation scheme mirroring that of private equity groups would be ideal. A salary and some type of carried interest (or an ability to invest alongside the fund) best links immediate decisions to long-run performance. But these schemes are relatively rare.

At the same time, a number of examples of creative structures have sprung up, with family offices leading the way. In many cases, these have been schemes where performance has been measured over three- to five-year time horizons: given staff turnover, decades-long schemes just may not be realistic. A compensation system that is excessively long-term may have difficulty retaining staff because the individuals foresee being gone before any rewards for their work are paid out. Some groups added a provision that provides an adjustment if a promising investment turns bad. For instance, some of the payment may be held in an escrow account, or actually "clawed back" from the team member if things turn south.

One certainty is that there is no right answer here. Groups differ in the extent to which

- Performance is linked to that of the overall organization, or just that of one's specific group. The benefits of a strong team orientation are easily understood, but at the same time, top performers should not be punished for the deficiencies of others.
- Good decision-making that turns out to be "unlucky" is nonetheless rewarded. For instance, an investor may decide to undertake investments with African private capital groups, even though it is likely that there will be some "rookie mistakes" along the way. Some groups have tried to craft a reward system that encourages creative strategy exploration.
- Bonuses are awarded on the basis of purely quantitative factors or are based on more subjective considerations. While the former option often seems to be chosen because of its perceived "fairness," a broad metric can capture important but hard-to-measure aspects of individuals' contributions.
- Negative nominal returns of the entire fund may trigger a cessation or dramatic curtailment of bonuses, even if benchmarks are exceeded. We personally are not great fans of the concept that poor short-term performance should lead to a dramatic curtailment of compensation. The motivation to avoid controversies is understandable. But this approach again sends a message that, ultimately, it is short-run performance that really matters.

But some other issues are much harder to address with a formal scheme, such as the danger discussed previously here and in chapter 3 that staff members will take actions that position themselves well for their next job. Moreover, many of the resources considered critical for executing a long-term investment strategy (travel to meet a team or money for research tools and training) are the first to be cut when budgets are squeezed. Meanwhile, the staff may be blamed if performance falls. As a result, they may be more risk averse than would be ideal, to avoid embarrassment and keep their jobs. As discussed earlier, for public and nonprofit investment organizations, compensation offers additional challenges. Due to political dynamics and public pressure, these groups generally cannot offer lucrative payouts. The possibility of substantial rewards for the team—even if it is conditioned on high realized returns—is often inconceivable.

This brings us to the distinction, long understood by psychologists, between intrinsic and extrinsic motivation. Intrinsic motivation is where people pursue activities out of the joy of the activity itself, rather than due to formal rewards or pressure; extrinsic motivation is the opposite. It is clear that intrinsic motivation is a powerful incentive for investors: many talented investment managers at long-term investment groups are compensated at far below market rates. And yet they remain, presumably because so many of their rewards are nonpecuniary. As humans, we have a strong desire for work that fulfills a broader mission.

As a consequence, many of the organizations that have been the best at recruiting talented investment staff have done so by emphasizing the organization's mission. For instance, Alexander Hetherington, a director and a 2006 Yale graduate noted, "To be interested in [working for Yale's Investments Office], it helps a lot if you feel a real connection to Yale and want to do something good for the University."[48] Similarly, the major Canadian pension funds have had considerable success with members of the "Canadian Diaspora" who are working overseas in major financial institutions, by offering the chance to live in Canada, pursue a global career, and make a difference to the lives and retirements of millions of Canadians, along with a competitive salary.[49] This observation is similar to the research findings of our colleague Teresa Amabile, who has found that in creative activities (and, certainly, long-term investing is one), an overemphasis on explicit extrinsic motivations can have a detrimental effect.[50]

Thus, one important—though often neglected—aspect of compensation is how to make the team connected to the broader mission. A shared sense of purpose, whether the mission is education or the provision of retirement security, can encourage pride in and commitment to an organization's work. Giving the team the chance to see the outcome of their work and to feel connected to others working in different ways to that end can go a long way. Other attributes of a successful and high-retention workplace include a clear promotion path, a stimulating work environment, and opportunities to learn and to grow.

It might also help going younger when building a team. A number of endowment heads told us that they have more success by recruiting young graduates, who have never yet "tasted the forbidden fruit" of Wall Street and are consequently willing to work for extended periods at modest salaries, rather than by dangling large pay packages in front of Wall Street veterans.

Sadly, many forces cut against the use of intrinsic motivation. Seeking to prevent scandals, public pension funds have in many cases so limited the discretion and roles of their staff that the sense of excitement and mission is lost. Some liberal arts schools have abandoned having investment teams teach in undergraduate classes, because the staff became demoralized after being berated by campus radicals for the perceived sins of the endowment, such as investing in companies that had something to do with oil and gas, Israel, timber harvesting, nonorganic farming, or an endless list of other perceived offenses. (Never mind the generous scholarships paid for by the same endowment.)

In short, incentive schemes can intrude on the best intentions of the individuals governing the investor. Unless the compensation system guards against it, incentives can send a message that is very different from the "vision statement" endorsed by the board and chief investment officer. And human nature being what it is, it is likely to be the incentives that most profoundly affect the team's behavior.

COMMUNICATION

We live today in an era of fishbowl-like transparency. Despite the best efforts of many long-term investors to stay "below the radar screen," public scrutiny is a fact of life for many investors. And if facts are not available, speculation will fill its place. The challenge in many cases is no longer how to stay out of the public eye but rather how to communicate effectively.

To illustrate how the world has changed, consider the experience of Harvard's endowment during the crisis of 1973. That year, the Arab nations imposed an oil embargo on the US, and small-capitalization domestic equities—a mainstay of the Harvard portfolio at the time—dropped by 31%.[51] Like many other institutions, Harvard's portfolio was adversely affected, and it needed to do some painful restructuring of holdings. Yet aside from a couple of brief mentions in the *Boston Globe*, the endowment's difficulties essentially passed without public notice—largely, it appears, due to adroit management of information by the endowment. Needless to say, the university fielded no calls about its financial position from reporters at Bloomberg Television or CNBC, because neither existed! By way of contrast, after the heavy losses associated with the crisis following the collapse of Lehman Brothers in mid-September 2008, the university felt compelled to put out a statement ten weeks later detailing its losses.[52]

Family offices may still be able to avoid scrutiny in many cases, as they often hide in plain sight behind generic names. But endowments, pensions, and sovereign funds do not enjoy the same luxury. Rather, one critical key to success has become communication, at least in two important ways.

The first communication challenge is to market the entity as a desirable investor. As we emphasized in chapter 2, we live in a world that is hungry for long-run investments. As a result, private capital groups with a successful track record can afford to be very choosy as to whose money they accept. Even first-time venture funds started by seasoned entrepreneurs and venture professionals have been besieged by investors looking to get in the door. The least pleasant manifestation of this phenomenon has been private capital funds that demand excessively favorable economic terms, confident that even if many of their existing investors are disillusioned by their greed, there will be others in line to take their place.

Thus, a counterintuitive challenge that many investors face is to convince fund managers to take their money—and to hopefully be invited to invest because they are seen as an attractive partner, as opposed to "dumb money" that is willing to agree to egregious and unfair terms! Even endowments and foundations, which prior to the financial crisis were seen as particularly desirable investors, are being forced in many cases to scramble to access funds. This reflects in large part the liquidity pressures that many endowments experienced during the crisis, and the consequent emphasis of many private capital groups of getting a diverse array of desirable investors.

So how does an investment organization become a desirable investor? The first step is just getting "out there." While the very largest private capital groups may be filled with specialists who have an encyclopedic knowledge of every money pot in the world, many teams are not. And many of the most exciting investment opportunities lie with these smaller organizations. The sheer number of faces in the crowd make it hard for investors to stand out without a concerted effort to attend and speak at conferences, visit private capital groups, and cultivate an image as a thoughtful industry actor. Thus, all but the highest-profile investors face the challenge of building awareness of themselves as an attractive source of financing.

What are the elements that are associated with a desirable limited partner? Among these are stability of the management team, considerable liquidity and resources, and an ongoing organizational commitment to long-term investing. The key criteria in this setting are a lot more like Match.com than Tinder.

Another dimension that factors into desirability is not to be too tough on terms. Certainly, as we explore at length in chapter 6, some of the recent economic changes by general partners have been unappealing. But it is important to remember that these are businesses still characterized by substantial dispersion in returns, as we discussed in chapter 3. An organization is likely to be at least as well off with the higher-performing but "greedier" group than with a generous underachiever.

The second communication challenge relates to the broader set of stakeholders, whether pensioners, family members, faculty, students, or alumni. In an ideal world, the boards of directors and chief investment officers should be willing to explain and defend their investment strategy to constituents.

This communication is important at all times, but never more than during market downturns that sharply affect the reported performance of the portfolio. Understandably, those with an interest in the success of the fund, whether it is pension contributors, alumni, or family members, become concerned when the value of the fund falls. These fluctuations can create huge public and political pressure, forcing managers to devote a lot of time to explaining the results and, sometimes, trying to save their jobs.

A common outcome is so-called panic selling and the rapid alteration of strategies. Panic selling refers to situations when managers and boards aggressively sell off their portfolios, usually at market bottoms due to a shift in investment strategy. This was especially evident during the Global Financial Crisis, when even some boards with a long history of long-term investments abandoned that strategy and instructed the staff to sell private assets on the secondary market. The consequences for returns over the next decade were in many cases substantial; the adverse impact for the investors' reputations even longer lasting.

A group with a set of long-term investment beliefs would respond, "It was worth X; it's priced at half of X." A truly long-term investor follows this with, "Let's buy more." But it takes a strong stomach and a supportive board to implement this strategy when journalists and politicians are complaining about losses in a pension fund. True governance and effective communication on the part of the board and the fund's upper management is critical at this time.

An extensive literature in social psychology and behavioral economics suggests that humans have evolved to go with the herd and to overvalue short-term information.[53] Both of these characteristics, it has been suggested, may exacerbate financial bubbles and crashes, making it difficult to convince a nervous board that a downturn is exactly the right time to buy secondary positions from distressed long-term investors. Without clear and confident communication, the outcomes of downturns are likely to be ugly.

This exhortation does not imply, of course, just disclosing information in crises. In many cases, poor performance during downturns has been driven by aspects of a fund's strategy that were hitherto obscured:

an internal hedge fund that was never disclosed, hidden leverage, and the like. In some cases, it appears that even some members of the investors' investment committee did not fully understand their position. Often the combination of the poor returns and the revelation of aspects of the fund's strategy that were previously hidden serves to dramatically undermine confidence. While we are not arguing that investors should display every position to the world at large, clear communication of strategy and tactics is important.

FINAL THOUGHTS

We began this chapter with the gold standard of the Yale endowment. The key elements of its program are no secrets, but its success has been difficult to replicate, as many investors who have attempted to do so have found. If there is a "secret sauce" to the Yale approach, it is not in the precise mixture of asset classes chosen. Rather, it is in the clarity of its investment philosophy and the rigorous and systematic way it has pursued its goals.

That message is why our second example, PensionDanmark, is so intriguing. This pension had none of the first-mover advantages that Yale did, nor a stellar alumni base to draw upon to staff or oversee its program. But they succeeded nonetheless in formulating a clear strategy, focusing on a set of opportunities where they had some advantages, and then executing their plan in a systematic way.

As we have highlighted here, successful long-run investing is much more a function of having a great organization than wizardry in stock picking. The building blocks delineated here—governance, measurement, incentives, and communication—may seem mundane, but they are truly essential to success.

In the next chapter, we shift our perspective to the other side of the table: the often mysterious world of private capital funds. These organizations are very different, from the nature of the employees to the incentive problems at work. But when we dig deeper, we find that many of the same fundamental challenges are present.

CHAPTER 5

The Genesis of Private Capital

In the next three chapters, we shift our focus from the long-term investors themselves to the funds that they work with. As we have discussed in chapter 3, as much as they want illiquid long-run investments in their portfolios, it is difficult for these investors to offer the incentives and the environment to do such investments internally on a sustained basis. With rare exceptions, it seems essential that the bulk of the heavy lifting in this arena be done by external investors.

Private capital organizations finance high-risk, high-reward companies and projects. They protect the value of their equity stakes by undertaking careful due diligence before making the investments and by retaining powerful oversight rights afterward. The arenas in which they invest differ, but can include start-up companies requiring substantial capital to grow, troubled companies that need to undergo a turnaround or restructuring, and projects to develop infrastructure, natural resources, and real estate. In each case, the risks surrounding the project are sufficiently large (often requiring intensive external supervision) and the capital needs great enough that the entrepreneurs are unlikely to be able to finance the projects exclusively through bank loans or other debt financing.

Private capital managed by dedicated funds today plays a critical role in the American economy and, increasingly, elsewhere around the globe. This influence can be seen most clearly in the financing of companies. At the end of the first quarter of 2018, the five most valuable companies in the world—Apple, Alphabet (Google), Microsoft, Amazon, and

Tencent—were all backed by venture capitalists. More generally, of all initial public offerings in the US between 1999 and 2009, over 60% of the entrepreneurial companies going public were venture-backed.[1] This is an extraordinary percentage considering that only one-sixth of 1% of all companies are backed by venture capital. Among buyouts, between one-quarter and three-quarters of a percent of the entire US private sector workforce has been involved in a buyout each year over the course of this century (with the exception of 2009).[2] Cumulatively, these transactions have had a profound effect on the economy across many dimensions, for better or worse.

In this chapter, we seek to understand the origins of these investors and their impact. This task is a big one, which could fill a volume many times the size of this book. Thus, we do so through five vignettes, which capture some of the representative dynamics as the industry has evolved from World War II until today.

THE PIONEER OF THE PROFESSIONAL LONG-TERM INVESTMENT

In its initial decades, the private capital industry was predominantly an American phenomenon. It had its origins in the family offices that managed the wealth of high-net-worth individuals in the last decades of the nineteenth and the first decades of the twentieth century. Wealthy families such as the Phippses, Rockefellers, Vanderbilts, and Whitneys invested in and advised a variety of business enterprises, including the predecessor entities to AT&T, Eastern Airlines, McDonnell-Douglas, and W. R. Grace. Gradually, these families began involving outsiders to select and oversee those investments.

The first formal private capital firm, American Research and Development (ARD), was not established until after World War II.[3] Because institutional investors were reluctant to invest, ARD was structured as a publicly traded closed-end fund (i.e., the number of shares issued by the fund was fixed) and was marketed mostly to individuals. The few other venture organizations begun in the decade after ARD's formation were also structured as closed-end funds.

Georges Doriot, born in 1899, served in the French Army during World War I before moving to the United States to get an MBA from Harvard Business School. After one year at Harvard, Doriot dropped out to get experience working on Wall Street. He returned to Harvard in 1925, though, to serve as an assistant dean. While at Harvard, Doriot taught a course titled "Manufacturing," in which he discussed the advantages and strategies behind venture capital investing.

After distinguished service managing logistics for the US Army during World War II, Doriot returned to campus, determined to put his ideas into practice. He founded ARD in 1946, with the express goal of exploiting the discoveries developed in New England's universities and research laboratories, which otherwise might languish for lack of capital. In this effort, he was joined by Vermont senator Ralph Flanders and MIT president Karl Compton, who supported the effort during its formative years.

Even before making the fund's first investment, Doriot laid out the template that venture investors have followed in large part to this day. First, he prioritized investing in forward-thinking companies focused on science and engineering. Doriot explained, "ARD does not invest in the ordinary sense. Rather, it creates by taking calculated risks in selected companies in whose growth it believes."[4] The word *selected* was a critical one: ARD funded only one out of every twenty-five proposals it received.

Second, Doriot emphasized the importance of the fund structure. Rather than pooling funds on a deal-by-deal basis, he sought to create a pool from which he could draw down funds as opportunities presented themselves. In this way, he could decide quickly, without second-guessing the worthiness of perceived opportunities.

It is worth emphasizing how much of a departure Doriot's conception of an equity fund to finance and govern companies was from the received wisdom. Immediately prior to the war, the New England Council, an assemblage of local business leaders, had appointed a committee to explore how financing young companies could offset the job losses associated with the departure of shoe-making and textiles to the South. The elders had recommended a revolving fund that was very different from venture capital:

> Funds to provide for further research in the small percentage of cases where competent opinion considers it warranted, for pilot production, for prosecution of patents, and the final commercialization through sale or licensing and, in rare instances, perhaps through the organization of a company, are necessary. . . . If such a fund could be created, it might, through administration by trustees, be utilized for carrying approved projects through the sequence of research, experimental production and finally, commercialization. It should be considered that this fund offers a source of permanent capital, but that it would be replenished through profits received from license fees or the sale of the product or process outright to an existing manufacturer.[5]

Yet despite the acuity and clarity of Doriot's vision, ARD struggled in its first decade. After the $500,000 it had raised from its initial backers, additional funding had been slow to come by. Its profile as a non-dividend-paying entity with losses stretching out for the foreseeable future did not excite many institutions. Moreover, the frequent articles about ARD's social goals of promoting economic development and entrepreneurship raised concerns among investors that financial returns were second-order. Early on, a decision was made to raise money by taking ARD public, when many of the seemingly natural investors, such as Harvard's endowment, State Street Bank, and numerous Boston-area insurers, declined to invest. Even then, no investment bank was willing to underwrite the offering, and it was largely sold off in small blocks to retail investors on a "best efforts" basis. In the initial public offering, the fund only raised $3.5 million, short of the $5 million goal. Moreover, the offering was heavily hyped by the brokers ARD had hired.

The reality was (predictably) different. A number of companies went bankrupt, such as Island Packers, a tuna fish–packing company. Others, like Tracerlab, which manufactured radiation detectors, eventually proved successful but were slow to move to profitability. Major shareholders, such as MIT, liquidated their stakes. Over time, the firm gained a better sense of which sectors were conducive to venture activity, with a move to earlier-stage firms and ones more dependent on novel technologies. But while the team refined its investment model, the lack of early success was inconsistent with the initial promises during the stock sales. During the course of the 1950s, Doriot spent much of his time personally dealing with disillusioned investors in the face of portfolio companies suffering from operational troubles and market turbulence. More generally, as the initial postwar wave of enthusiasm for venture capital cooled, ARD struggled to maintain interest in the entity.

Doriot attributed his struggles to the short-term nature of investors: "Bankers, investors, brokers, etc. generally speaking... have come to the conclusion that creative venture capital was a fanciful idea of the past which should be mostly discarded on account of the fact that it cannot be made to pay very quickly."[6] But Doriot did not help his cause with numerous pronouncements suggesting that financial considerations were far from paramount. One example was his 1967 statement, "We are really doctors of childhood diseases here. When bankers or brokers tell me I should sell an ailing company I ask them, 'would you sell a child running a temperature of 104?'"[7] The experience of "zombie" firms like Ionics raised the question of whether the evergreen structure that characterized the ARD fund was appropriate. Once the capital was raised, ARD had no obligation to ever return the capital, and could keep on investing until the firm ran out of money or was acquired. As Spencer Ante succinctly explains, "Much of Wall Street still viewed ARD as a freak philanthropic enterprise dreamed up by a strange mélange of Harvard professors and State Street financiers."[8]

ARD's structure as a closed-end investment fund also proved problematic. In addition to the pressures from investors to generate steady streams of cash, which was inconsistent with the underlying nature of the investments, other issues emerged. For much of its life span, ARD traded at a discount to its net asset value (not uncommon for publicly traded closed-end funds), which was a distraction to management.

But despite these limitations, ARD proved to be a savvy investor. ARD's annualized return from 1946 to 1971 was 14.7% per annum, significantly above the compound return of 12.8% for the Dow Jones Industrial Average for the same period.[9] Consistent with the feast-or-famine nature of venture capital ever since, the bulk of the return was driven by an investment of $70,000 in Digital Equipment Corporation (DEC) in 1957, in exchange for 70% ownership of the company. The minicomputer manufacturer experienced explosive growth in the ensuing years, and this single investment sealed ARD's legacy. By the time of ARD's final distribution to its investors in 1971, the investment had created gains of $355 million for the investors.

ARD's validation of the success of a venture capital firm, however, contained the seeds of its own destruction. Its triumph generated numerous competitors. These included the government-backed Small Business Investment Companies (SBICs) established in 1958, many of which featured inexperienced but cash-rich investment teams. More formidable were the early investment partnerships that soon followed.

As these new firms proliferated, other weaknesses of ARD's status as a publicly traded entity became apparent. The Securities Act of 1940 prohibited investment managers at publicly traded funds from taking equity stakes or receiving options in either their investment company or their portfolio companies. These limits on incentive-based compensation resulted in staff defections. These became particularly acute as the amount of wealth created by the DEC deal became apparent to the team.

Not only did competing funds siphon off many of the most promising team members, but they also had more investment flexibility. ARD was forced to frequently use debt or debt-like instruments to ensure a steady cash flow to satisfy investors. As alternative financing options proliferated, ARD's deal structures were rejected by a number of entrepreneurs, who (reasonably) believed that all their cash flow should go into advancing the growth of the business.

ARD was never able to overcome the limitations engendered by its structure. The combination of staff defections, increased competition for investments, and ARD's inability to restructure itself proved overwhelming. Ultimately, Doriot sold the company to the manufacturing conglomerate Textron in 1972, and ARD soon ceased to be a factor in the venture industry.

CREATING THE FUND MODEL

The first venture capital limited partnership—Draper, Gaither & Anderson—was formed in 1958. Imitators soon followed, but limited partnerships accounted for a minority of the venture pool during the 1960s and 1970s. Most venture organizations raised money either through closed-end public pools (like ARD) or the federally guaranteed SBICs that proliferated during the 1960s. And while the market for SBICs in the late 1960s and early 1970s was strong, incentive problems ultimately led to the collapse of the sector. As a result, the annual flow of money into private capital during its first three decades never exceeded a few hundred million dollars and usually was substantially less. During these years, while a few funds made a considerable number of investments in buyouts, real estate, and distressed situations, private capital organizations were universally referred to as venture capital funds.

General William Draper, a long-serving military officer and occasional industrialist, founded Draper, Gaither & Anderson (DGA) in 1958 along with Rand Corporation founder Rowan Gaither and Air Force general Frederick Anderson.[10] DGA was notable for its location (it was one of the pioneering firms in Silicon Valley) but particularly for its structure. With a small number of private backers—of its $6 million fund, the venerable investment bank Lazard Frères contributed $1.5 million and the Rockefellers and two other leading families nearly as much—it eschewed the publicly traded structure of earlier funds. Rather, it adopted the model that would become standard in the industry, the limited partnership.

In making this choice, the partners were swayed by the difficulties that Doriot had faced with ARD: for much of ARD's first fifteen years, Doriot had struggled to raise capital. While much of this dissatisfaction may have reflected the naiveté of inexperienced investors, even knowledgeable investors criticized ARD's tendency to stick with troubled firms too long.

The limited partnership structure that DGA introduced to the venture capital industry addressed several concerns. By raising funds up front, the venture capitalist firm received all the money it needed for the life of the fund. There would be no need to go "back to the well" every year or two for another tranche of capital, as Doriot had been required to do. (To be precise, investors in venture capital limited partnerships are not typically required to put in all the capital that they commit to the fund up front. Rather, they promise the funds, and then the general partners draw down the capital as needed.)

Moreover, the new firm's founders felt that the ARD structure had brought about excessively conservative thinking. As Pete Bancroft, one of the junior investment professionals at DGA, noted of their predecessors, "They did not dare as greatly or as well."[11] Much of this could be attributed to the compensation scheme at the Boston firm: everyone, including Doriot, received a salary—there was no explicit link of compensation to performance. Instead, at DGA, not only were the partners major investors (contributing $700,000 of the capital, or more than 10% of the funds), but they also got a significant profit share. In particular, the DGA partners received 40% of the capital gains (well above the 20% to 30% standard in the industry today), in addition to their proportionate share of the amount going to the limited partners.

But at the same time, there were advantages of the new structure for the limited partners. The venture capitalists only raised funds for a set period, typically seven to ten years, with the possibility of an extension for a few more. This stipulation provided a distinct time limit for the venture capitalists' activity: there would be no nurturing sick firms indefinitely. Moreover, the investors had the assurance that, ultimately, they would get back whatever money remained. While it would be very hard to dislodge the manager of an evergreen fund like ARD without an expensive battle for control of the board, limited partnerships simply wind up. Unless a venture firm can convince investors to ante up for a new fund, they will go out of business.

The partnership structure also addressed investors' concerns by drawing a sharp line between the limited and general partner. The limited partners were limited in the sense that their liability was capped by the amount they invested. For instance, if the fund invested in a biotechnology company whose drug unfortunately ended up killing several people during a clinical trial, the general partners running the fund might face many millions of dollars of claims for damages,[12] but the investors would not. This was important to many investors, as an investor putting a few million dollars into a venture fund does not want to have to worry about the risk of losing many millions more if something goes wrong with a high-risk investment.

At the same time, the fact that the general partner needed to return to the limited partner for funds meant that the institutional and individual investors who provided the capital could have a lot of power. Bill Draper, General Draper's son and the eventual founder of Sutter Hill and a number of other venture groups, related how, while working for his father at DGA, they were approached about investing in the first condominium development in Hawaii.[13] The investment appeared to be highly promising. But midway through the due diligence process, Draper was summoned to Rockefeller Center, and dressed down by one of the family office's partners for investing outside of their promised mandate and expertise. He was told in no uncertain terms that the Rockefellers could access such investments through much more knowledgeable, real estate–focused intermediaries. As a result, they were forced to turn down the investment, which ultimately provided a higher return than any of the deals in DGA's portfolio.

Ultimately, Draper and his colleagues had limited success, and the fund undertook its final distribution to its limited partners in 1966. But in the years between Draper, Gaither & Anderson's inception and its dissolution, the limited partnership had been demonstrated to be a powerful way to invest venture capital. Two of the most successful groups launched in these years were Greylock (which we discuss in chapter 7) and Davis & Rock (Rock would go on to fund, among other firms, Apple, Intel, and Scientific Data Systems, venture capital's first billion-dollar exit, while Davis would go on to found the Mayfield Funds, which continues to be a leading venture group to this day).

Undoubtedly, the creation of the venture capital limited partnership represented the fund's most important legacy, which addressed many of the drawbacks of publicly traded closed-end funds such as ARD. But limited partnerships also posed issues of their own, as subsequent fund managers discovered—among them that these partnerships too could be swayed by the whims of investment fashion.

THE BROADENING OF PRIVATE CAPITAL

Activity in the private capital industry increased dramatically in the late 1970s and early 1980s. Industry observers attributed much of the shift to the US Department of Labor's clarification of the Employee Retirement Income Security Act's "prudent man rule" in 1979. Prior to this year, the legislation seemingly limited the ability of pension funds to invest substantial amounts of money into venture capital or other high-risk asset classes, and pension fund managers consequentially shied away from these funds. The Department of Labor's clarification of the rule explicitly allowed pension managers to invest in high-risk assets, including private capital. Numerous specialized funds—concentrating in areas such as leveraged buyouts, mezzanine transactions, and such hybrids as venture leasing—sprang up during the years following the rule clarification.

The subsequent years saw both very good and trying times for private capital investors. With the limited number of funds and investors, the structure of the deals was shaped by supply-and-demand conditions. A sudden increase in demand for private capital investing services in the early 1980s increased the bargaining power of the fund managers, allowing them to enter into agreements with more freedom and also with higher levels of fees. The fund managers were definitely in the driver's seat.

That said, the 1980s saw venture capitalists back many of the most successful high-technology companies, including Cisco Systems, Genentech, Microsoft, and Sun Microsystems. Numerous successful buyouts—such as Avis, Beatrice, Dr Pepper, Gibson Greetings, and McCall Pattern—garnered considerable public attention during that period. At the same time, commitments to the private capital industry during this decade were very uneven. The annual flow of money into venture capital funds increased by a factor of ten during the first half of the 1980s but steadily declined from 1987 through 1991. Buyouts underwent an even more dramatic rise through the 1980s, followed by a precipitous fall at the end of the decade.

Much of this pattern was driven by the changing returns from these investments. Returns on venture capital funds had declined sharply in the mid-1980s after being exceedingly attractive in earlier years. This fall was apparently triggered by overinvestment in a few industries, such as "Winchester" computer disk drives, and the entry of many inexperienced venture capitalists. Buyout returns underwent a similar decline in the late 1980s, due in large part to the increased competition between groups for transactions. As investors became disappointed with returns, they committed less capital to the industry.

The dynamics of the private capital business during this period were perhaps best captured by Kohlberg Kravis Roberts & Co. (KKR), which captured the power—and the potential pitfalls—of the private capital model like no group before.[14] Although the term *leveraged buyout* may have been new, the transactions that KKR championed were not. Some point to J. P. Morgan's assemblage of the International Mercantile Marine Company in the early days of the twentieth century as the pioneering buyout, an effort that floundered on debt and the decline of world trade around World War I.[15] Others highlight Henry Ford's debt-fueled "take private" of his eponymous automaker in the late 1910s.[16] In any case, by the 1960s, it had become commonplace for publicly traded holding companies to be used to undertake leveraged acquisitions. While some of the pioneers of these transactions are still active today (for instance, Berkshire Hathaway and Onex Corporation), many more, such as Victor Posner's DWG Corporation and Malcolm McLean's McLean Industries, are largely forgotten.

The vast majority of buyouts in the years before KKR's formation were far less glamorous affairs than the Ford or Morgan transactions, often involving small family businesses that were undergoing generational transformations. Small investor groups would purchase shares of the business, often with a small slice of their own equity and the remainder borrowed from banks and insurers. When the business was later sold at a premium, the heavy leverage would mean that the profits of the equity-holders were multiplied manyfold.

KKR grew out of the activities of Jerry Kohlberg on the Bear Stearns trading desk, beginning with Stern Metals in 1965. Joined by George Roberts in 1969 and Henry Kravis shortly thereafter, they undertook transactions using the investment bank's capital. The marriage of this activity and investment banking was an uneasy one (as many subsequent deal-doers would discover). Not only was the time frame of these transactions very different from those typically pursued on the trading floor, but they required an increasing amount of the banking partnership's capital, which became a source of tension once the market slumped in 1973. These tensions—along with personality clashes—led the three to depart in 1976 to begin their own firm.

Starting with the $26 million buyout of A. J. Industries, the partners began pursuing transactions. Before long, the firm was bagging much larger game. The 1979 buyout of Houdaille Industries was a $380 million transaction that was financed with a mere $25 million of equity (most of which came from coinvestors and management, given the small size of the 1976 fund).[17] This transaction set KKR on the route to ever larger and more audacious deals over the next decade.

One of the critical innovations by KKR was coupling buyouts with the limited partnership structure that had primarily been used by venture funds to date. Beginning with the $31 million 1976 fund, KKR raised progressively larger pools of capital. Several set records for the largest pools of capital raised to date, including the $357 million 1980 fund, the $1 billion 1984 fund, and the $6.1 billion 1986 fund. This sharply distinguished KKR from many of its predecessors, who had to assemble the equity for these transactions on a deal-by-deal basis or rely on the good humor of the financial institutions that employed them. (Of course, given the extraordinarily leveraged nature of the 1980s deals, plenty of attention was devoted to relationships with the banks.) It also allowed the firm to invest in building a real institution, with a distinct culture and worldview.

Like many financial entrepreneurs, the success of Kohlberg, Kravis, and Roberts was in part due to the skills of the team but also to being in the right place at the right time—because these years coincided with two major realizations by American business.

The first of these was that the conglomerate model, which had proliferated during the "go-go" 1960s, was deeply flawed. In many cases, the companies consisted of a loose confederation of entities with too many lines of business to be effectively overseen. Corporate managements, which often owned little equity in the entity, appeared more concerned about their own compensation and perks than the returns to investors. Meanwhile, the boards were frequently "toothless tigers": the directors frequently had little personal financial stake in the firm's success but were anxious not to endanger their own sinecures by asking too many probing questions. Private equity investors could thus create value by carving off underperforming divisions. The combination of a more readily managed, focused business, intense monitoring by equity owners who dominated the board, and the provision of generous option grants to management could affect dramatic transformations.

The second of these realizations related to the power of leverage. As a long-lingering consequence of the Great Depression, many US corporations had eschewed the extensive use of debt. KKR and its peers argued that this conservative approach was problematic. Not only was debt financing cheaper than equity, due to the tax deductibility of interest, but it had additional benefits. Foremost among these was the way in which leverage could create pressure for change in a way that no amount of pounding on the boardroom table could. In particular, the required interest and principal repayments would vacuum up what financial economists termed *free cash flow* that otherwise might go to pet projects or corporate jets. Moreover, the debt amplified the returns to the equity investors (although also amplifying its risk).

Of course, if the business lost value, the equity-holders—and perhaps some of the debt-holders—could be wiped out. Indeed, while KKR's first funds generated very attractive returns—the first six funds generated returns of 24% after fees and carry—many of the first funds were characterized by one transaction in which the entirety of the firm's equity was lost. These failed transactions also had wrenching impacts on the stakeholders. (While a thorough discussion of the extensive literature of the effects of private equity on the companies they back would take us too far afield, we have written extensively on these issues elsewhere.[18])

As with their venture capital predecessors, KKR and its pioneering peers were victims of their own success: their spectacular performance in the late 1970s and early 1980s attracted ever more capital to the industry and spurred many imitators. As a result, not only did the investors pay increasingly more for transactions, but the intensity of the competition led to heavily indebted balance sheets with little room for error.

There was no more dramatic illustration of this than RJR Nabisco. Clearly, this was a firm with plenty of fat to trim: the country club memberships for executives, the fleet of corporate jets, and a (could-be) team of athletes on six- and seven-figure retainers stand out. But control of the firm turned into a battle royal between virtually all the major buyout groups of the day, as well as RJR's own management. It was as far from the "proprietary deal" that groups like to boast about as can be imagined.

Without wading into the discussion of whether the $31.4 billion transaction could be justified at the time, it is clear that the deal soon encountered difficulties. In part, this can be attributed to the collapse in the junk bond market triggered by the troubles of Drexel Burnham Lambert, which prompted an upward revision of interest rates and greatly exacerbated the financial pressures associated with its indebtedness. In addition to the sheer amount of debt that RJR had assumed, the number and dueling agendas of the creditors posed grave issues. Ultimately, the buyout group undertook a complex series of restructurings that ultimately salvaged the equity invested in the deal (and a little more). And KKR itself went on to live another day, raising much more capital and doing many other transactions and initiatives.

KKR's experiences in its first fifteen years illustrate several key points. They showed how the limited partnership model employed by General Draper, Arthur Rock, and their peers could be adapted to very different kinds of investments. They also highlighted the way in which the partnership model could scale to accommodate much larger and more complex transactions. At the same time, their experiences in those years illustrated in a particularly dramatic form—though neither for the first nor the last time—the way in which private markets seemed particularly prone to booms and the consequent disruptive busts.

PREMATURE EXPANSION

The boom and bust of the 1980s was repeated in the 1990s on an unprecedented scale. Much of the decade saw dramatic growth and excellent returns in almost every part of the private capital industry. This recovery was triggered by several factors. First, the industry stabilized following the exit of many inexperienced investors at the beginning of the decade, ensuring that the remaining groups faced less competition for transactions. The healthy market for initial public offerings during much of the decade meant that it was easier for all investors to exit private transactions. Meanwhile, the extent of technological innovation—particularly in information technology–related industries—created extraordinary opportunities for venture capitalists. New capital commitments to both venture and buyout funds rose in response to these changing circumstances, increasing to record levels by the late 1990s and 2000.

But as is often the case, the growth of private capital increased at a pace that could not be sustained. Institutional and individual investors—attracted especially by the tremendously high returns enjoyed by venture funds—flooded money into the industry. In many cases, funds grew rapidly in size. In other cases, venture groups that should not have raised capital at all succeeded in garnering considerable funds. Excessive growth led to overstretched partners, inadequate due diligence, and, in many cases, poor investment decisions.

One clear example of the dangers of overreaching was the experience of 3i.[19] The oldest private capital group in Europe, 3i stood out from its peers along several dimensions. It had been founded in 1945 by the UK government and funded by a consortium of banks to provide capital for small- and medium-sized businesses in the post–World War II rebuilding effort. 3i initially used both debt and equity to fulfill its mandate, and expanded into far-flung product lines like consulting, securities underwriting, and ship financing. Over time, it became a more traditional private equity group, focusing on buyouts and growth capital and shedding many of its ancillary activities. It also expanded its footprint into continental Europe and elsewhere. These efforts yielded some real successes, including investments in Bond Helicopters, Caledonian Airways (later British Caledonian), and Oxford Instruments, the pioneer of magnetic resonance imaging.

In July 1994, 3i made a transition that was virtually unheard of in Europe at the time: the firm went public on the London Stock Exchange. In this way, the banks could unwind their shares and 3i could attract a new investor base. The offering was initially seen as a success: by September of that year, 3i's market cap had risen enough that it was included in the FTSE-100 market index of leading British firms.

As the decade progressed, however, 3i's management became increasingly frustrated with its perception and valuation in the market. The market viewed the firm as, in the words of one observer, more of a "quaint throwback than a go-ahead investor."[20] As the technology market had soared, 3i appeared to be left behind: its stock price had increased by only 39% between the beginning of 1996 and 1999, even as the tech-heavy NASDAQ had more than doubled and even the staid FT-100 firms had gone up by nearly 50%.[21]

At the behest of Brian Larcombe, who became 3i's CEO in 1997, the firm sought to address the market perception. Beginning in 1999, the investment company began aggressively moving into early-stage investments. 3i increased its pace of start-up investments tenfold in three years, and directed much of its later-stage investments from its traditional transactions involving mature firms to follow-on investments in technology companies. Meanwhile, in 1999 it opened offices in Silicon Valley and Boston to increase its exposure to early-stage deals there. The result was undoubtedly successful—in the short run. Its stock price nearly tripled between January 1, 1999, and mid-2000, breaking the thousand-pence mark in August 2000. The *Boston Globe* even dubbed it "the biggest venture firm you've never heard of."[22]

But dark clouds were gathering. In March 2000, the market for new offerings of technology companies—and the valuation of those firms that were traded—began collapsing. Many seasoned venture capitalists, having been through such market cycles before, began pulling back from new investments, instead focusing on nurturing the existing companies in their portfolio. Meanwhile, 3i, convinced it was giving the market what it wanted, plunged ahead. In mid-April 2000, it launched a £400 million (about $600 million at the time) European technology fund quoted on the London Stock Exchange. Its investments in start-up firms actually peaked in the fiscal year ending March 31, 2001, a year in which technology stocks (and venture returns) had been in a virtually continuous state of decline. Even as late as May 2001, the firm expressed its desire to keep investing at least half its new capital in the technology sector. Larcombe professed, "This is not a time to be shy of making new investments—I have little doubt that the fastest growing businesses will continue to be technology companies."[23]

By the end of 2001, however, the optimistic tone was gone at 3i. The extent of the folly was apparent. The firm reported a loss of almost £1 billion for the fiscal year ending March 31, 2002 (at the time, $1.5 billion), driven by the poor performance of its technology portfolio. Needless to say, its stock price plummeted as well, falling below £3 by the first quarter of 2003 from its peak of nearly £18 in September 2000: it had given back all the gains from the giddy years of 1999 and 2000, and was trading below where it was at the beginning of 1996. The firm responded by dramatically curtailing its new technology investments, laying off 17% of its staff, and entering a "triage" process to salvage its portfolio.

In 2004, the venture capital group, which accounted for as much as 50% of the firm's investment value at the peak of the bubble, was still recovering from the 2001 crash. Lacombe retired as CEO, and Phillip Yea took over. One of Yea's first priorities was to increase the selectivity of the venture business line while working down the size of the portfolio. Managing partner Rod Perry cut back venture investments and closed numerous offices and sector groups. The team also cut the portfolio of four hundred companies to a hundred and reduced its staff by 75%. Philip Yea explained, "Early-stage has not been an easy place. It is a natural evolution, because there is more value for us in later-stage companies internationally and that is what we have been doing more and more."[24]

But the biggest cost to the firm may have been the distraction in the ensuing years posed by this troubled portfolio. The process of working out the portfolio of doomed technology companies proved to be a tortuous one: it was not until 2008–2009 that it closed down its Silicon Valley office and sold its remaining holdings to a consortium of secondary funds. While management struggled with these issues through the early and mid-2000s, opportunities abounded in 3i's traditional market: equity investments in mid-sized European firms. 3i's later-stage funds showed attractive returns during this period, but younger rivals such as Montagu and Permira had superior returns and more rapid growth. It is hard not to feel that the distraction of dealing with the portfolio of troubled technology investments—brought about by a desire to please the public markets—led to 3i not being able to fully take advantage of the opportunities when conditions in its core markets were best.

While 3i was one of the pioneers in turning to public markets, and did a strategic detour of epic proportions, it was certainly not unique. Numerous other groups would seek to raise capital in subsequent years from public sources, first in the late 1990s and then again beginning in the middle of the next decade. Even more ubiquitous were efforts by groups to expand across asset classes, geographies, and transaction sizes. Few of these groups, it is true, rivaled 3i in the audacity and the futility of their expansion efforts. But there were certainly numerous disappointments and mixed outcomes alongside the successes. Many of the problem cases had much the same drivers as 3i's, such as a desire to provide the "flavor of the moment" to investors (whether or not it fit the group's skill set well) and the absence of careful strategic planning about what would be required for success.

Although overshadowed by the venture capital boom, the 1990s also saw innovation in the types of private capital raised. The most important of these was the rise of real estate private equity.[25] While institutions and families had long invested in real estate, many of these deals were done through direct transactions or publicly traded real estate investment trusts. Many credit Sam Zell with forming the first real estate private equity fund, Zell-Merrill I, which was raised in 1988. In establishing this fund, modeled directly after venture and buyout funds, Zell was motivated by the excessively leveraged transactions that characterized the deals of the day. He correctly anticipated that there would be ample chances for an "opportunistic" fund that could swoop in and buy distressed properties once the market collapsed.

Keeping with the adage that success breeds imitation, Zell was soon joined by others, first by Goldman Sachs and the Whitehall funds, and then by a plethora of others. These included dedicated groups (for instance, AEW, Colony, Lone Star, and Starwood), investment bank affiliated funds (CSFB and Lehman soon joined Goldman in sponsoring funds), and buyout groups that crossed over to offer products (Angelo Gordon Apollo, Blackstone, and Cerberus, to name a few).

THE SCALING OF PRIVATE CAPITAL

The first years of the twenty-first century saw the emergence of "financial supermarkets" for institutional investors that offered wide ranges of alternative investment products. Private capital funds, while in the business of funding innovations of many kinds, had been remarkably steadfast in retaining their structure since the mid-1960s. In recent years, however, a flurry of experimentation has taken hold in the industry, as firms try to resolve the question of structure and scale. Among the changes have been the establishment of affiliate offices and entire funds in different regions, and the expansion of the offerings of buyout firms to include real estate, mezzanine, distressed debt, and bond funds.

The increased diversity of the types of funds being raised was an innovation in itself. One dramatic example was in real estate private equity, which, as we mentioned, had been dominated in the 1990s by opportunistic funds that sought to buy distressed or deeply discounted assets. Over the course of the first decade of the 2000s, it became commonplace to see funds devoted to core assets, which featured safe properties with limited upside; value-added funds, which undertook development projects; and core-plus funds, which sat in between the two on the risk-reward spectrum.

These patterns were repeated elsewhere. For instance, trading in secondary interests in private funds (i.e., stakes in already seasoned funds), hitherto a modest backwater, exploded as both existing firms and new entrants raised substantial capital. Similarly, the volume of capital devoted to funds investing in natural resources, such as farmland and timber, expanded dramatically. In addition, the decade saw the creation of new categories. In perhaps the most striking examples, funds that employed the standard private capital structure to invest in infrastructure (with some modifications) were introduced by the Australian bank Macquarie in the first days of the new millennium. Again the category soon attracted other players, such as Alinda Capital Partners and Global Infrastructure Partners.

The expansions in firm scope were accompanied by increases in the amount and types of private capital raised. Most dramatic was the buyout sector, which underwent a tremendous boom in activity between 2004 and 2007. Fueled by the increased appetite of institutional investors for alternative investments, a greater willingness of boards of directors and managers to sell to private capital groups, and—last but not least—a wave of debt on generous terms and with few protective covenants, the industry experienced explosive growth. As in many earlier booms, as the influx in capital continued, valuations rose, and standards for undertaking deals in many cases fell. It was not surprising to industry observers, then, that the financial crisis of 2007–2008 triggered a major downturn in the market. What was more surprising was the speed of recovery: by the early 2010s, many of the troubled investments had been restructured, and a considerable number of transactions were being exited through secondary buyouts or initial public offerings. Collateralized loan obligations (or CLOs) and covenant-lite lending had returned with a vengeance.

So, what explains the sudden changes in the structure of private capital groups in the twenty-first century? We believe that this reflected a more fundamental shift in the industry, as groups struggled to address the increasing efficiency of the markets in which they invested. Facing increased competition, they sought new ways to differentiate themselves.

Evidence of the increased efficiency of these markets can be seen in many places. While private capital for much of its first decades had the flavor of a cottage industry, with a considerable number of relatively small firms working alongside one another, today it is much more competitive.

Given this changed competitive environment, the leading firms are increasingly seeking to differentiate themselves from the mass of other investors. They are employing a variety of tools to build up and distinguish their "brands" from their competitors. These steps include the strategic partnerships, international operations, provision of additional services, and aggressive fund-raising described above, as well as many other initiatives to extend their visibility in the US and abroad. (Of course, these steps by themselves are no substitute for the ability to build better companies and to generate superior investment returns!)

To be sure, private capital is not unique in this transformation. For instance, the investment banking industry, the financial supermarket for corporations, had undergone a similar transformation several years earlier, as the leading "bulge bracket" firms solidified their leadership positions. The gap between the leading banks and the following ones greatly increased in the 1970s, as the leading groups enhanced their range of activities and boosted their hiring of personnel. Similarly, the management of the major banks was transformed during these years, as procedures were systematized and management structures formalized.

Undoubtedly, the firm that has encapsulated this trend is the Blackstone Group.[26] The Blackstone Group was founded in 1985 by Stephen Schwarzman and Peter Peterson following their departures from Lehman Brothers. "The story of Blackstone was really the story of the failure of Lehman," said J. Tomilson Hill, vice chairman, president, and CEO of Blackstone's approximately $68 billion hedge funds business, who joined the firm in 1993.[27] Previously, Peterson had been chairman and co-CEO of Lehman, chairman and CEO of Bell and Howell Corporation, and secretary of commerce for the Nixon administration. Schwarzman had been global head of Lehman's mergers and acquisitions (M&A) practice.

As a way to get started and generate revenue, the founders looked to build an M&A advisory business with a more entrepreneurial spirit and with a different culture than Lehman's. Each put up $200,000, and they opened Blackstone's first office on Park Avenue in New York City in the autumn of 1985. In 1987, Schwarzman decided it was time to augment Blackstone's M&A advisory business by raising a $1 billion leveraged buyout fund. Neither Schwarzman nor Peterson had experience on the principal side of buyouts. Their first few marketing pitches, including those to the Massachusetts Institute of Technology endowment board and the Delta Airlines pension fund, failed. Finally, Peterson secured a meeting with the chief investment officer at Prudential Insurance, with whom he had a good relationship from previous dealings. Prudential committed $100 million to the fund, becoming the lead investor, and was followed by the Mitsubishi Industrial Group, General Electric, General Motors, and others. Soon Blackstone had raised $635 million, closing the fund-raising round the day before the stock market crash of 1987. By 1988, the fund had grown to $850 million, the largest first-time fund at the time.

In 1989, Blackstone made its first deal, a $640 million buyout for the transportation subsidiaries of USX, U.S. Steel's parent company (later Transtar). Blackstone invested $13.4 million of its own capital, acquiring a 51% stake in the new company, improving operations, and weathering economic cycles over the fifteen-year course of the investment. When

Blackstone exited in 2003, the deal had earned their investors twenty-five times their investment. "It was the best single deal ever done at the firm," said Hill. "It proved the point that if you had relationships and were clever, you could turn lemons into lemonade."[28] Other early deals included a buyout of the railroad company Chicago and Northwestern (CNW) in 1989 for $1.6 billion; a $177 million acquisition of Great Lakes Dredge and Dock Company in 1991; and the purchase of Union Carbide and Mitsubishi's joint venture, UCAR, in 1994 for $1.2 billion, on which Blackstone earned 3.6 times its investment by its 1997 exit. Of course, not all early deals succeeded. In 1989, Blackstone's $122 million investment in Collins and Aikman and $330 million leveraged buyout of Edgcomb Metals Company both turned sour. Nevertheless, although some deals struggled, the firm generated solid returns overall.

Blackstone was among the first firms to focus on product line diversification. In 1990, Blackstone began expanding beyond private equity and advisory services, starting with a "fund of hedge funds" that began as a high-risk-adjusted return vehicle in liquid alternatives for the partners to invest their own money. Next came the launch of an opportunistic real estate fund in 1992 that blossomed under the leadership of Jon Gray, an alternative credit business in 1999, the opening of a European office in 2000, the launching of senior debt funds in 2002, a proprietary hedge fund in 2005, an Asian office in 2006, the acquisition of GSO—an alternative asset manager specializing in credit products—in 2008; the list goes on and on. From its humble roots thirty years ago as a two-person M&A boutique, Blackstone became the most diversified private equity firm, with $434 billion under management at the beginning of 2018, nearly two times larger than its biggest competitor.

Another key change in this century was a shift in ownership structure, with several large private equity firms becoming publicly traded entities. Once again, Blackstone was one of the earlier private capital groups to go public. In 2006, Schwarzman and Blackstone's president, Tony James, began discussing an initial public offering (IPO), which could bring an influx of capital as well as a liquid security for acquisitions and stock-based compensation. In addition, it would facilitate an orderly generational transition as Peterson exited the firm, providing him "a share of the value that he'd created in Blackstone without selling the firm," said Schwarzman.[29] The exposure brought on by an IPO could also help cement Blackstone's premium brand in the industry. But going public meant becoming subject to increased transparency and filing requirements, expanding corporate legal and compliance staff, and having to weather the volatility and changing tastes of the stock market.

A key attribute of the offering, they decided, had to be the publicly traded partnership (PTP) structure, which maintained much of Blackstone's existing governance and minimized interference with the firm's traditional way of operating. In addition to crafting the PTP to maintain the firm's culture and his own authority over operations, Schwarzman went so far as to warn public investors about his ultimate priorities: "We had a section of the prospectus titled: 'We Intend to Be a Different Kind of Public Company.' I wanted our new public investors to understand that we place the interests of our investment funds first, even if that adversely affects our near term results."[30] As Schwarzman's company hinted, and we discuss at length in chapter 6, the structure introduced a conflict: the limited partners naturally desire high returns while shareholders are likely to welcome more assets and fees, even if returns suffer to some extent. Nonetheless, in June 2007, the company sold 14% of the equity in the general partnership, raising $5 billion, the biggest IPO in the US in five years.

The future success of Blackstone is of course not guaranteed. We have seen many examples of investment groups that, after enjoying an extended run of success, go "off the rails" and encounter difficulties. In particular, generational succession, the surfeit of uninvested capital in many alternative investment areas, and increasing competition from institutions that want to "go it alone" can all be highlighted as challenges. But so far change has been smooth, including the replacement of James by Jon Gray as president and chief operating officer in February 2018, reflecting Blackstone's strong culture and shared approach to doing business.

FINAL THOUGHTS

We began by noting that the history of private capital could fill many volumes. These five snapshots of particular firms can neither do justice to the industry nor even to the firms themselves. That being acknowledged, the vignettes presented in this chapter highlight the challenges in finding an appropriate structure for private capital investing, the many strengths of the limited partnership model, the way in which the model has come to encompass many more types of companies and projects, and the increasing complexity of the investment groups themselves.

In the next chapter, we turn to looking more systematically at the challenges of the limited partnership model as currently practiced.

CHAPTER 6

The Fund Manager's Challenge

As we emphasized in chapter 5, the private capital partnership was created as a solution to the problems posed by the illiquid and highly uncertain nature of long-term investments. The deferral of much of the compensation, which is linked to performance, until the investments are realized helps alleviate the information problems in these settings.

But in many cases these partnerships do not work in the ways that the pioneering capital investors envisioned. A whole series of deleterious behaviors can creep in, as fund managers make decisions that reflect their own interests rather than those of their investors. In some cases, these distortions seem quite deliberate, where investors exploit the information gaps to make decisions that seem clearly wrong.

Consider the case of Mike Rothenberg.[1] Rothenberg founded his eponymous venture firm while still at Harvard Business School, from which he graduated in 2013. His concept was to undertake an alternative approach to venture capital, drawing on his network of buddies from his undergraduate days at Stanford, his business school classmates, and his globe-trotting friends to generate deal flow. Initially, the effort seemed to be working. Early investments included Revel, Robinhood, and SpaceX. With an investment style that featured quick decisions—sometimes after no more than an hour's conversation—Rothenberg built the fund's portfolio. Moreover, Rothenberg undoubtedly mastered the visionary (or perhaps we should say hype-ridden and overwrought argot) of Silicon Valley. He pitched his fund, for instance, as the combination of "the service-model approach of Andreessen

Horowitz, and the founder-first community building offline and online approach of First Round Capital, with the processing power and reach of Silicon Valley Angels, and the discretion of Floodgate and the judgment of Sequoia."[2]

Playing a not small part of the Rothenberg Ventures' hype was the founder's willingness to spend lavishly at a level only approached by rap stars, which earned him the title of "[Silicon] Valley's Party Animal." The firm had as many as sixty employees (including three personal assistants and a driver), many times those of its comparably sized peers. This was just the beginning: luxury boxes at San Francisco sports events, an annual party that entailed renting Giants Stadium, a Rothenberg Ventures–sponsored race car in Global Rallycross meets, a private jet club membership, and a Super Bowl suite (billed as essential for fund-raising).

Not surprisingly, whispers soon began surrounding the firm. Rothenberg was seen as hopelessly overcommitted, and more interested in hanging out with Hollywood royalty than in the grinding process of seeking out new investments. Staff members began complaining—and then suing—about unpaid wages and expenses. Media accounts raised questions on how a group that had raised less than $50 million could afford the extravagant spending it was undertaking.

And then came the federal investigators.[3] A number of the allegations surrounding Rothenberg related to the use of investors' funds, including undisclosed loans of the investment funds to the founder's personal bank accounts. But perhaps the most serious allegations revolved around a company that Rothenberg himself founded in 2015 called River Studios, whose primary accomplishments to date seemed to be shooting virtual reality videos for Björk and Coldplay. This company was funded by $5 million from Rothenberg Ventures—much larger than its typical $100,000 investment—but apparently investors were never informed that the fund was undertaking this transaction. According to the SEC's charges in late 2018, "over a three-year period, Rothenberg and his firm misappropriated millions of dollars from the funds, including an estimated $7 million of excess fees." Rothenberg Ventures settled the charges without confirming or denying the allegations.[4]

There are many other none-too-pretty stories where partnerships have gone wrong. In many cases, the root of the problems seems to be the very process of growth itself, or the failure of the firm to adjust as it grows. Mistaken judgments, overconfidence, and an inability to relinquish control can have equally devastating effects on a firm's success. Consider, for instance, the story of Forstmann Little.

Forstmann Little was one of the true private equity pioneers.[5] Founded in 1978, the very dawn of the modern buyout age, by Theodore (Ted) Forstmann, his younger brother Nick, and Brian Little, the firm did a number of early, highly successful transactions. For instance, in its 1984 acquisition of Dr Pepper, Forstmann Little's limited partners are said to have earned 8.5 times the original amount in under three years. These spectacular gains were achieved by cutting overhead, boosting marketing, selling off unrelated subsidiaries such as a textile company and a television station, and splitting off the bottling plants and the Canada Dry subsidiary. Ted Forstmann was a pioneer in raising a mezzanine fund to finance his deals, allowing them to close transactions faster, pay fewer fees, and consume less of Forstmann Little's equity.[6] Despite occasional setbacks associated with Forstmann's unwillingness to use high-yield debt—a decision that led to the loss of transactions such as Revlon, Duracell, and RJR Nabisco (although this last loss was probably for the best)—the firm prospered in its first two decades: until the late 1990s, Forstmann Little had annual returns rumored to be close to 60%. Investors flocked to the fund, as it expanded from its original $400,000 fund to $300 million in 1983 and a then record $2.7 billion in 1987.

The three partners were a study in opposites, with Ted the controlling visionary, Little the detailed financier, and Nick managing public relations, not only with investors but also with his abrasive brother. Ted needed to control all aspects of the deal, even to the point of precluding the firm's participation with others. As one journalist wrote about Ted, "He needed to be in charge of everything. Nor did he seem to have much appreciation for his partners: When it came to dealmaking, he liked to say, he was Picasso, and the others guys were holding the ladder."[7]

In the late 1990s, though, Forstmann Little shifted strategy. The partnership had changed with Little's retirement. A new partner, Erskine Bowles, had been recruited in Little's place. The firm had successfully exited the Gulfstream investment, but still had more than $3.6 billion to deploy.

At a time of a lot of media attention to telecommunications and software, Forstmann Little invested $2 billion in McLeod USA and XO Communications, both venture investments in areas in which Forstmann had little investment experience. In early 2001, Nick Forstmann died, Bowles left the firm, and the telecom bubble burst, leaving McLeod and XO on the brink of bankruptcy. The following year, the state of Connecticut sued Forstmann Little for breach of contract for investing in the two companies. After a long trial, Forstmann Little was convicted on violating details of their partnership agreement, but was not found liable for monetary damages. Forstmann decided not to raise another fund and instead managed out the last of the portfolio companies.

At its heart, we believe that Forstmann Little's troubles cannot be attributed to the kind of ethical issues that allegedly tripped up Mike Rothenberg. Rather, the pioneering firm stumbled on the difficulties faced by rapidly growing private capital groups that underinvest in building organizational structure and investment capabilities. Perhaps as a result of an inability to deploy the capital that it was raising in its traditional kind of transactions, the firm undertook an abrupt change of focus. The firm was leanly staffed, having not built up the kind of deep bench of investment professionals and industry practice areas that its rivals such as the Blackstone Group and Kohlberg Kravis Roberts were already constructing. As it moved into areas and deal types where it had little or no experience, it was uniquely vulnerable to the shock of the telecom bubble's bursting. What specific steps the firm could have taken to avoid its meltdown can be debated. It is clear, however, that Forstmann's personality was such that no strong second-in-command existed, either to help make decisions or to contest those that might have been ill advised.

In chapters 3 and 4, we saw that there were many obstacles that precluded family offices, pensions, and sovereign funds from successfully pursuing long-run investments. These two sobering stories suggest that private capital groups also face challenges, which we explore in this chapter. We highlight three sets of concerns: the design of incentives, the effects of increasing firm size, and the issues around generational succession. While important concerns are raised here, in the next chapter we address how they can be solved.

THE DESIGN OF INCENTIVES

The first concern for private capital groups has to do with the nature of the incentives offered by the private capital funds. Almost all private capital funds, whether focused on farmland or real estate, infrastructure or new ventures, employ a similar compensation scheme. An annual fee to the investment professionals is complemented with a share of the profits. Both the level and the nature of the rewards frequently raise concerns for investors.

The origin of the compensation schemes employed by private capital has been lost in the mists of history. Some have pointed to the contracts entered into by whaling crews and their backers in colonial Massachusetts. Others have traced back to the fourteenth century *commenda* contracts of the Genoese and Venetian trading families, or even further back to the Byzantine *cheokoinonia* or the Muslim *muqarada*.[8] Many of these earlier agreements established the principle that the providers of capital pay some sort of fee or salary over time to their partners who provide the labor, in addition to a share of the profits. In a surprisingly large number of cases, the split of the profits between capital and labor has been set at 80:20.

Whatever the origins, the structure that has emerged is frequently referred to as "two and twenty." The annual fee is frequently set at 2%, often calculated as a share of the total amount raised by the fund, though the percentage typically goes down (or the base on which the fees are calculated shrinks) as the fund reaches its final years. Larger groups may charge smaller amounts, as do those specializing in areas such as infrastructure.

The profit share, or carried interest, may be calculated in a myriad of different ways, but typically entails provision to the investment professionals of one-fifth of the proceeds after the capital invested has been returned to the investors, or else 20% of the profits from each deal as it is exited. The latter scheme allows the investment group to share in the profits sooner, but may create problems if some of the last companies end up being worth less than originally believed. In these cases, the investment partners may have received more than 20% of the profits and must repay the investors, termed a *clawback*. This process can be a little awkward if the money has already been spent and is currently in the wine cellar and the art collection! In many buyout funds, as well as those specializing in real assets, the profit sharing may not begin until the capital providers have gotten back not just their initial capital, but also some set return on that capital (often 8% per year).

So far, this may all seem reasonable. And indeed, for many smaller funds, this scheme appears to be a perfect way to focus the attention of the investment professionals on the task at hand. The expenses of running the firm—rent, travel to visit companies, an office manager, and modest salaries for the investment professionals—rapidly consume the management fee. In fact, for the smallest funds, it is often a struggle to make ends meet on the fee income. If there is to be any significant compensation for the partners, the carried interest is how it is attained. And this is paid out only if and when (or even after) the investors get their payout. Thus, this scheme achieves an alignment of incentives.

In larger funds, the story is very different. The fee income, rather than being sufficient to "keep the lights on" and little more, now becomes a major part of the story. This change reflects the extent of economies of scale in private equity. While it is more expensive to write a $1 billion check than a $1 million one, it is certainly not a thousand times more expensive. The transaction may get more exhaustive due diligence, the legal negotiations may be harder fought, and so forth, but at its heart the investment process is quite similar. And as we highlighted in the previous chapter, what was once an industry dominated by $20 million funds is now one where $20 billion funds (that is, funds that command $300 to $400 million in annual fees) are no longer extraordinary.

The extent to which new compensation schemes have changed the game is highlighted in an analysis by Andrew Metrick and Ayako Yasuda.[9] Working with a large investment consulting firm, they looked at 238 partnerships raised in the run-up to the financial crisis. These were among the largest venture capital and leveraged buyout partnerships raised during this period, with an average fund size of over $300 million and $1.2 billion, respectively. The authors collected the detailed information about the economic terms of these contracts. They then made a set of assumptions, based on historical data, about how quickly the funds were invested, the speed with which the holdings were sold, and the attractiveness of the resulting exits.

The modeling allowed Metrick and Yasuda to compute the ultimate returns to the investment professionals. In their most provocative analysis, they computed the payments per partner, reflecting the fact (as we discuss below) that the overwhelming majority of the economic gain in these funds goes to the partners. They expressed this amount as a net present value per partner per fund: essentially, a check showed up in the mailbox of each partner on the day the fund was established. (Of course, the funds actually trickle in over a period of a dozen years or so, with the exact amount received a function of the investment performance, but this is the expected amount in today's dollars.)

Their results, reproduced in table 6.1, are remarkable for two reasons. The first is the size of the overall compensation: $17 million and $33 million, respectively; numbers that are even more striking when one recalls that during this period, many of these groups were raising funds every two years. This line of the table alone would be enough to give Senator Bernie Sanders heartburn.

But even more disturbing—at least to our eyes—is the way in which they are earning these funds. The incentive compensation is present, with carry of $6.5 million and $10.1 million, respectively. But in each case, the carried interest represents only about one-third of the total compensation. The rest is in the form of fees, which the fund managers are going

TABLE 6.1. Average Payment per Partner per Fund, Based on 238 PE/VC Partnerships ($USD)

	Venture capital	Leveraged buyout
Carried interest	$6.5 million	$10.1 million
Management fees	$10.6 million	$18.5 million
Other fees	—	$4.1 million
Total	$17.1 million	$32.7 million

Source: Compiled by the authors from Metrick and Yasuda, "The Economics of Private Equity Funds" (see note 8).

to receive regardless of how well the fund does. Even in years where the private equity investments struggled, the partners were sure to be doing very well for themselves.

The analysis was focused on funds in what has been termed "the golden age of private equity": the years leading up to the financial crisis. But most analyses suggest that the postcrisis rate of adjustment in the economic terms of private capital partnerships has been modest. The share of profits accruing to the investment group (depicted in figure 6.1) remains 20% in most cases, just as it has been historically. And as figure 6.2 depicts, Preqin's annual survey found real estate management fees bunched at about 1.5%, levels very similar to those before the financial crisis. Meanwhile, private equity fees bunched around 2% for all but the largest ($2 billion plus) funds, which were around 1.5%. While there has been some modest downward movement of fees among the largest funds, the picture is one of stasis rather than disruption.

We must acknowledge that these figures are a simplification of a complex reality. On the one hand, as we noted in chapter 2 and explore in more depth in chapter 8, more and more asset owners are not paying the "list price" denoted in the partnership agreements. Instead, they bring down their average cost by coinvesting, structuring special investment vehicles, and the like.

On the other hand, desirable investment groups are increasingly adjusting less visible terms, which can substantially improve their economics. For instance, Advent Global Private Equity VIII, a $13 billion fund raised in 2016, featured a management fee of 1.5%, akin to their large

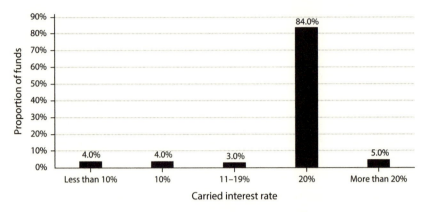

FIGURE 6.1. Carried interest rate used by direct private capital funds.
Source: Compiled by the authors from *2017 Preqin Global Private Equity & Venture Capital Report.*

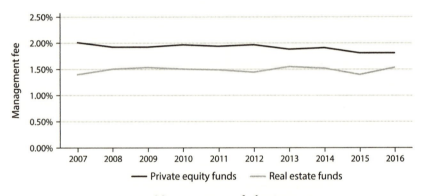

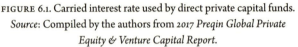

FIGURE 6.2. Mean management fee by vintage year.
Source: Compiled by the authors from *2017 Preqin Global Private Equity & Venture Capital Report.*

peers.[10] But they chose to abandon their 8% hurdle rate, the amount that their investors must receive in addition to their capital back before profits are shared with the general partners. While this shift has the effect of driving some investors away, others—attracted to Advent's strong performance in prior funds—stepped in. Similarly, in its seventh fund, European-based EQT altered the "waterfall," or the way in which profits were divided from that used in its 2011 fund, which ensured the partners were paid sooner.[11] This pattern is an age-old one: when times are good, private capital groups will adjust the terms, often in less visible ways, to favor themselves at the expense of their investors.[12]

Moreover, the fee calculations above actually understate the compensation the general partners receive. Historically, fund managers have also charged fees to the portfolio companies themselves. These fees have included, among others, charges for initiating the deals, for sitting on the boards, and for doing add-on transactions. Never mind that these activities might be thought to be covered already by the management fees that the investors are paying directly!

Most notorious have been the "accelerated monitoring fees." These charges kick in when groups have sold firms before an agreed-upon holding period (often as long as ten years). In these instances, the investment group gets what is truly "money for nothing": the fees they would have received for providing monitoring, had they held the firm for the entire period. It is as if LeBron James demanded that the Miami Heat continue to pay his salary, even after he had chosen to leave the team to play for the Cavaliers! In some cases, the groups did not disclose their practices clearly to their investors. Moreover, while partnership agreements often called for such fees to be rebated to the limited partners, in many cases, the rebates were not fully honored.

Consider, for instance, the case of Fenway Partners.[13] This group had encountered mixed investment success, and had announced its intention to wind down its third fund and not raise additional capital: in the industry argot, it was a zombie fund.[14] Shortly thereafter, in late 2011, the firm undertook a seemingly subtle shift. In particular, rather than having the private equity firm provide management services to its portfolio companies, such as offering advice and serving on the boards, it directed them instead to enter into consulting agreements with an entity called Fenway Consulting Partners LLC.

This change might have seemed benign, as the new entity was owned and run by the partners of Fenway. It involved the same people providing the same services to the firms in Fenway's portfolio in exchange for the same payment from the companies. But according to a US Securities and Exchange Commission (SEC) analysis, the catch lay in what happened to the funds. Under Fenway's agreement with its limited partners, it had to reimburse to its investors 80% of the payments that the fund received from its portfolio companies. But the funds received by the consulting company—almost $6 million over the course of 2012 and 2013—did not need to be shared in this manner. The full nature of the shift, and the implications for the limited partners, were not fully disclosed to the investors. Ultimately, the SEC settled with the partners in exchange for a $10 million payment.

It might be hoped that this was an oddball case, perhaps a consequence of the firm's zombie status. But as Andrew Bowdon, director of the SEC group responsible for enforcing these rules, noted: "When we have examined how fees and expenses are handled by advisers to private equity funds, we have identified what we believe are violations of law or material weaknesses in controls over 50% of the time. This is a remarkable statistic."[15]

It should be noted, however, that these practices are not universal. Important classes of private capital, such as venture capital funds, traditionally have not charged transaction fees. Even within private equity, the range of transaction and mentoring fees charged varies dramatically. An ingenious analysis by Ludo Phalippou, Christian Rauch, and Marc Umber sought to back out the fees charged by the leading buyout groups by examining the financial statements of the firms in their portfolio.[16] (Even though the fund managers historically have not disclosed these payments to their investors, companies that must undertake public securities filings while held by private equity often include information about the fees they paid in these documents.) They highlighted an enormous discrepancy across groups.

While the compensation of private capital professionals remains high relative to their peers managing, for instance, mutual funds and exchange-traded funds, it is natural to wonder whether the most problematic behaviors delineated above have been eradicated. Those inclined to view the glass as half empty argue that many of these abuses were not unearthed until the SEC was given fuller authority to review private capital funds as part of the Dodd-Frank Act, signed into law by President Obama in 2010. Whether these provisions will survive the Trump administration is unclear: the Financial Choice Act that passed the US House of Representatives in June 2017 proposed to eliminate these provisions, but the bill died on the Senate floor. As Dan Primack, private equity blogger extraordinaire, noted about an earlier Republican legislative effort:

> When private equity firms were first required by Dodd-Frank to register with the SEC, I wrote about my yawning ambivalence. . . . I actually believed that most private equity firms were complying with their own limited partnership agreements. Yup, smack me with the naiveté hammer. . . . In short, private equity registration has turned out to be a *very* big deal. . . . What is particularly troubling right now, of course, is that there are GOP-led (and PE industry-backed) congressional efforts to repeal private equity registration requirements. . . . Several years ago, I would have been on board with such repeal. After all, it was a misguided rule to begin with. But not today. The genie is out of the bottle, even if it isn't the genie we were expecting.[17]

A more optimistic industry observer would point to industry-led efforts to increase disclosure and transparency about compensation. In particular, the Institutional Limited Partners Association (the leading trade group of pensions and other long-run investors) in 2016 unveiled a template to track all fees flowing into private equity funds.[18] Numerous groups have indicated that they intend to employ it in their reporting, including Apollo, Blackstone, Carlyle, KKR, and TPG. If this standard is seriously and consistently adopted, it will go a long way to addressing concerns about disclosure.

The cynic might counter that this agreement was only obtained in the shadow of SEC enforcement. Moreover, investors have historically found it hard to coordinate with each other: their efforts to "hold the line" are frequently undermined by their burning desire to get into the hottest funds. The optimist might respond that, ultimately, this is an industry where the groups with the highest net returns are rewarded with more capital. Behavior that unfairly transfers wealth from the investors to the fund managers will lead to poorer returns and ultimately will be punished, whatever the regulatory regime in place. And so on!

As we have seen here, the level, composition, and disclosure of fees all pose substantial issues for the private capital industry. The one certainty is that the debate about fees and their role is not going away soon.

THE IMPACT OF GROWTH

A second challenge that private capital groups face is the siren call of growth. Growth has several potential benefits. But if executed poorly, the consequences can be quite devastating. This point has never been as important as it is today, when many limited partners are pouring money into alternative asset classes in hopes of undoing the damage of a decade of depressed returns.

Managers of funds have many reasons to welcome growth. In many cases, growth has consequences that benefit everyone associated with the fund. In others, the benefits are confined to the fund managers, who gain in the following areas:

- *Visibility.* In many market segments, there are a large number of private capital firms competing with one another. Investment groups struggle to stand out among the competition, and attract high-quality entrepreneurs, investors, and managers. A larger fund is likely to be a more high-profile one, with the kind of visibility that makes it easier to find quality partners.
- *Recruiting and retention.* The lifeblood of an investment group, like any service organization, is its people. And to renew the organization, the group needs to recruit and develop new people. Numerous funds that have eschewed growth find that young people, eager to make their mark, look elsewhere. Growth creates numerous opportunities for promotion, the promise of which can help attract the best and the brightest.

- *Fund-raising.* Investors are increasingly seeking to reduce the number of their private capital relationships. This trend has led to more money in fewer hands. For instance, $10 billion in aggregate commitments were made by TRS to KKR and Apollo, and the New Jersey Division of Investment committed $2.5 billion to Blackstone in what are termed "separately managed accounts."[19] Overall, about a quarter of the aggregate capital raised in 2016 went to the ten largest funds, and the average fund size reached a record $471 million, or 11.7% of the fund-raising pool, up from 10.7% in 2011. The share represented by the top thirty private equity funds over the same period went from 28.7% to 31.9%.[20] As a result, groups may find that staying the course in some cases is not a viable strategy. Their investors are moving up-market, and they must either join them or be left behind.

- *Compensation.* As the calculations we ran through above illustrate, being a senior partner at a major private capital fund is a recipe for the good life, at least financially speaking. Moreover, the compensation is largely independent of fund performance. A similar role at a small firm is much less economically compelling. Thus, there are powerful incentives for partners to steer their firm on a high-growth path.

Despite these apparent benefits, growth is frequently not beneficial to fund performance. The most immediate way to see this is in figure 6.3, which presents an analysis by Andrea Rossi of the relationship between the increase in fund size between two funds and the change of the funds' ultimate performance, based on all private capital funds in the Preqin universe.[21] The line is the predicted effect from a regression analysis: thus, it presents the central tendency across thousands of funds. The regression approach allows him to include controls for such considerations as the year of the original and new fund, the type of fund, and the size of the original fund.

The results are striking: the greater the increase in size between two funds, the more dramatic the fall in performance. Groups that do not

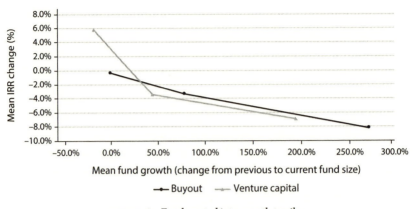

FIGURE 6.3. Funds sorted into growth terciles.
Source: Compiled by the authors from Rossi, 2017.

increase their size continue to perform at the same level (in fact, in the case of venture capital, they improve their performance). But those whose fund size increases sharply experience sharply lower returns: a doubling of fund size (i.e., a 100% increase) translates into a reduction of IRR by roughly four percentage points: for example, from 16% in the previous fund to 12% in the next one.

Note this pattern continues to hold when controlling for the years in which the funds were raised. In other words, the results are not just a consequence of large funds being raised in frothy years. Many of the largest increases in fund size occurred in years with large influxes of funds into private capital, like 1999 and 2007, which subsequently, typically, had very poor performance. But the patterns still hold when looking at increases in fund size over and above the increases that everyone else was doing at the same time. Put another way, we are studying the deleterious effects of drinking by examining the membership of the ΔKE fraternity. We are not comparing the frat boys with the members of the Mormon Students Association.[22]

While figure 6.3 suggests that growth poses a challenge, it does not answer the question of why. Perhaps we can find some clues in the story of the Buenos Aires–based Exxel Group.[23] Exxel was established in 1991 by Juan Navarro, a veteran of Citibank who had first led the bank's efforts to swap its troubled Argentine loans for equity, and then maximized the value of these stakes. His first-time fund raised $47 million from sophisticated investors, and deployed the money in small buyouts. Examples were a $22 million consolidation of consumer cleaning product firms, a $15 million stake in a paper products company, and other modest-sized transactions. Exxel closed its $150 million second fund in 1995, and continued with deals that followed the same template.

Shortly thereafter, however, the firm started aggressively pursuing larger transactions, including the $136 million Argencard transaction and the $440 million purchase of Norte Supermarkets. Exxel used three methods to finance these deals. First, it raised special-purpose funds that provided equity for individual transactions. Second, it raised progressively larger and more frequent funds, most notably the $867 million Exxel Capital Partners V, which closed in 1998. Finally, it borrowed aggressively from global banks and the bond markets. On the equity side alone, Exxel raised seven partnerships totaling over $2 billion in special-purpose and traditional funds in the four and a half years through 2000.

With the benefit of hindsight, the timing for this fund-raising binge was problematic. In the early 2000s, Argentina experienced an economic cataclysm, with a dramatic economic collapse, a wrenching devaluation, and hyperinflation. But the investor money was plentiful right before the grand reversal. Chapter 5 provided several examples of such ups and downs of private capital more generally along these lines. The crisis in Argentina pushed many of the nation's most established firms into bankruptcy, much less companies that had been recently acquired in highly leveraged transactions. But Exxel's relentless pursuit of capital accentuated the difficulties that companies in the portfolio suffered. Among the problems was the need to finance transactions with dollar-denominated debt, which meant that the amounts the companies owed exploded when the Argentinean peso was devalued. The portfolio's size and complexity may have exceeded the fund managers' ability to manage it. There is also a strong likelihood that in their eagerness to do deals, Exxel overpaid for some of the portfolio companies. While it is impossible to know how well Exxel would have done had it grown at a more modest rate, it is hard not to feel they would have far exceeded the annualized rate of return of −45.4% that Preqin records for Exxel Capital Partners V as of March 31, 2017 (with only six cents of every dollar raised paid back to investors).

More generally, what lies behind the seemingly deleterious impact of growth on performance? This question is a difficult one to answer definitively. One possibility is that these firms simply become very difficult to manage as their *scale* grows. Groups begin doing substantially more investments, making it harder for senior management to keep track of the deals and impose a uniform quality standard. The number of partners may not grow proportionately with the capital under management, leading to pressures across the firm. If the private capital firms respond by undertaking progressively larger transactions, returns may also suffer. The new markets they are competing in may be more competitive, or the partners simply less familiar with the market dynamics.

These suggestions are supported by the work of Florencio Lopez-de-Silanes, Ludo Phalippou, and Oliver Gottschalg, who studied the growth trajectory of 250 private equity funds.[24] They found that groups that experienced an increase of portfolio complexity, frequently associated with growth, suffered poorer returns. In particular, investments made at times when a portfolio was already bulging substantially underperformed. The economic magnitude of the scale effect was large: investments by the least busy 10% of groups earned a median IRR (PME) of 36% (1.65), while those by the busiest decile earned a median IRR (PME) of 16% (1.08).

Another possibility is that the deleterious effects of growth are driven by the increasing *scope* of the funds' portfolios. Groups with investments in a single industry may perform better. A Cambridge Associates analysis compared the returns from private equity transactions in various industries by funds that were specialists in that area with similar investments by those who were generalists.[25] The disparities are substantial: for instance, health care investments by specialists generated a rate of return of 25.1%, as opposed to 17.3% for similar investments by generalist funds. Similar patterns emerged with consumer, financial services, and technology deals.

A complementary picture emerges from an analysis of the venture industry by Paul Gompers, Anna Kovner, and Josh Lerner.[26] Growth and maturation of venture firms leads, in general, to portfolios that include companies in more industries. This pattern is true not just for venture groups as a whole but even in the portfolios that individual partners are responsible for. And again, more diverse portfolios perform less well. One interesting note is that the effects of diversification are not nearly as severe if the partners resist the temptation to dabble individually in different areas, and each stays focused on their own area of expertise.

These studies, of course, only show the central tendency. Private capital has examples of firms that have grown with considerable success. The real standout in this regard is Blackstone, which we discussed in chapter 5. Of course, the future success of Blackstone and its peers is not guaranteed. We have seen many examples of investment groups that, after enjoying an extended run of success, go "off the rails" and encounter difficulties. (After all, at the turn of this millennium, few imagined that landmark financial institutions like Lehman Brothers, Bear Stearns, and Merrill Lynch would soon cease to exist.) As we have mentioned, generational succession, the surfeit of uninvested capital in many alternative investment areas, and increasing competition from institutions who want to "go it alone" can all be highlighted as challenges.

Thus, growth is clearly a two-edged sword. There are compelling reasons to grow, both for the good of the firm and for individual partners. And there are examples across all sectors of firms that have done so while showing attractive returns. At the same time, there are clearly substantial pitfalls.

What explains the reluctance of investors to resist demands for larger funds or higher fees? In some cases, new staff members may not really understand exactly how problematic some features of the industry are. Staff may fear that rocking the boat would limit their own ability to get a high-paying position at a fund or an intermediary in the future. In yet other cases, they may fear that developing a reputation as an activist would jeopardize their organization's ability to access the best funds.

The last potential motive, it should be noted, is a highly reasonable one. A consortium of nine major pension funds pushed for an overhaul of the relationship between investors and private capital funds in the mid-1990s. The report they commissioned from William M. Mercer, *Key Terms and Conditions for Private Equity Investing*, highlighted a number of concerns, many of which continue to resonate two decades later.[27] For instance, they asked that general partners contribute more than the traditional 1% to the fund in the hope of having better alignment, that the role of advisory boards be clarified and strengthened, and that provisions for the early winding up of the partnership be reconstituted to give more power to investors. While not all the conclusions were on target—their suggestion to reduce the level of carried interest would have had the effect of reducing alignment—the report was in general a serious and thoughtful effort.

Yet even at the time of the report's release, the sponsors were nervous about its consequences. As one anonymously commented, "All nine of us went out on a limb, since we don't want to be perceived in the marketplace as difficult investors."[28] And that is precisely what happened, particularly to the report's lead sponsor, CalPERS. The giant pension spent many years living down a reputation as a china-breaking activist that limited its access to desirable venture and buyout funds alike.

PASSING THE BATON

A third challenge for private capital groups relates to the sticky issues surrounding generational succession. In many sectors of private capital, the industry has until recently been dominated by first-generation firms: their founders remain firmly in control of the economics and the decision-making. This pattern partially reflects the relative youth of this sector, as we noted in chapter 5. Only in the past year have the very largest groups undertaken major transitions, including KKR, Carlyle, and Blackstone.

It is not necessary to dig deep to find numerous accounts of groups coming to grief over these issues.[29] Already in the late 1990s, industry observers were attributing the dissolution of Golder Thoma Cressey Rauner into multiple firms to "its history of losing bright associates to competitors willing to share equity."[30] More recently, the internal pressures related to these issues seem to have escalated. According to news accounts, "future ownership of the firm" was a major factor that drove president and successor-designate Justin Wender away from Castle Harlan.[31] In 2015, the twenty-eight-year-old private equity firm gave up trying to raise capital following a dispute over succession, despite substantial success in its earlier funds.[32] In 2014, twenty-three years after its inception, Weston Presidio suspended its fund-raising after a group of partners left to start a new investment firm.[33] In 2015, Doughty Hanson's demise was explained by one investor as follows: "Historically there was an issue with the top guys having all the power and the economics, so there were quite a few spinouts in the past." According to another investor who chose not to invest in the firm's funds, "One of the things that we never got comfortable with was the economics between the two founders and the rest of the team, and as far as I'm concerned that did cause [staff] turnover to a large extent."[34] Earlier that same year, Charterhouse, "the elder statesman of British private equity," was exposed to be "a scene of frictions, involving both how its earnings are divided among the staff and how to hand power to a new generation."[35]

Because of the opaqueness of partnerships and the difficulty of determining individual contributions—the very reasons that the literature suggests private capital partnerships exist in the first place—the founders of partnerships may not appropriately reward other contributors, and instead take for themselves a disproportionate share of the economic gain generated by the firms. Many accounts suggest that when nonfounding partners leave to begin their own funds, they frequently find it difficult to attract capital due to concerns about "attribution": whether their past performance was really due to their effort or to the reputation of their former firm and its founding partners. For instance, Probitas Partners notes the following:

> Even with emerging managers, few investors are willing to back groups unless they have an attributable track record of successful private equity investing. However, the process of vetting such a track record for an

emerging manager can be much more difficult. . . . Since private equity investing is a collaborative effort, it is often difficult to sort out responsibility for individual transactions and the issue can be very contentious.[36]

Due to this "lock-in" effect, in many cases younger partners may be compelled to remain in unhappy situations—at least until they can develop enough visibility to break apart. To the degree that such departures reveal problems at the firms to asset owners and lead them to anticipate further departures may result in subsequent reduced fund-raising. Nonetheless, founders may prefer to extract a "larger slice of a smaller pie": that is, even if it ultimately retards the long-run growth of their groups, founders may prefer to hold onto a lion's share of the returns.

These patterns are exactly what we saw when we looked at approximately 700 private equity partnerships. The economic splits in these partnerships had been captured by a major institutional investor in the course of deciding whether to invest in these funds. In each case, the investors shared with us the detailed (and highly sensitive) data on how the economics of the fund—in particular, the carried interest and ownership of the underlying management company—is split between the individual partners.

Three core findings emerged from our analysis:

- First, even among the most senior group of partners, the allocation of fund economics was far from even. Rather, it was typically weighted toward the founders of the firms. As figure 6.4 depicts, the typical founder had twice the share of carried interest than the typical senior partner who was not a founder. Meanwhile, the factor that we might think would matter most—individual investors' past performance—had little association with economic allocation.
- Second, individual senior partners with a smaller economic share were more likely to leave the partnership. At a broader level, partnerships with a more unequal distribution of economics appeared less stable, at least in regard to the mobility of the junior partners. The

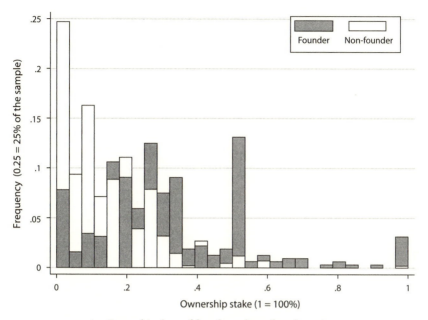

FIGURE 6.4. Ownership share of founder and non-founder senior partners.
Source: Compiled from Ivashina and Lerner (see note 28).

majority of the departing partners remained in the private equity industry and had investment track records as successful as their former partners, suggesting that the departed were not under-performers who were unable to make successful investments.

- Finally, partners' departures negatively impacted private equity groups' subsequent ability to raise additional funds.

These patterns, it should be acknowledged, are not universal in private capital. Some groups have succeeded in passing the baton not just once, but multiple times, with investment success before and after. Many—though not all—of the examples are concentrated in the venture industry. For instance, the leadership of Sequoia, which frequently tops the leaderboard in rating of venture firms, has passed from Don Valentine to Michael Moritz to Doug Leone. At Kleiner Perkins, Tom Perkins was followed by John Doerr and then a triumvirate of Ted Schlein, Beth Seidenberg, and Mary Meeker. Pioneering buyout group Clayton

Dubilier & Rice initially relied on the joint leadership of its founders, followed by Joe Rice as the sole chairman and CEO in 1991, who was in turn succeeded by Don Gogel in 1999.[37] Interestingly, many of the buyout groups that have made successful leadership transitions, such as Bain Capital and Silver Lake, had a significant venture influence in their early years, which may have subtly affected their "organizational DNA."

Why might venture groups have been particularly successful in managing these transitions? Based on our interviews, one potential explanation is that the norm within venture firms is for founders to hand off their ownership of the firm without compensation, or in exchange for a modest amount of carried interest in the first postretirement fund. This attitude reflects a perception that the senior partners "earned enough" during their years as an active partner. Such an approach is certainly not unique to venture funds: Marvin Bower, for instance, used a similar scheme for one of the foundations of McKinsey & Co.[38]

At many other private capital groups, however, the attitude of many founders seems to be that they have created something of value and want to be paid for it. The value that they perceive in the partnership is often far more than the next generation of partners is able or willing to pay. These attitudes and constraints may lead to the dynamics we described above.

RECENT INITIATIVES: IS THE CURE WORSE THAN THE DISEASE?

In the past decade, this conundrum has stimulated two responses. Both have positive aspects but also create a whole set of problems in their own right and have proved to be quite controversial. To tip our hand, we are on the side of the critics here.

The first of these—raising capital from the public markets—is not a new idea. To review some of the key aspects of chapter 5, early private capital pools were generally structured as publicly traded closed-end funds. This structure was adopted out of necessity, not choice, as most traditional institutional investors were reluctant to invest. The funds struggled during the 1950s and 1960s. In part, this reflected the fact that the shares were often sold to unsophisticated investors at market peaks. Once the initial enthusiasm faded, these funds moved from trading at a premium to their underlying assets, to a discount. In many cases, the underlying companies in the portfolio struggled. The results were takeovers and restructurings led by the early hedge funds, difficulties in raising any follow-on capital, and, when capital was raised, substantial dilution to the earlier investors. Many of the early public groups ultimately were acquired and went out of business.

A second wave was seen during the Internet bubble of the late 1990s. Internet Capital Group (ICG), CMGI, and MeVC are examples of firms that raised public money for venture investing. Many of these funds, such as MeVC, dissolved in acrimony and lawsuits once the bubble burst.

Europe, on the other hand, had a long history of publicly traded funds.[39] We discussed the story of 3i in the last chapter. Listed on the London Stock Exchange (LSE) in 1994, 3i pursued a hybrid strategy, investing both off its corporate balance sheet, which was publicly traded, and from outside-raised funds.[40]

Beginning with the initial public offering of the Fortress Investment Group in February 2007, a number of private capital groups went public. They did so by selling portions of the management company rather than raising a publicly traded fund, as earlier groups often did. Fortress was followed, among others, by Blackstone (June 2007), KKR & Co. (July 2010), Apollo Global Management (March 2011), Oaktree Capital (April 2012), the Carlyle Group (May 2012), and Ares Management (May 2014).

The process of going public has undoubtedly provided some real benefits to private capital organizations (though not always to their investors). Foremost among these has been facilitating acquisitions and entrepreneurial ventures within the groups. While privately held groups can—and do—undertake acquisitions, the fact that the partners are digging into their own pockets for funding limits the pace of activity.

Raising a large pool of cash, and being able to issue more shares that can be readily traded, has allowed groups to be more aggressive. Examples of such activities include:

- Exploring new areas. KKR made balance sheet investments into areas where they did not have a fund with an existing mandate, in order to explore their promise. Examples include its investments into Israeli software and semiconductor transactions such as Clicktale and Optimal+, which helped pave the way for the firm's 2016 $711 million next-generation technology growth fund (though of course the investment success of this strategy remains to be proved).

- Undertaking acquisitions to expand into new product lines. In 2011, Carlyle acquired AlpInvest, one of Europe's largest private equity investors, focusing mostly on funds for institutional investors; while Blackstone acquired credit manager GSO, which had roughly $8 billion of debt-oriented funds. While GSO has grown spectacularly in the ensuing decade, some acquisitions have been more mixed: for instance, hedge funds acquired by Carlyle, KKR, and Blackstone have been closed after disappointing performances.

- Seeding new operations. One highly visible and successful effort has been Blackstone's Tactical Opportunities group, which seeks to identify investments across its platform that do not fall under mandates of existing funds and managed $17.5 billion in assets as of midyear 2017.

- Providing a cushion. Permanent capital on a private capital group's balance sheet provides protection against economic downturns when fund-raising may be more difficult. Any number of groups reached into their balance sheets to shore up struggling companies after the financial crisis of 2008–2009, injecting equity into the firms that may have been impossible to raise elsewhere, or only on very expensive terms.

Going public may arguably also allow the firm to cultivate a "one firm" culture. A number of groups have shifted compensation schemes to emphasize more equity in the firm as a whole, rather than carry for the particular fund that the individual works for. In theory, this compensation scheme gets staff members to focus on what is good for the firm as a whole—such as cooperative endeavors like the Tactical Opportunities effort described above, where a number of group heads are actively involved—rather than what is best for an individual's own group.

Such territorial thinking can be a real danger. We have seen groups where a compensation scheme based on deals done has led industry groups to promote subpar deals to the investment committee, withholding negative information in hopes of getting credit for the deal. Equally ugly are cases where partners have reserved wide swaths of potential deals for themselves, blocking their colleagues from approaching them even though they do not have the bandwidth to do the deals themselves. To the extent that the use of equity compensation eases this problem, going public has real advantages.

But it seems that the problem of territoriality could be addressed in other ways, such as giving parties carry in multiple funds. Moreover, the stock price may be determined by many things, of which the success of the firm is only a modest consideration. Historically, the valuations of publicly traded private capital groups has been deeply discounted: for instance, an analysis of ninety-seven listed private equity funds (mostly UK or European funds) between 1992 and 2007 suggests that they traded at an average discount of 26% to underlying value, far more than closed-end mutual funds.[41]

These discounts have also affected the private capital giants that have gone public more recently. For instance, during its 2014 Investors Day, Blackstone argued that its share price should be above $100 per share, rather than the $31 it was trading at then.[42] Carlyle's cofounder, David Rubenstein, made this observation in 2016: "I can't imagine why any private equity firm would ever want to go public. . . . Private equity firms that are public have underperformed virtually every other publicly traded stock."[43] Steve Schwarzman observed that the market appeared to be only valuing Blackstone's ability to collect fees, not to earn carried interest from its investments:

> It's ridiculous empirically, but psychologically, people want to believe that it might never happen again. Is it a miracle when LeBron James scores 37 points? Not really . . . he is the best basketball player. The guy scores more than anybody. Each shot is unique, but over time, some teams win and . . . that's like [carried interest] for us.[44]

Another possibility, of course, is that the market is right! In particular, the complexity of the structures pose substantial issues. We highlight three issues here.

The first is the fundamental misalignment between the limited partners and public investors. One of the beauties of the partnership structure is that everyone is—more or less—on the same page. But a public private capital group is the servant to two masters. While a home run investment that generates huge returns benefits both the limited partners and the unit-holders alike, fees are a different story. The higher the fees that are charged to the funds, the happier the public shareholders but the grumpier the limited partners.

Recent public offerings of private capital groups, it should be noted, have sought to develop governance structures that insulate the firm from public market pressures. In particular, the investment professionals have been assigned special shares with extra voting rights, and can out-vote the unit-holders on any matters that might come to a vote. The firms have also sought to undertake clear communication to the marketplace about their long-run orientation, as we saw from the discussion of Blackstone's IPO prospectus in the last chapter. Having drawn such a line in the sand, it was easier for Blackstone's management to signal their unwillingness to deviate from its principles, even in periods such as the winter of 2009, when the stock was down 90% from the price at which it went public. While the common unit-holders might technically be partners, the fund managers are still driving the bus. In this way, private capital groups limited the pressures from hedge funds and potential raiders that other publicly traded funds without these protections (as well as countless other concerns) have faced, most recently illustrated by the replacement of the board and the investment manager of Britain-based Electra Private Equity.

The second, related concern is that being public can create pressures to do the wrong thing. History is rife with examples of firms that took disastrous steps in a bid to appease analysts and hedge funds, only to bitterly regret them later. It is not clear that private equity is exempt from this temptation. For instance, the tale in chapter 5 of 3i's disastrous deviation from its European middle-market focus to Silicon Valley venture investing can be attributed to its desperate desire to please investors.

For most groups, these pressures may lead to less dramatic but still deleterious decisions. One example is illustrated by the study of transaction fees discussed earlier in the chapter: a driving factor behind fee increases appeared to be whether the private equity groups were shortly about to go public. Three groups that filed to go public in 2007 (or flirted with doing so) increased their monitoring fees by 55% in the years before, while a matched set of firms that did not seek to do so actually cut these fees by 32% over the same period.[45]

The third, most profound concern is that the process of going public typically begins the liquidation of management stakes. The idea that managers would not want to have all their eggs in one basket is understandable. But as we have highlighted in earlier chapters, one of the unique aspects of private capital funds is the need for strong alignment: because it is difficult for investors to monitor what the general partners are doing, they must rely on the carrot of high-powered incentives. And the more that the ownership of the management company moves from the investment professionals to institutional and individual shareholders, the more this alignment breaks down. We might worry as well that as founders with large share holdings age and their involvement with their firms fades—indeed, with their shares eventually passing to their heirs—the potential for misalignment accelerates.

Perhaps because of these issues, the tide today seems to have shifted against going public. In particular, in a dramatic reversal, the first of the mega private equity firms to go public, Fortress, became in 2017 the first to be bought.[46] Originally formed as a private equity business in 1998, Fortress Investment Group also developed into a hedge fund business.

On the day of its 2007 IPO, Fortress's shares soared from $18.50 to $31. The firm said that it planned on using the $634 million raised from the public offering to branch into alternative investment strategies, such as real estate, structured debt, and other specialized funds. But the subsequent performance of the firm was underwhelming. During the financial crisis, the firm suffered heavy losses from being slow to exit the subprime loan business and challenges in its private equity portfolio. Both sides of the Fortress house failed to recover from the financial crisis to the same extent as many of its peers. For instance, its major 2004, 2006, and 2007 private equity funds—representing collectively over $10 billion of capital—are all reported by Preqin as being in the bottom quartile, as are the associated coinvestment funds.[47] Major performance trouble on the hedge fund side began in 2014, when Fortress's macro funds—like many of its peers—began to falter. The macro hedge fund once managed $8.1 billion before poor trades led to clients withdrawing their money, which led to further underperformance. In 2015, Fortress shuttered the hedge funds, and the key leader, Mike Novogratz, left.

The lackluster performance and redemptions inflicted pain on the firm. Major earnings drops in 2011 and 2014 tested investor confidence. As figure 6.5 depicts, beginning in 2010 the firm remained stuck at between 20% and 25% of its IPO price, even as the public market benchmarks soared. Fortress's price-earnings ratio was largely in the single digits over this period. A variety of strategies to boost the share price, such as a $100 million share buyback, failed to ignite investor interest.

After a decade of frustration, Fortress's founders sold out to SoftBank, the eclectic (a less kind description is frequently "baffling") Japanese software and telecommunications conglomerate. The announced acquisition price was $3.3 billion in cash. While the price was a 39% premium compared to current market valuation (to the surprise and bemusement of some analysts), it was a steep drop from the initial valuation of $7.4 billion when Fortress went public or the $14 billion valuation the group reached within a few minutes of its market debut.

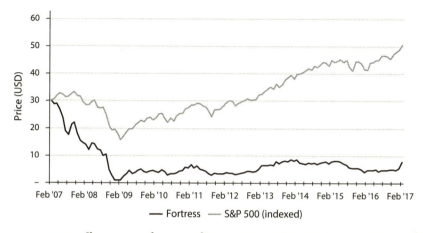

FIGURE 6.5. Share price performance of Fortress. *Note*: S&P 500 Index is normalized to be $30.17 as of February, 2007, the opening trading month for Fortress. *Source*: Compiled by the authors from Bloomberg.

While the enthusiasm of funds going public appears to have slackened, an alternative has sprung up: the sale of minority interests in management companies in private transactions. Over a dozen such transactions took place in 2016 and the first half of 2017.[48] While some of these stakes have been undertaken by sovereign wealth funds and pensions, the bulk of the activity has been driven by funds dedicated to these transactions. Most notably, the market leader, Dyal Capital Partners, closed a $5.3 billion fund in 2017, with Carlyle's AlpInvest, Goldman Sachs's Petershill, and Blackstone also raising (or considering raising) funds.

The main critique of these exits is very similar to those of public offerings. In order to provide returns to the holders of the management company, private capital groups may need to undertake steps that are not in the best interests of the limited partners. As one aggrieved investor noted, "You need firms to double their [assets] for the math to work," which, as we have discussed earlier, is not necessarily the recipe for sparkling returns. "[LPs] don't want GPs' attention diverted by a minority stake sale, which forces a firm to figure out how to grow assets under management to make such transactions valuable to minority investors."[49]

FINAL THOUGHTS

As in chapter 3, we must end with a caution. It is far easier to identify problems and sources of tension in investment management than to solve them. As complex as some of the issues identified here are, identifying the issues is the simple part.

One potential answer, which certainly some of the more vociferous critics of the industry would be likely to agree with,[50] is that the private capital arena is too slanted in favor of the fund managers. They would argue that the best strategy for investors would be simply to stay away. As much as we respect these critics for their dogged work ferreting out problematic behavior in the industry, we would respectfully disagree with this conclusion. We believe that the issues identified here can be addressed and that a stronger industry will result. This is the focus of chapter 7.

CHAPTER 7

Revisiting the Private Capital Partnership

As we highlighted in the introduction to the book, the private capital model is a very powerful one, and much needed to address broad societal issues. And, certainly, these issues only affect part of the industry. Many private capital groups have succeeded in delivering attractive returns to their investors over extended periods. We believe a better industry can be created in their likeness.

In this chapter, we offer a number of suggestions as to how the private capital model can be refined. These suggestions relate to the organization of funds, the way in which they are overseen, the measurement of their performance, and the nature of the rewards to private capital fund managers. We are heartened by the innovation and reforms that we have seen in recent years. We discuss these signs of change as we lay out our recommendations.

We begin by looking at two organizations. Both have tried to approach private capital investing in a way that is different from the norm, and they highlight the opportunity inherent in thinking differently. One is very much "old school," with a well-proven track record; the other, an up-and-comer with promise but also uncertainty.

We then turn to four areas where we see the greatest opportunity for change: fund structure, governance, performance measurement, and compensation.

A BENCHMARK AND AN UPSTART

Greylock was founded in 1965 by Bill Elfers, who had been only the second employee hired at ARD.[1] Having seen the pioneering venture firm's struggles with the public markets, when he founded his own firm, Elfers eschewed this route. He was also unenthusiastic about having a single limited partner, an approach that many other venture groups took at the time. Venrock, for instance, was solely backed by the Rockefeller family and Bessemer by the Phipps. Rather, Elfers emulated the approach of some of the leading California groups, such as Draper, Gaither & Anderson and Davis & Rock, in forming a limited partnership with multiple investors. Starting with $10 million raised from six families, Greylock over time expanded in both size and the diversity of its investors, including additional families and leading university endowments.

In the ensuing decades, Greylock established itself as one of the premier venture capitalists worldwide. Among its home run investments have been a rich array of biotechnology, communications, software, and web companies, including (to name a few) Avid Technology, Continental Cablevision, Prime Computer, Red Hat, Stryker, Teradyne, United Healthcare, Vertex Pharmaceuticals, and Zipcar. Despite its venerable history, the firm has evolved with the times. Its investment scope expanded from the Northeast United States to around the globe. Motivated by the success of its investments in Facebook and LinkedIn, the firm moved its headquarters from Boston to Menlo Park, California, in 2009.

How is it that Greylock enjoyed such success over so long a period, from the era of the pioneering cable television providers to the advent of social media? Of course, its extended run reflected the quality of its investment choices, as well as the caliber of the people working for the firm. But digging a level deeper, the firm made from its earliest days some fundamental choices that shaped the organization.

One defining element of Greylock was an emphasis on alignment and communication with its limited partners. While many private capital groups use such language in their marketing materials, the group's actual behavior—as we pointed out in chapter 6—is frequently different.

Greylock's philosophy had several manifestations. One aspect was limiting fund size to what could actually be deployed successfully. As Elfers commented in 1994:

> Currently, some large pools of venture capital with 2 to 2-1/2 per cent financial fees on assets place too much emphasis on income for the general partners rather than capital gains, where it belongs. Size alone does not produce performance; quality and depth of general partner experience does.[2]

A second critical element for Greylock was eschewing management fees in favor of a negotiated budget. This principle was codified in its original operating plan in 1965 and has been retained ever since. As the firm's website recently explained their approach: "We meet with our LPs twice a year and we share details about our operating budgets and our expectations of future fund performance. We do not distribute excess fees to our partners, we send them back to the LPs."[3]

This approach does not mean that Greylock's partners are living exactly in penury. The firm, like its elite Silicon Valley brethren, charges a carried interest of 30%. And to be sure, the returns from investing in LinkedIn in 2004—which was ultimately acquired by Microsoft a dozen years later for $26 billion—were doubtlessly attractive, as were any number of their other home run transactions. The key benefit of the structure is thus not about saving the limited partners money on fees. Rather, the goal has been ensuring that everyone is aligned around the same goals. The importance of getting everyone on the same page, and eliminating the layer of worry about whether the partners are getting rich regardless of investment performance, cannot be overstated.

A third element of critical importance was having frequent meetings with its limited partners. For its first decade, while the firm's concept was being proved, the firm met monthly with a board consisting of representatives of each of its limited partners. While the board did not have decision rights, the meetings gave the investors a very detailed look at the progress—and the reversals—that Greylock's portfolio was experiencing. The firm later scaled down the number of meetings in favor of other forms of communication, but investor communication remains a hallmark of Greylock to this day.

A final important aspect of Greylock's formula has been a focus on succession within the firm. This attitude was evident as early as 1976, when Elfers decided to step down as chairman and CEO of Greylock in favor of Dan Gregory. In making this decision, he was swayed by the experience of ARD, where Georges Doriot remained in charge until the sale of the company to Textron in 1972, when he was seventy-three years old. During the prior years, numerous key investment managers had defected from ARD to form competitors, including Fidelity Ventures, Palmer Partners, and of course Greylock itself. Elfers's own comments in his biography are revealing:

> I have been asked many times whether I handed over the reins and a larger financial interest too soon. Perhaps, but I think not. From a financial viewpoint, my subsequent [outside investor] status has been rewarding. Also, the environment of a venture partnership organization involves more than money. Productive young partners should be given added responsibility and recognition as soon as possible.[4]

This philosophy has continued to this day. On its website, the firm recently characterized its approach to intergenerational issues as follows: "We make succession planning a priority for the firm, and invest heavily in the development of our newer partners. We ... understand that how we treat our own team is a direct reflection of how we will treat the entrepreneurs we back."[5]

A much less well-known group is Teays River Investments, an Indianapolis-based group specializing in agricultural transactions.[6] Obviously, the firm today does not have the decades-long track record of Greylock. But like that venerable firm, they have shown a willingness to go against the grain, to build an organization conducive to long-run investing.

The predecessor to Teays River was established in 2006. After exploring a number of alternatives, including a fundless structure and a traditional limited partnership, the partners decided to try something different in 2012. Their dissatisfaction with the fund structure had to do with the nature of their holdings. For unlike many of their peers, the team did not simply focus on a subsegment of agriculture, like holding farmland or owning a distribution company. Rather, their approach entailed identifying an entire agricultural production chain that was short on investment, choosing an appropriate initial investment (a "platform"), and then working with carefully built management teams to expand both the breadth and depth of the company (in economics parlance, to horizontally and vertically integrate).

Given the complexity and duration of this process—not to mention the fluctuations in commodity prices that put a premium on being flexible as to when to sell investments—the partners realized another model would be ideal. As a result, they undertook a restructuring in conjunction with their high-caliber roster of investors. They designed an organizational form that was conducive to the long-run nature of their holdings. In particular, they raised over $1 billion of new capital, which was largely added to the investment pool. The fund was reconfigured as an operating company, with no distinct end date. In this way, they could pursue long-run transactions without the pressure of a ticking clock.

As part of this change, Teays River introduced a number of other important—and indeed radical—innovations. Foremost were those involving corporate governance. The firm created a board of directors that includes four large investors (shareholders in the new corporation), two independent outsiders, and its CEO, Richard Haldeman. The board has extensive powers, including a review of the annual budget (as at Greylock, the fees are based on the actual expenses incurred) and the decision to exit transactions and reinvest the capital in another transaction. In fact, a supermajority of the board can even trigger a dissolution of the company.

This active role of the board—and especially the investors—in running the firm is in sharp contrast to almost all other private equity groups. For instance, at Blackstone, the investment professionals occupy five out of the twelve seats on the board, with the remainder held by independent directors (and none by investors). At the time of the IPO, Blackstone's insiders had 87.3% of the voting power. In this respect, they were similar to other groups that have gone public: for instance, at the time of its IPO, Apollo put 86.5% of the voting rights with the insiders; KKR, 75%; and Oaktree, 98.2%.[7]

Teays River has also introduced a variety of other innovations. Given the long-term nature of the holdings, one concern has been ensuring liquidity to the investors who need to get out due to changing circumstances. As a result, they have developed a procedure where the shares are first offered to the management company and then to the other shareholders, at a price that is determined annually through an objective process involving both investors and management. Similarly, they have designed a process for rewarding the investment team based on the performance of the underlying investments over a three-year period, where the size of the option grants are a function of the return on equity. The fact that their investments are businesses generating positive cash flows makes the valuation and liquidity issues easier to address; were they investing in young start-ups with negative cash flows, the challenges would have been more substantial.

As alluded to earlier, while the Greylock model is certainly proven, we will not be able to complete the report card on Teays River for a number of years, given its relative youth and the long-term nature of its portfolio. The Teays model may yet evolve: for instance, the share of outside directors on the board might increase over time. Nonetheless, it has distinguished itself by its creative and thoughtful innovations that fit its long-run goals.

BUILDING FLEXIBILITY

One of the interesting conundrums about private capital is that even though it is all about funding change and innovation, its own structure has been remarkably constant. Nowhere is this truer than when it comes to partnership structure, which is the first of the four areas of opportunity for change that we explore in this chapter.

The eight- or ten-year fund life was, as we suggested in chapter 5, largely borrowed from earlier partnerships and has been with us ever since. Moreover, a ten-year fund life has somehow evolved to mean funds raised every three or four years for most groups, with the associated pressure to deploy capital rapidly and to have exits to impress prospective investors.

In some cases, this number may well make sense. For instance, many social media companies either rapidly prove to be successful or flop. Indeed, many are either shut down or sold only a few years after being formed. But in many other cases we see companies that are pushed into the public market or sold to a corporation too soon. One obvious example is biotechnology. The Pharmaceutical Research and Manufacturers Association reports that it takes at least a decade and costs several billion dollars to develop and obtain approval for a new drug.[8] Thus, it is not surprising that an overwhelming number of biotech companies have gone public well before their products reach the marketplace, with the associated uncertainties about the valuation that the market will assign and even the ability to complete the offering at all. Another example is infrastructure, where projects can be difficult to sell due to their scale, yet often have a life span of decades.

But this is a much more general problem. An example of a firm in a more prosaic industry is Eight O'Clock Coffee.[9] The coffee company was owned by A&P, a struggling US grocery chain. Not only was the retailer unable to invest in the business, but Eight O'Clock's captive status limited its ability to sell to competing grocery outlets. Moreover, convenience-hungry shoppers were apparently too impatient to grind the whole beans in store in the traditional manner.

In 2003, A&P, by then on the verge of bankruptcy, sold Eight O'Clock to the private equity group Gryphon Investors. Gryphon implemented a wide-ranging operational revamp of the firm, including a new information technology system, an incentive system for its union workforce, an emphasis on quality improvement, and a major marketing effort. Three years later, Gryphon sold Eight O'Clock to Tata Global Beverages for a very attractive three-times return.

In the ensuing years, Tata reaped the rewards of Gryphon's work. Helped by recognition of its quality improvements (for instance, Eight O'Clock won *Consumer Reports*' Best Buy rating), social trends (post-2008, cost-conscious consumers increased at-home coffee consumption), and product innovations (e.g., a collaboration for single-serve cups with Green Mountain/Keurig), sales boomed. By 2014, Eight O'Clock was 18% of Tata Global's revenues. One of Gryphon's partners, observing the firm's progress, noted that they "would have liked to keep it, but we had to sell."

Another manifestation of this phenomenon is the fact that, for many years now, selling to another private equity firm has been a prominent form of exit for private equity transactions. If the buyer finds it attractive to make the purchase, it implies that there is "more juice in the lemon" that the first group did not extract. In some cases, the second group may have a set of capabilities that the first group did not, as when a modest-sized industry specialist sells its stake to a much larger private capital fund who can presumably inject much more capital into the firm.

But many transactions involve the sale of the firm between groups that are largely similar. To cite one example, the Fojatasek Companies (later renamed Atrium Windows and Door) was a family-owned manufacturer in Texas founded shortly after World War II.[10] It was first bought out by family-specialist buyout shop Heritage Partners, then sold to TPG, then bought by New York buyout shop Ardshiel and GE Asset Management in 1998, and finally sold to Kenner & Company, who had the misfortune of owning the by-then highly leveraged entity when the financial crisis hit. They were required to bring in a new investor, Golden Gate Capital, as part of a restructuring in 2010, during which the company's debt load was slashed from over $650 million to a much more manageable $300 million. By then, the firm was undoubtedly a much larger and better managed concern than it was when first purchased by Heritage in 1995. But it is hard to argue that the same or better results could not have been accomplished—with a lot less distraction, banking and legal fees, and compensation to general partners—had there been just one or two chefs in the kitchen during this period, rather than six.

The academic literature paints a similarly nuanced picture as the discussion in the two previous paragraphs. Work by Francois Degeorge, Jens Martin, and Ludo Phalippou suggests that the minority of secondary buyouts made by buyers under time pressure to spend capital underperform. Others do well, especially when the buyers and sellers have complementary skill sets.[11]

One natural response to these concerns would be to introduce more flexibility in fund length. There is no reason why a large fraction of funds should have lengths of eight to ten years, regardless of the investments they are making.

For the private capital manager, the benefits of flexibility are clear. Such a structure reduces the painful and very inefficient process of fund-raising, by locking in capital for a longer period of time. Moreover, there is no pressure to exit investments prematurely, whether before the business has matured sufficiently, the value creation plan has been fully executed, or market conditions are optimal. Thus, the danger of leaving money on the table is less. Potentially, the private capital group with such a fund may be able to attract entrepreneurs to accept their capital who otherwise would be reluctant to get involved with an investor using a traditional fund structure.

For the investors in these funds, substantial advantages are also present. The fees are likely to be lower if a single group holds a transaction for fifteen years, rather than three groups over the same period: each sale of the company triggers transaction fees payable to the intermediaries and often to the private capital groups. Such an approach also avoids the dynamic where the third or fourth buyer—having paid a stratospheric price—must make extremely aggressive financial and strategic decisions, in the hope of eking out a sufficient return. Moreover, such a fund brings the time frames of the private capital groups into better alignment with those of the institutions.

We have seen a few examples along these lines. The first type of experimental funds that have been offered in recent years are longer-lived funds, typically with a fifteen- or twenty-year time frame. These funds typically lure investors with lower fees and carry; for instance, some groups have charged fees of between 0.5% and 1% of invested capital (rather than a higher rate on all funds committed, even if not drawn down yet) and a carried interest of 10% or 15%. At the same time, however, many of these funds target lower returns.

An example is Altas Partners, a Toronto-based firm founded by Andrew Sheiner.[12] During his years at the Canadian buyout giant Onex, he was impressed with their success with Sky Chefs, which the group held for fifteen years and built into the largest airline caterer in the world. With his cofounders, Sheiner raised an informal initial fund in 2012 and a follow-on fund in 2016, each totaling a billion dollars. One distinguishing characteristic of the group is undertaking a few large bets, with no more than five transactions per fund. The fund has the right to hold these investments for up to seventeen years, thereby giving them the freedom to maximize value over the longer term. In their initial transactions, which have ranged from a salt producer to a provider of support services of optometrists, the fund has found that managers react positively to "the notion of having a more stable, more long-term capital partner," as Sheiner related.[13]

Farther out have been the evergreen funds. These funds are actually an old idea, dating back to Sutter Hill (formed in 1962), General Atlantic (1980), and Golden Gate Capital (2000). In recent years, they have been joined by groups such as Cranemere, Maverick, and Public Pension Capital Management. Typically, these funds operate in four- or five-year cycles. At the beginning of each period, investors commit to provide a certain amount of capital to the fund. During the next few years, the fund manager invests the capital, calling for the committed money from the limited partners on an as-needed basis. As deals are harvested, the funds are either reinvested by the fund or disbursed to the investors. At the end of the four- or five-year period, the investors can adjust their commitments by exiting the fund or by changing their investment amounts for the subsequent four-year period. These transactions are done at a price that is determined around the time of these anniversaries. Groups employ a variety of techniques to ensure that the prices are fair, such as an advisory committee of limited partners that reviews and approves the proposed valuations, the use of independent third parties to review the largest or most contentious transactions, and so forth.

But these funds very much remain the exception. In part, the reluctance to raise or invest in long-term funds reflects the challenges that they present. For the private capital group, foremost are the compensation issues. For the senior partners who have already been successful, a long-lived fund may be fine. But for the younger investment professionals working on the fund, waiting two decades for their first real payout is not an appealing option.

One possibility is to emulate hedge funds and pay the investment professionals on value created before the deal is exited. But valuing private companies, as we have highlighted, is a tricky endeavor. Moreover, the very process of paying private capital professionals substantial sums before the investors see any profits is likely to raise the blood pressure of limited partners concerned about the appropriate alignment of incentives. Finally, the junior investors are likely to want to be associated with an undisputed winning investment to help solidify their reputation in the industry. A privately held investment may not give them the visibility they crave.

One recent manifestation relates to the tendency of large groups, such as Blackstone and Carlyle, to raise long-lived funds that invest alongside their traditional funds. The groups have argued that they will be able to successfully sort the "quick hits" into their traditional funds, while placing lower-yielding plays that will create value over an extended period into the long-lived funds. A natural, though surmountable, concern is ensuring a disciplined sorting process.

GOVERNANCE

If funds with flexible or long-lived time frames are to be successful, we believe that they will need to be associated with reforms of governance. As we have repeatedly emphasized, while private capital providers are experts at governing the firms in which they invest, their arrangements with their own investors are problematic. Not only do investors have very modest control as limited partners, but exercising even these rights can be painful. The case of Bay Partners illustrates this point. In 2010, three of its younger partners resigned due to their frustrations with the behavior of senior partners.[14] (Red flag!) Making this situation even more tenuous, the three partners were relatively recent hires, brought in to replace a set of partners who had left (or had been pushed out) after several investment disappointments. On top of that, while the companies in the fund's portfolio were quite promising, they were still early stage. But even though, on paper, the limited partners had a variety of tools, including rights under a "key man provision" and the ability to trigger a "no-fault divorce," salvaging the fund proved to be an incredibly time-consuming exercise for them.

The fact of the matter is that the ability of investors to provide governance to funds is likely to be highly constrained. One need only walk into the office of a typical investment professional responsible for private equity at a major pension fund to understand the issue: they are likely to be surrounded by piles of pitch documents and quarterly updates. Many pensions, whether corporate or public, keep an extremely careful eye on costs. This affects not only operating expenses, as we discussed in chapter 4, but also staffing levels. Many of these pension executives face a major struggle to keep up with the flow of new investments coming in the door, much less to oversee existing portfolio relationships with the level of scrutiny that may be warranted.

Another complexity is introduced by the commonly employed limited partnership structure. The limited partners are "limited" in the sense that they can lose no more than the amount they invest. But limited liability comes at a cost. If the endowment is too active in the operations of the fund, it may be construed to have forfeited its protected status.[15] Investors are naturally wary of any activity that will take them too close to this line.

Despite these limitations, there are a number of changes that can and should be undertaken: if investors are to be asked to tie up their capital for decades, having more voice in the key decisions is essential to success. Teays River provides one illustrative approach. Another approach might be to lower the hurdles to limited partners' interventions as the funds mature. In many partnership agreements, the barriers for the limited partners to fire the general partners without well-documented misconduct (which can be very difficult to prove) are very high and quite costly. Adjusting the contracts between limited and general partners so the barriers to such "no-fault divorces" fall as the funds mature may be a way to make investors comfortable about tying up their funds for extended periods.

One of the crucial areas for discussion between limited and general partners has to be succession. As we discussed in chapter 6, the private equity industry is at a relatively early stage in thinking about these issues, particularly when contrasted with venture capital. The limited partners should play an important role in these discussions since they have a considerable amount at stake in the conversation as well.

MEASURING PERFORMANCE

As we highlighted in chapter 3, a third substantial issue is the inability for investors to get accurately calculated performance data. The alternative ways to compute returns have led to a lot of "junk science" being presented to investors as performance numbers. The imprecision by which performance has been measured is, at its heart, a subsidy to underperforming firms by the winning groups. In that sense, private capital is very similar to a college where grade inflation is so rampant that the median grade is an A–. In such a world, it is of course the most committed and talented students who are harmed: their accomplishments do not stand out from the efforts of their peers hanging out at their fraternities who barely bother to look at a textbook between cocktails.

A natural response to these issues would be to create a central body charged with laying out clear rules as to how performance should be calculated. A preliminary effort along these lines is the Institutional Limited Partners Association (ILPA), a trade association of large investors that has laid out some broad guidelines and templates for reporting. Another is the AltExchange Alliance, a nonprofit private equity industry group that has sought to define, maintain, and promote a single data reporting standard.

But the broad principles and templates laid out by these bodies only go so far, due to the complexity of assessing performance. For each private capital group is different, which leads to demands to compute performance in different ways. Consider a few scenarios:

- One group may have done a large number of transactions on a deal-by-deal basis before forming a fund, which they may want to include in their track record alongside deals done by the fund.
- Another may feel that a few large investments in their earlier days, which were mostly funded by coinvestors, would have been done by the fund had they had more resources. Thus, they are likely to argue that the entire sum invested should be included in their track record.
- Yet another may have undertaken some experimental deals outside their main area of specialization that went poorly, and propose to exclude them from the calculations on the grounds that they were "noncore."

Some of these requests may be reasonable; others less so. For instance, is the desire to exclude companies on the part of the group in the third bullet motivated by the fact that the transactions really are different in nature from the others they have done, or because these were poor performers? The complexities of the stories makes defining a "one size fits all" process for assessing performance very challenging.

Given the limitations of broad guidelines, an alternative would be to have third parties actually do the dirty work of assessing and ranking performance. Advisers such as Cambridge Associates already assess the groups that the investors they consult with are considering. Taking this a step further would be to do a documented analysis of the performance of individual general partners.

Here, bond-rating agencies are both a model and a caution. The leading rating agencies—Fitch, Moody's, and Standard & Poor's—are mandated to provide investors with reliable advice on the quality of various debt offerings. The need for these organizations reflects the severe information problems surrounding bond offerings. It is often hard for investors to assess whether a complex security issue is a good one. Rating agencies in theory should be able to do the heavy lifting of assessing whether the offering is an attractive investment and overcome these information problems. Moreover, once this information is gathered, it can be shared with hundreds or thousands of investors, thus obviating the need for much duplicate effort.

But as is well understood today, the rating agencies during the mid-2000s went off the rails. Put bluntly, they ended up giving far too positive evaluations of very risky securities based on precarious structures involving dicey mortgages. Investors relying on these ratings to buy securities were badly burned. Moreover, these overly favorable ratings were far from innocent mistakes. Much attention has focused on the "issuer pays" model that the largest three rating agencies employed. In this approach, the firms issuing the bonds bear the entire cost of the original rating and follow-on monitoring. In many cases, the rating agencies also provided consulting to extract even more revenue from the issuers, who found the favorable rankings that the agencies handed out enormously valuable. (Many institutional investors are prohibited from holding low-rated securities.) The public (and the investors) can then access these ratings free of charge.

As numerous postmortems have pointed out, this structure—as well as demands for profits by the management and investors of the rating agencies—led to irresistible pressures on the bodies to abandon their mission.[16] The various checks on such behavior, such as concerns about their reputation and future business, were abandoned in response to these forces.

One possible solution would be the creation of one or more nonprofit bodies to undertake these assessments, where the commercial pressures would presumably be reduced. Similar bodies are commonplace in the technology world, which faces complex issues of harmonizing new technologies. Literally thousands of standard-setting bodies seek to represent the interests of technology developers and users in industries such as telecommunications, computers, and software. Standards developed and approved by these bodies are ubiquitous, whether allowing individuals to communicate seamlessly across wireless networks or manufacturers to procure goods across complex global supply chains.

It is not hard to imagine that a similar body, overseen by investors and fund managers alike, could play the role of an intermediary that fairly assesses and certifies fund returns. Establishing the group as a nonprofit entity would dampen some of the financial pressures that led the rating agencies astray. Undertaking and certifying a series of return calculations, such a body could go far to addressing the mystery and ambiguity that surrounds performance assessment.

At the same time, the experience with technology standardization has been somewhat mixed, which suggests the need for care here.[17] In particular, efforts of standard-setting bodies to ensure the orderly development and deployment of new technologies has been challenging at best. In particular, in most technology areas, there are multiple standard-setting bodies seeking to make a name for themselves by promulgating a new approach. This competition can lead to a "race to the bottom."

In particular, if a standard-setting body does its job scrupulously, it may seriously annoy a major patent owner. For instance, it may decide not to employ the firm's proposed technological approach, leading to the potential loss of millions or even billions of dollars of licensing revenues for the firm. Or it may insist too intensely that the firm honor its commitments to the standards body to license their patents at a reasonable price if they are included in the standard. In these cases, there are frequently consequences for the standards body. In particular, the firm can find another standards body that is more willing to employ their technology or does not constrain their freedom to license patents as they see fit. In extreme cases, firms have sought to undermine or get decertified standards bodies whose decisions they disagree with, or which they feel are too scrupulous in enforcing agreed-upon commitments.[18] In short, we cannot expect standards bodies to mandate rules by themselves or the powerful entities being regulated to cooperate.

These same difficulties are likely to manifest themselves in private equity. If there is a single body to assess returns, it may serve as an honest broker. Otherwise, competitions between certifiers—even if nonprofits—are likely to have deleterious effects. The pressures to do the wrong thing are likely to introduce distortions into the evaluation process. While we are enthusiastic about the prospects for such a body, the devil will truly be in the details of design and execution.

STRUCTURING REWARDS

The last topic in our discussion is the most sensitive one. Allowing groups more flexibility in structuring funds would help investors and fund managers alike. Similarly, at least the subset of high-performing private capital firms would likely benefit from greater clarity around the measurement of performance. But when it comes to splitting the proceeds between the limited and general partners, feelings seem almost certain to be bruised. Indeed, as we discussed in chapter 6, the formula for rewarding private capital groups has changed little, even as the funds have grown much larger and despite the presence of economies of scale in fund management.

Much of the concern has centered on management and transaction fees. As we have seen, these charges themselves became a major profit center for larger firms. But such steady profits may create unappealing incentives: the temptation to raise too large a fund at the expense of lower returns, the lure of doing a subpar deal so money can be put to work quickly and a new fund can be raised sooner, and a tendency to do excessively safe investments that will not have as much upside but pose less possibility of a franchise-damaging visible failure.

What makes this state of affairs particularly frustrating is that an alternative model beckons: the way that venture capital groups used to operate. Early venture capital groups, such as Draper, Gaither & Anderson, negotiated budgets annually with their investors. The venture capitalists would lay out the projected expenses and salaries, and reach a mutual agreement with the limited partners about these costs. The fees would be intended to cover these costs but no more. While a few "old school" groups like Greylock stick to such an arrangement, these are very much the exception rather than the rule.

Such negotiated fees greatly reduce the temptation to grow at the expense of performance. Better alignment, in turn, should lead to better performance. But this well-proven approach nonetheless remains quite rare. The objections outlined by the Mercer report two decades ago still seem to play:

> Budgeted fees were viewed very negatively from the majority of the general partners we surveyed. Comments included concerns that limited partners would be micromanaging the partnerships; negotiating budgets would not be a good use of time; budgets create "cost plus" thinking; and, "our budget is proprietary information."[19]

Left unsaid was the likelihood that a negotiated budget was likely to lead to a wealth transfer from general to limited partners. One doesn't need to be a devotee of Elizabeth Warren, our firebrand senator deemed by the US Chamber of Commerce to "represent a greater threat to free enterprise" than any other American politician, to feel that such a shift might be appropriate.[20] As the research reviewed in chapter 3 highlighted, however extraordinary the performance of certain funds, aggregate private equity performance has lagged in the past decade.

But even a change that left the split of fund proceeds between investors and fund managers unchanged might be very beneficial, if it was accomplished by lowering fees and raising carried interest. The greater alignment of incentives should lead to a greater focus on what really matters: adding value to portfolio companies and creating wealth.

A second area of compensation that is ripe for reform is hurdle rates. Hurdle rates ensure the investors get paid first. That is, with a typical hurdle rate of 8%, there are no carry distributions—although there are certainly fees—until the limited partners receive an 8% return on their capital. After that, general partners are typically allowed to catch up, until they earn their full share of the carry.

For a successful fund, a hurdle scheme such as this would have no impact on the amount of money paid out to each party. The only change is that the investors get paid earlier. But for a poorly performing fund, there would be no returns to make catch-up payments with, so the payouts would disproportionately go to the providers of capital.

Today the overwhelming majority of private equity funds have a hurdle rate of 8%, while 9% has been the most common rate for real estate funds.[21] (Most venture capital funds dispense with these entirely.) The rationale for these hurdle rates seems lost in the mists of history, but they may have been chosen because they reflected the prevailing government bond rates of the early 1980s, the time that private equity partnership became commonplace. Certainly, this is a "high" rate relative to inflation today, a rationale that has been used to justify efforts by fund managers to reduce these rates.

But more to the point, private capital is typically an equity investment, and a rather risky one. It seems to us that the appropriate hurdle rate would be closer to 13% or 14%: that is, the annual rate of return that would fairly compensate investors for the risks that such an investment would pose, at least if the bulk of recent academic research is to be believed. Such a change would introduce greater alignment.

FINAL THOUGHTS

As we highlighted in the introduction, altering the workings of the private capital industry is a tall order, due to the multiple parties at work here and their varying incentives. Despite these challenges, the recent years have seen encouraging signs of initial change. In this chapter, we highlighted several areas ripe for evolution and offered a variety of suggestions for avenues to pursue.

CHAPTER 8

The Best (or Worst) of Both Worlds

We have explored at some length over the course of this volume the challenges that both investors and funds face. In this penultimate chapter, we turn to efforts that seek to bring these two actors together: where investors create internal teams to undertake investments directly.

Today investors of every stripe and size are embracing direct investments in private capital, whether a coinvestment in a new start-up alongside a venture capital fund or the purchase of a pipeline by a sovereign wealth fund. A few statistics illustrate this point:

- Preqin found that 50% of surveyed investors were actively or opportunistically coinvesting, while another 22% were actively considering doing so. Just under one-half of the respondents planned to increase their level of activity, while only 2% expected to scale back.[1]
- Another indication of the scale of these activities is the estimates by the adviser Triago that between 2009 and 2015 the amount of capital committed to traditional fund investment increased by 78%. Meanwhile, the amount going to what they term "shadow capital"—coinvestments, solo deals, and separate accounts of various types—grew twice as quickly, by 155%.[2]
- The growth of direct investment is also evident in the reports of individual investors, such as the Canadian Pension Plan

Investment Board (CPPIB), whose portfolio of such investments climbed from under C$0.5 billion in 2006 to over C$50 billion in 2017.[3]

There are few that can escape the temptation. The passion for these transactions has spread to family offices, pensions, and sovereign funds alike. Even small family offices that do not have enough bargaining power to negotiate coinvestment rights up front are frequently asked by large private equity firms to participate in coinvestments when the funds find themselves scrambling for extra cash to complete a deal.

The appeal of going it alone is understandable: it is the promise of the benefits of alternative investments, with few of the downsides of funds that we highlighted in chapter 6. Moreover, many of the private capital–backed companies and projects that have literally changed the lives of millions of people, from Alibaba to Uber, relied on coinvestors since these ground-breaking investments often seem not to fit neatly with the traditional fund structure.

But as we highlight here, it is far from clear that these programs are always (or even usually) the best of both worlds. The same structural flaws that can make it hard for institutions and families to select the best funds at the best times can make it impossible to successfully undertake individual transactions. In this chapter, we explore both the pluses and minuses of direct investment pursuits. We end with suggestions for success when going it alone.

WHY GO DIRECT?

Over the course of the industry's history, investors have taken two primary routes to investing directly. The first is through coinvestments. In this case, a private capital group offers part of a transaction that it is undertaking through the fund to some of the investors in its funds. In other words, it allows select investors to increase their exposure to some investments that the fund makes. Such an arrangement has several potential benefits.

First, the investors can opt either in or out regarding the additional investment, unlike the fund investments. (With the fund, the manager typically has the freedom to invest the committed capital as it sees fit, subject to some general restrictions in the partnership agreement. For instance, the fund agreement may contain prohibitions against investments in gambling or vineyards, or putting more than 20% of the fund's capital into any single transaction.) This opt-in feature is itself a powerful lure to many investors, as they may have strong preferences regarding which sectors and geographies they need more exposure to.

The primary rationale for pursuing direct investments, however, is to reduce the management cost, since coinvestments typically feature more favorable economics. This is very attractive given that, as we explored in chapter 3, the returns to traditional private capital funds in recent years (particularly when adjusted for illiquidity and risk) have been disappointing. Much of the blame has been directed toward carried interest and transaction fees (as discussed at length in chapter 6). For instance, Oliver Gottschalg and Ludo Phalippou estimate that, for the typical fund, the gap between gross and net returns due to fees and carry is about 6% per year.[4] As table 8.1 illustrates, a 6% annual return gap results in a thirteen-fold difference in investor wealth after fifty years. If investors could bypass this hefty compensation, and instead get close to the prefee returns from these investments by accessing them directly, many of their problems with private capital would be alleviated.

In a coinvestment arrangement, the investor may be able to invest on a no fee/no carry basis or (as has become more common in recent years) only pay an up-front fee of a few percentage points of the amount invested and a modest share of the profits. While not as good as free, these terms are considerably more attractive than the "two and twenty" terms that partnerships typically charge. In exchange for these fees, the investor benefits from having a big brother—the private capital group—willing to do the heavy lifting of sitting on the board and guiding strategic decisions.

Typically, the private capital group retains the right to decide when to sell the company in a coinvestment. Even if the coinvestors would like

TABLE 8.1. Wealth Impact of a 6% Annual Investment Cost (Fees and Carry)

Investment horizon (years)	Gross return (before fees and carry)	End of horizon wealth (A)	Net return (after fees and carry)	End of horizon wealth (B)	Wealth gap (A/B)
5	20%	$2.5 million	14%	$1.9 million	1.3×
10	20%	$6.2 million	14%	$3.7 million	1.7×
50	20%	$9.1 billion	14%	$700.2 million	13.0×

Note: Assuming the initial investment is $1 million.

to remain investors in the firm for a longer period, the investment group frequently has "drag-along rights" that ensure that all the shareholders sell. This provision is important to the private capital group, as corporate acquirers typically want to buy all of a firm. But as we have discussed before, the private capital group may want to exit before their investors do.

The second route commonly seen in practice is the "solo" investment. In this case, the investor puts its money into the company alone, or in conjunction with another investor. Thus, the institution or family forsakes the counsel, help, and cost of a private capital group entirely. For the investor, the discretion is the greatest: the party can decide when to enter and exit the deal as it sees fit. This freedom to hold the investment until a time of the investor's own choosing may be a real plus, especially for long-lived assets such as toll roads or bridges. Rather than being forced to sell when an investment partner does, a pension or a family can hold the transaction for twenty to thirty years or more. Moreover, there are no fees or carried interest to be paid to any partner, though of course the investor will need to reward its own employees who select and oversee the investment. Despite the increased compensation pensions pay to manage investments in-house, it is often far cheaper than hiring outside managers.[5]

It should be noted that there are, as is so often the case, many alternatives to these two basic models. Some of the most sophisticated investors—for instance, Canadian groups like the Canadian Pension Plan (CPPIB) and Ontario Teachers—increasingly seek to "colead" rather than coinvest in deals. That is to say, they are involved with the analysis of the transaction alongside the private capital firm from the very early stages, rather than being presented an almost-completed transaction on a silver platter. At the other extreme, many private capital groups are raising coinvestment vehicles, which invest alongside the fund when the opportunity arises.

One way or another, these investments are normally cloaked with mystery. While tracking private capital is challenging, nowhere is this truer than in direct investments taking place outside the traditional fund structure. Institutions such as sovereign wealth funds, university endowments, and family offices—and even many pensions—are typically under no obligation to disclose the nature or performance of their direct deals to outsiders. While databases such as Capital IQ list some of these transactions, their coverage appears to be highly selective. Just like people, investors seem far more eager to brag about their successes than to talk of their failures.

Thus, our ability to draw definitive conclusions about direct investing is somewhat limited. But from our case-writing, research, and work with investors, we can highlight some lessons about what the major challenges are and how they can be addressed.

WHAT ARE THE CHALLENGES?

It might be thought that as an investment strategy, direct deals would be a slam dunk. Coinvestments might be seen as particularly advantageous: if an institution is investing in the same transactions as a fund, but paying less, what can go wrong?

Unfortunately, the counterintuitive answer is "plenty." In particular, three problems rear their heads in this setting: (a) constraints, lack of financial sophistication, and adverse selection in coinvestments that defeat a good deal selection; (b) an inability to set the right incentives in-house to attract talented managers and ensure the achievement of investment objectives; and (c) difficulty in resolving the investors' often conflicting objectives. We explore each of these in turn.

Deal Selection

The fundamental problem for investors who wish to undertake investments directly is that the selection of appropriate direct deals is far from trivial. This problem has several dimensions.

The first issue is that the selection of deals is not a blank slate. Many groups are highly constrained in terms of the types of investments they can consider. The constraints can be self-imposed: for instance, a sovereign wealth fund of an Islamic nation may understandably want to steer away from alcohol- or gambling-related investments. But these policies can be taken to extremes: for instance, as of 2011, CalPERS had adopted 111 different policy statements regarding ESG (environmental, social, and governance), all of which restricted how funds can be invested.[6]

Similarly, political considerations may block promising investments. This problem is not just a consideration confined to sovereign wealth funds or to Middle Eastern and Chinese entities. A dramatic example was the proposed transaction in which the CPPIB was to buy a 40% stake in Auckland's airport.[7] One might think that Canadians and Kiwis—being fellow members of the Commonwealth of Nations with quite parallel histories—would be about as close as residents of any two nations. Moreover, Canada is perennially highly ranked on compilations such as the "World's Most Reputable Country"[8]: it is hard to imagine the pension pursuing some duplicitous strategy to advance Canadian global hegemony. Nonetheless, the proposed purchase of a 40% stake of the airport at a 50% premium to the market valuation ignited a firestorm of protests and was ultimately blocked by the government.

In some cases, political considerations have led to groups being unable to pursue attractive investments; in others, groups undertook transactions they should not have. A dramatic example of the latter was the experience of Norway in the 1970s and 1980s.[9] In the oil surge of those years, the government received a tremendous windfall of funds from its numerous rigs in the North Sea. The money was largely spent immediately on direct investments. Some of the spending benefited physical and social infrastructure. For instance, Norway rebuilt its excellent system of roads and bridges and provided free health care and higher education to all residents. While these expenditures may have had social benefits, the direct financial returns were very modest.

Meanwhile, much of the remaining funding for the industry was earmarked for dying sectors, such as the Norwegian shipbuilding industry. This support allowed facilities to remain open for a few years more, but could not reverse the industries' inexorable decline as production moved to Asia. Other funds for new ventures went to friends or relatives of parliamentarians or bureaucrats responsible for allocating the funds.

Moreover, the policy of aggressively spending the government's petroleum revenues introduced chaos into public and private finances when the oil price plunged in the mid-1980s. The government's oil revenue dropped from about $11.2 billion in 1985—or about 20% of Norway's gross domestic product—to $2.4 billion in 1988. The resulting retrenchment of public investments and tightening of credit led numerous banks to fail. The downturn also led to an unprecedented wave of bankruptcies by private citizens.

Even in the absence of investment constraints or political motives, examples of poor investment choices and their devastating consequences are abundant. Many asset administrators are essentially nonprofit or governmental institutions, where the leadership may have neither exposure to the world of investing nor an appreciation of its complexities. Indeed, their success in other arenas may lead to a fatal hubris when it comes to deal selection. Moreover, they may in many cases be seeing the leftovers—deals on which other, more sophisticated institutions have passed—making it even easier to make mistakes (we return to these issues shortly).

Perhaps the clearest example of this is the ignominious experience of Boston University, which put more than two-thirds of its endowment into a faculty-led biotechnology company, Seragen.[10] The decision to make this investment was personally made by the university's visionary but frequently tyrannical president, John Silber, who held a PhD in philosophy. In making this selection, Silber was not swayed by negative signals from the market about the firm's prospects: the school bought out the stakes of several independent venture capital investors, who had apparently concluded after a number of financing rounds that the firm's prospects were unattractive. Silber may have instead been swayed by the importance of Seragen's mission: it was developing a new type of drug that had the potential to cure cancer.

Between 1987 and 1992, Boston University provided at least $90 million to the private firm and added another $17 million in debt financing in 1995 and 1997. (By way of comparison, the school's entire endowment in the fiscal year in which it initiated this investment was $142 million.) Silber himself invested his own money in the firm and successfully persuaded dozens of trustees, fellow administrators, friends, and even retired faculty members to do likewise. His ability to engage in this behavior was a function of the organizational culture, described by one observer as "resembl[ing] that of the court in a 17th-century monarchy, with courtiers jostling among themselves to curry royal favor."[11]

While the company succeeded in completing an initial public offering, it encountered a series of disappointments with its products. The same issues that led Seragen's venture investors to walk away a decade before were still present: the complexity of cancer resisted the company's efforts to design therapeutics to address it. By late 1997, when the university's equity stake was worth only about a few cents on the dollar, it liquidated its investment in the shadow of public investigations into financial mismanagement. The realization of the university's investment was only about $4 million.

This huge, undiversified investment created a large loss for the debt-ridden university. One might have anticipated that this miscue would have led to Silber being asked to resign in disgrace. Instead, he was appointed chairman of the state board of education of Massachusetts!

All of the above only discusses one side of the deal selection problem: that of the investor. But the selection issue in coinvestments is a double-sided problem, as only *some* of the investments are available for coinvestments. And these are not always the best investments!

What drives a fund manager's decision to open a particular deal for coinvestments? Below we describe what we have found in our own research, but the adverse selection problem that the coinvestment programs face is not a new problem: in 2001, George Akerlof, Michael Spence, and Joseph Stiglitz received the Nobel Prize for showing that in markets with extensive information problems, these types of "lemons problems" were likely to emerge.[12] And coinvestments are indeed transactions with big information problems. While the private capital groups have been working on the transactions for months or even years, the coinvestors frequently have to plow through a massive amount of information in a data room and decide in two weeks' time whether they want to invest.

Compensation

We have already highlighted the difficulties that many investors face when recruiting investment professionals to the role of choosing funds. When it comes to dealmakers, the challenges of compensation are even greater. Put bluntly, it is hard to recruit and retain a team with the same skills as those of Blackstone or KKR if the investor can only pay them a tenth as much (or even less). Moreover, even their below-market compensation may trigger public outrage, as the distinction between the 1% and the 0.01% of income earners is lost.

To illustrate this point, unfortunately, we do not have to look further than our own backyard. Harvard Management Company (HMC), responsible for investing Harvard University's $35.7 billion endowment, has been plagued by management and strategic instability for the past dozen years.[13] While the set of issues behind HMC's turmoil cannot be boiled down to one factor, it is clear that the compensation of key managers has been a critical problem.

During the tenure of Jack Meyer, nicknamed "Harvard's billion-dollar man" by the *Boston Globe*, Harvard's endowment grew from $4.7 billion in 1990 to $22.6 billion in 2005, with an annualized return of 15.9%. Unlike Yale's model, Meyer instituted a hybrid investment management approach that involved not only allocating money to external managers but also investing a sizable portion of the endowment in-house.

In 1974, Harvard's endowment had been made into a wholly owned subsidiary (HMC) of Harvard University. HMC thus had the power to construct its own compensation structure different from that of the university. This allowed Meyer to set attractive compensation levels—certainly, very different from university pay scales. High performance started to go hand in hand with high pay. For instance, in 2003, David R. Mittelman earned $34.1 million for managing $2.9 billion in domestic bonds, and Maurice Samuels earned $35.1 million for managing $2.1 billion in international bonds. Both, it should be noted, far outperformed their benchmark index. Mittleman and Samuels added $777 million and $580 million to the endowment, respectively.

The release of these compensation numbers lit a slow-burning fuse. Grumbles in faculty lounges in such otherworldly departments as Inner Asian and Altaic Studies and Romance Languages and Literatures and among the ex-hippie alumni of the class of 1969 turned into critical articles in the *Harvard Crimson* and ultimately into stories in the major national papers. The ensuing controversy ultimately led to the departure of many of Harvard's key investors, as well as the exit of Meyer himself. Harvard's willingness to invest in the new funds established by the departing staff (albeit on favorable terms for the university) may have hastened the process.

Once the apple of discord brought about expulsion from the garden of financial Eden, the Harvard endowment faced a very challenging time. A revolving door of successors followed Meyer: four full-time endowment heads in the next eleven years, with as many interim heads. Not only was the turnover disruptive to the investment staff, but it led to strategic instability. The heads struggled with the question of how much of Harvard's hybrid model to preserve, with inconsistent answers. The result of this extended period of rapid flux was, not surprisingly, one in which Harvard underperformed its top endowment peers. The newest chapter began in early 2017, with the arrival of N. P. (Narv) Narvekar, previously chief investment officer of Columbia's endowment.

Drawing an unambiguous conclusion from the Harvard experience is challenging. The argument by university administrators that Harvard was getting a "bargain" from its investment staff was in some senses legitimate. Harvard would have paid in many cases far more to outside managers had they invested in funds that generated the same performance, with a 20% profit share going to the manager. Just think of Accel, with their 30% profit share and nearly $6 billion in capital gains from Facebook. (Harvard itself was not a direct early-stage investor in Facebook, despite Mark Zuckerberg's stint as a student.)

Yet the compensation of the internal team was far more visible than the fees paid. HMC, as a university affiliate, had to report the amount paid in compensation to its investment team on its Form 990 filings to the Internal Revenue Service. Meanwhile, the endowment—like the vast majority of other investors—only reported the net returns of its fund's investments, not the total amount paid out in fees and carry. And the very visibility of the internal compensation can create challenges (see, for instance, Michael Sandel's thoughts on the consequences of injecting market-oriented thinking into aspects of life traditionally governed by nonmarket norms[14]).

It is worth noting that the developments over the past decade have validated some of the concerns about the compensation at HMC. First, some—though certainly not all—of the managers who were very successful within the Harvard umbrella proved to be significantly less so after they spun out. This pattern suggests that a considerable portion of their success may have been driven by structure and financial backstop provided by their former employer.

The poster child for this argument would be Sowood Capital, founded by Jeffrey Larson, who was responsible for foreign equities at HMC until 2004.[15] Freed from the HMC structure, Larson leveraged his fund aggressively (the $3 billion of equity from outside investors, including HMC, was supplemented by $18 billion of debt). For several years, this strategy worked fine. But once markets began experiencing stresses in the lead-up to the financial crisis, Sowood's arbitrage strategy stopped working. As the value of the portfolio fell in the spring of 2007, lenders began demanding more collateral. Unable to meet these capital calls, Larson was forced to sell his portfolio in a fire sale to another hedge fund, leaving Harvard with a $350 million loss. Even Convexity Capital Management, founded by former endowment head Jack Meyer to great fanfare in 2006, has struggled in recent years.[16]

A second corroboration of these concerns was a 2015 internal report for the endowment by the consultants McKinsey & Company, which ended up being leaked.[17] The report highlighted the contradiction between the size of the bonuses for purported outperformance paid out at Harvard and the endowment's lagging performance relative to its peers. In many cases, the report suggested, the benchmarks for bonus payouts at the endowment were "easy to beat, inconsistent, and often manipulated"—in other words, "slow rabbits."

The Harvard experience poses a variety of questions without easy answers. Is it really feasible for a nonprofit to pay $100 million in annual bonuses to five individuals, even if this is a discount to their true "market price"? Would the endowment have been better off recruiting less pricey talent and developing their skills in-house? Or would such a developmental strategy have exposed the endowment to too much risk from poor investment choices? And would this kind of employee strategy have been feasible anyway: What would have stopped the staff from leaving for elsewhere once they had become savvy investors? Does it make sense for an investor to pursue these kinds of investments internally at all?

Setting competitive compensation is even harder for public institutions in Western democracies, where the media may be overeager to engage in sensationalism. The challenges here can be illustrated by looking at the recent experience of CPPIB; as it were, the sequel to the vignette in chapter 2.[18] The architects of the modern CPPIB created a structure that allowed the public pension unique freedoms, including the ability to set salaries and bonuses completely outside the Canadian civil service scale. With multimillion-dollar bonuses—as well as the ability to live in Toronto, work in a congenial setting, and contribute to the betterment of the nation—CPPIB attracted a high-caliber investment team, many of them Canadians, eager to move home after a stint on Wall Street. "We're not the top payer but we're not bound by government pay scales. We pay fair market compensation, with carry-like compensation even to associates.... Our pay scale is close enough; not only are we not losing people, we're getting people I never would have thought we could have gotten," remarked then-CEO Mark Wiseman.[19]

But implementing this scheme has been challenging. The fund was bitterly criticized for proposing to pay bonuses totaling $7 million to four top executives for 2008–2009, after the fund had lost almost 19% of its value during the financial crisis. The *Toronto Star* ran mug shot–type pictures of the leadership team and their compensation.[20] Opposition politicians were quick to pile on. For instance, New Democratic Party leader Jack Layton noted, "I don't know how they can look themselves in the mirror and (then accept) cheques of Canadians' money for millions of dollars for such a pathetic performance. Remember, their salaries are already higher ... than the Supreme Court justices, higher than the Prime Minister."[21]

The institution's explanation was that (a) the compensation scheme was based on performance relative to a market-adjusted benchmark computed over a four-year period, and (b) the 2008–2009 compensation represented a 30% cut from earlier years. This rationale fell on deaf ears, whether due to its complexity or the political feeding frenzy, and the board ultimately adjusted its compensation policy downward.

But again, in 2013, Jim Leech, Mark Wiseman, and Ron Mock claimed the top three spots on a list of the highest-paid pension CEOs, all representing Canadian public pension funds. Jim Leech of Ontario Teachers' Pension Plan topped the list with $7.4 million in pay that year.[22] The same year, Anne Stausboll, then the CEO of CalPERS, the largest American public pension fund, made a little over $400,000.

As in the HMC case, eventually, much of CPPIB's leadership team left for jobs elsewhere. To cite a number of examples, CEO Mark Wiseman departed to become a senior managing director and chair of the global investment committee at BlackRock; senior managing director Mark Jenkins took a senior position with the Carlyle Group; senior managing director and global head of private investments André Bourbonnais left CPPIB to become CEO at the Public Sector Pension Investment Board; and managing director and head of principal credit investments Adam

Vigna left to join activist equity manager Sagard Capital.[23] While such turnover is inevitable, the pace of change in recent years suggests some of the challenges of retaining staff in a public setting with constraints on compensation and intense media scrutiny.

In sum, designing appropriate compensation schemes for direct investment teams can be very hard in the nonprofit or public sectors. But in our experience, numerous family offices, which operate completely below the radar of public and media attention, nonetheless have struggled with exactly these same issues.

Governance

The conversations above regarding deal selection and compensation structure naturally lead to a discussion of governance. As we have highlighted, investment committees and governing boards of many funds have been far too eager to jump on the bandwagon of the hot idea of the moment. In many cases, the board members—whether the schoolteacher representative, a local bank president, or a successful entrepreneur—have enthusiasm and dedication. But to successfully steer a long-term investment program, these attributes are not enough. Skills and experience of the team, and not just one individual, are also essential. These requirements are particularly critical when it comes to steering direct investment decisions, rather than just making broad asset allocation and fund selection decisions.

The sophistication of the governance of these efforts varies tremendously. On the one end, there are families that have been investing for decades in certain industries, often closely related to their own holdings. Not surprisingly, the family members and investment professionals often bring a great deal of expertise, discipline, and shared understanding to this task. Conversely, we have encountered investors at the other extreme: for instance, a sovereign fund with a team devoid of transaction (or even private capital) experience, which is expecting that private capital groups will somehow see fit to bring a plethora of attractive transactions to them.

It is challenging, however, to isolate the consequences of effective and ineffective governance of direct investment programs without being a fly on the wall and seeing how decisions are made. Thus, we take here a higher-level view, speaking to all three of the issues outlined above based on the work we have done with Lily Fang. To do this, we worked with seven large investors, who provided us with the detailed cash flows for all of their direct investments between 1991 and 2011.[24] During this period, these investors put $23 billion to work in 391 direct investments, ranging from early-stage venture investments to massive buyouts. About $14 billion was in the form of coinvestments, with the remaining 39% as solo transactions. The investors included some of the most sophisticated institutions from North America, Europe, Asia, and Australia.

When we dug into their investment results, four surprising conclusions about this mysterious realm emerged. First, the performance net of fees of the direct investments was not very different than that of the average investment partnership. Because the direct transactions have less of a "haircut" associated with fees and carry than the partnership investments, this means that on a gross (prefee) basis, the direct transactions did worse. If investors were looking for a free lunch by going direct, it does not appear to be there!

Second, direct investments in venture capital transactions performed far worse than those in buyout deals. This discrepancy may be bad news for institutions such as Saudi Arabia's Public Investment Fund, which in 2016 placed $3.5 billion as a direct investment into Uber at a stratospheric valuation of $62.5 billion.

Why might direct investments into venture capital firms particularly languish? One possibility is that these investments are simply harder to value. Established companies and existing infrastructure assets have cash flows that can lend themselves to a reasonably straightforward valuation analysis. But venture capital is a horse of a different color. Consider Uber, for instance, which has grown from losing "just" $20 million in its 2011 fiscal year to $1.5 billion of losses in the third quarter of 2017 alone, even as its valuation has skyrocketed.[25] In order to justify Uber's current valuation, a number of assumptions need to be made about how long it will take the firm to become profitable, how much of the market it will capture (e.g., will its scope be limited to ride hailing, or will its moves into trucking and food delivery, among other areas, be successful?), and whether new innovations like self-driving cars will bring great opportunities or mortal threats to its business model. These questions do not have easy answers, yet are critical to successful venture investing.

Another possible explanation for the poor performance of venture direct investments is the timing of these deals. In buyouts, all parties usually invest at the same time and at the same price. Of course, this is no panacea—just ask the investors who eagerly piled in to coinvest with KKR and TPG in TXU, the giant Texas utility that spectacularly imploded in the face of declining natural gas prices. But at least the "everyone into the pool at the same time" approach avoids the problems associated with venture deals, where the venture capitalists dominate the early investment rounds completed at relatively low valuations, leaving the later, higher-priced rounds to the coinvestors.

Consider again the case of Uber. The last two rounds led by traditional independent venture capital groups were in 2011, when Benchmark Capital led an $11 million round that valued the firm at $60 million and Menlo Ventures spearheaded a $37 million round with a $300 million valuation.[26] But once the valuation of the firm crossed the billion-dollar threshold, the venture investors turned the financing reins over to others: corporations such as Google and Microsoft, public fund managers such as Fidelity and Wellington, and a United Nations of individual, corporate, and government investors from places as diverse as China, India, Qatar, Russia, Saudi Arabia, and the United Kingdom. Given the great disparity in the entry prices across rounds, it would not be surprising if returns of the various classes of investors were to differ dramatically. The early insiders would likely do far better than the institutions that followed. Thus, it is not surprising that when Softbank sought to buy shares in January 2018 from the existing investors at a 30% discount to the valuation in the last financing, it was the earliest investors who were eager to sell and lock in their still-gigantic profits in a company facing many headwinds.[27]

The third surprising pattern that emerged from our research was the extent to which performance had deteriorated over time. For instance, the annual rate of return for the transactions made during the 1990s was about 5% above the Preqin global private equity benchmark; those during the 2000s, about 4% below. Much of this poor performance was concentrated during the years leading up to the financial crisis, when direct investments had an initial surge in popularity. This pattern suggests that direct investing is like many other aspects of private capital: the more popular a strategy is today, the less attractive the returns to investors are likely to be. This finding clearly augurs poorly for any investors rushing to do direct investments today.

Finally, the performance of solo and coinvestments differ substantially. It would be natural to assume that coinvestments would do better, because a professional is in the pilot seat there. But the investments alongside private groups actually *underperform* the solo deals. The average public market equivalent (PME) of the coinvestments over the entire sample was 1.26 (or a 26% greater return over the public market), while the solo deals had a mean PME of 1.35.

Why did coinvestments perform relatively worse? As we dug into the track records of our seven institutions, two patterns became clear. First, these institutions tended to concentrate their investments at exactly the wrong times. Of course, it takes two to tango: it is likely that coinvestments become more widely available during booms, and limited partners may not adjust their selection criteria to reflect this fact. Investors generally have a bad sense of when to get enthusiastic. Consider venture capital, where investors poured capital into funds in record amounts (still unbroken) during 1999 and 2000. Venture funds formed in these two years ultimately proved to be among the poorest performers ever. But coinvestments display this pattern on steroids. Somehow, reading headlines about an asset class for weeks on end in the *Financial Times* seems to cause investment committees to lose their collective minds. Huge amounts of funds flowing into coinvestments follow. In other words, coinvestments occur most frequently when market interest is the highest, which typically is a bad time to invest.

Second, coinvestments tend to be made in the largest deals being done at the time. To see this, we looked at all the deals in the private capital funds with which our institutions did a coinvestment. If we compare the typical (median) deal in the fund into which our institutions put their own capital with the ones where they did not, the coinvestments were three times larger in size. At one level, this is not surprising. The private capital funds are likely to need help completing their largest deals, due to formal limits in their partnership agreements regarding how much capital they can put into any one transaction (or else they may desire to diversify or face informal pressure from their investors to do so). Thus, the largest deals are where they need help "filling out their dance card." But the consequences of having a portfolio consisting of the largest deals done at market peaks is ugly. These transactions—like the aforementioned TXU or Webvan, the profligately spending online grocer that collapsed in the wake of the dot-com bust in 2001—are not the road to riches.

Meanwhile, when we turn to the solo investments, what is behind their relative success? Being local is a critical factor. For every additional sixty miles between the target firm and the investor, the ultimate PME of the investment falls by about 0.15. To put it another way, Canadians investing in Canada have considerable success with their solo transactions, but Canadians investing in China on average fare far worse. This pattern is not surprising. Due diligence should be much easier when an investor is evaluating a transaction in their own backyard. Similarly, well-connected public pensions and sovereign funds should find it easier to add value to local firms. But as wonderful as Canada is, there is a limit to the number of investment opportunities it can offer.

These results have not been uncontroversial. In a 2017 working paper, Reiner Braun and Christoph Schemmerl of the Technical University of Munich, along with Tim Jenkinson of Oxford's Saïd Business School, looked at a sample of 1,016 coinvestments made by 458 LPs, submitted to the CapitalIQ database.[28] In contrast with our findings, the paper saw no difference between the gross (prefee) returns of coinvestments and the deals made by funds only. Thus, their results suggest that coinvestors perform better for investors, once their lower fees and carried interest are accounted for.

One of the concerns about this counterresult, however, is which transactions end up in CapitalIQ. In particular, one could readily imagine that limited partners would be far more willing to publicize coinvestments that turned out well than those that struggled. Indeed, Josh Lerner's subsequent work, along with Antoinette Schoar of MIT and Jason Mao and Nan Zhang of State Street, using State Street's custodial data (which captures all private market activity by over one hundred major investors representing close to 10% of all commitments to private capital over the past few decades), underscores questions about adverse selection in coinvestments and biases in public data sources.[29] Consistent with our earlier work, these new findings confirm that, even factoring in the lower fees, the coinvestments actually underperformed the main funds.

Taken together, these findings suggest that going direct does not appear to be the cure-all that it is seen to be by many investors today. While such investments are "cheaper," in the sense that fees and carry are lower, they are not necessarily bargains. The inability of these investments to achieve outperformance, the declining performance over time as more investors have adopted this strategy, and the limits to the most successful strategy (direct investments locally) all raise concerns about the likely success of this approach going forward. It certainly suggests the need for caution on the part of investment committees and supervisory boards.

BEST PRACTICES

We have spent a lot of time on the challenges of direct investment. One conclusion that the skeptical reader might draw from this discussion might be, to reverse the Nike motto, "Just Don't Do It."

But this conclusion may need some nuance. After all, for good reasons or bad, investors may still desire to invest directly:

- Many private capital investment professionals have a strong mandate from their overseers to undertake these programs.

- Moreover, this may be the only way for investors with very large pools of capital to put "enough" capital to work in long-term investments.
- Finally, our research does not suggest that, over the long term, direct investments have underperformed partnerships net of fees: rather, the net performance is virtually indistinguishable.

Given the likelihood that direct investing will be an important part of the private capital landscape for the years to come, what hallmarks of successful programs featuring these types of deals can we point to?

We believe that five recommendations are clearest. While many of these echo the principles we highlighted for the success of patient investment programs more generally, because of the greater tensions in this setting, they are particularly important here:

- Define a clear strategy as to what kind of direct investments the organization will be pursuing. In other words, understand why you are special, as well as what your weaknesses are. Successful private capital groups often have a shared understanding of the characteristics of a transaction that is a good fit with the firm. Having this agreement allows them not only to come to consensus about doing deals quicker but also to quickly eliminate inappropriate transactions from consideration. In this way, their energies can be concentrated on the most promising transactions. In many cases, however, the strategy of investors doing direct programs has been essentially confined to "let's see what deals the private capital funds send us." A clear strategy can avoid these pitfalls. For example, PensionDanmark (discussed in chapter 4) had distinct experience with renewable energy technology, as well as numerous local collaborative partners, which provided important edges when investing directly. Other groups have similar sources of "unfair advantage" that should be exploited.
- Mitigate the lemons problem. This is of paramount importance. If adverse selection were not a problem, coinvestments would be a winning strategy. It is the presence of this problem that makes the

process much more difficult. The lemons problem may be addressed in a number of ways:

- First, one common element of successful programs is to co-invest only with familiar groups, groups with superior track records, and groups with strong incentives to continue raising funds from their existing limited partners. Incorporating data and more qualitative insights about the potential investment partner into the decision-making process can help in the evaluation of transactions.

- Consistent with the first point, one way that groups can respond to this problem is by limiting the scope of the deals in which they will coinvest to certain geographies and industries, where they perceive themselves as having a deeper understanding of the issues.

- Third, the lemons problem can also be mitigated through having deal-level due diligence capabilities, so that the investor can evaluate the prospect of potential investments on an independent, stand-alone basis. At the same time, it is important to recognize that even the best-skilled staff cannot fully assess a transaction in the few weeks that the private capital groups often have many months to carefully study.

- Fourth, while this may be hard to accomplish, the lemons problem can be mitigated through the contractual agreements between investors and private capital groups. If the private capital groups cannot "cherry-pick" which deals to offer as coinvestment opportunities, the lemons problem is removed. One danger here is that fund managers have been known to make promises during the fund-raising process and then not deliver.[30]

- Undoubtedly, one of the most vexing set of management challenges associated with coinvestment programs is the determination of appropriate compensation levels. Few limited partners can (or are willing to) offer compensation that matches that in private equity groups. Yet in many cases coinvestment programs are asking team members to play a role similar to partners in these groups. This difficult issue can be at least partially addressed in several ways, recommendations that we realize are far easier said than done:

- Realize that undertaking a coinvestment program is a major effort. This involves a substantial departure from an indirect investing approach, in terms of the number of staff required, their skill sets, their compensation levels, and so on. To be successful, this type of effort requires a consensus at all levels of the organization, and a substantial financial commitment.
- Accept that, at least at the junior level, turnover will be part of the process. Many successful groups that have coinvestment programs operate these in a manner akin to a training academy, where high-quality analysts and associates join the firm for a few years, then "graduate" to work at a private equity group.
- Strive very hard to keep stability among the senior staff of the coinvestment program. Among the most promising steps involved are (a) carefully choosing team members who are not just motivated by financial returns and who can operate well in this environment, (b) offering compensation, while below that of private equity groups, that is substantially greater than that paid elsewhere in the organization, and (c) as highlighted in chapter 4, proactively communicating the reasons for this approach to stakeholders.
- Ensure that the work environment is a rewarding one. Some endowments and other limited partners have achieved continuity of investment staff over many years, even with relatively modest compensation levels. They have done so by ensuring that the investment professionals have a high degree of autonomy and that the broader objectives of the organization's mission are frequently emphasized.
- Be careful in scaling up too quickly. Even if competitive compensation is feasible (and talent is abundant), growing too fast can put a strain on the culture, affecting the work environment.
- These programs are unlikely to bear fruit immediately. Just as first-time funds have a much greater range of outcomes than subsequent ones, the success of institutions as coinvestors appears to increase as they become more experienced. It is important that the investor's leaders understand these dynamics, and not terminate a direct

investment program prematurely. At the same time, as we highlighted in the discussion of best practices for investors more generally,
a process of evaluation and course correction is also important.

Direct investing is a challenging territory. While it is seductive, investors have discovered that alongside the beautiful blossoms are sharp
thorns. Given the level of enthusiasm in this arena, we offer these suggestions for approaches that may have a greater chance of success against
the odds. But all in all, Nancy Reagan's "Just Say No" slogan might be a
simpler and more effective answer to coinvestment challenges.[31]

CHAPTER 9

The Future of Long-Term Investing

We began this book by outlining the case for patient capital: many of the most pressing needs in the world today, whether in developed or developing nations, require long-term investors. While not all investors need to be long-term, those who adopt such an orientation will likely play a critical role. The odds seem low that governments will be able and willing to address these profound challenges facing our society. Unless large investors can do so, while at the same time hopefully garnering attractive returns for the ultimate owners of the assets (such as pensioners or students and professors), the prospects for future generations are bleak.

Throughout this book, we have traced the growth of the concept of long-run investing among institutions and families, as well as the evolution of their partners, the groups managing private capital funds. We have highlighted that, despite the massive amounts of dollars being targeted today to these arenas, there have been numerous barriers to success that have proved daunting to overcome during the past few decades. The chapters have laid out critical problems and suggested potential solutions.

In this last chapter, we seek to draw together our previous thoughts by discussing how long-term investing is likely to evolve over the next decade. As we have highlighted above, the past decade has seen extraordinary changes to the status quo in this arena: from investors seeking to move more activities in-house to private capital groups transforming themselves from specialists to alternative investment supermarkets. While it is hard to have a definitive answer about how long-run investing

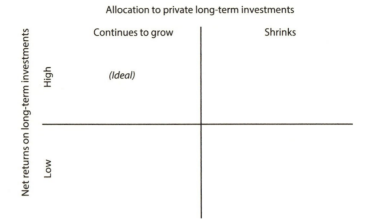

FIGURE 9.1. Future of private capital: Potential scenarios.

will evolve, it is important to understand the implications of the trends discussed in the earlier chapters.

Thus, in the initial part of this chapter, we consider four scenarios along which long-term investing may evolve. We conclude by outlining some of the key recommendations we believe have the power to positively shape the evolution of the industry.

One way to organize these scenarios—in a tried-but-true business school manner—is as a two-by-two matrix, as depicted in figure 9.1. On the horizontal axis, we contrast cases where, on the one hand, the investor base (the providers of capital) and their allocations to long-term investments continue to grow and, on the other hand, where they shrink substantially. The vertical axis distinguishes between scenarios where the returns to private equity funds going forward are attractive—that is, they are commensurate with the risks that investors take on—and those where they are disappointing.

Of course, the two dimensions are not independent, as more capital flowing to the same investment strategies is bound to lower the gross investment returns (and vice versa). Needless to say, higher returns tend to attract the capital. These inflows can have dramatic effects and sow substantial chaos in both the operations of the private capital funds and the portfolios of their investors. Over the course of the volume, we have highlighted the booms seen before the financial crisis of 2008–2009, the dot-com crash of 2000, and the stock market and junk bond collapses of 1987–1989. However, in what follows, we want to distinguish between these factors and the fundamental drivers of long-term investing.

A HEALTHY PRIVATE CAPITAL INDUSTRY

The first scenario envisions a return to the condition that has characterized the industry for most of the past three decades: an attractive risk-return profile. While the years since the financial crisis have seen relatively modest returns for many subclasses of private capital, these changes and upheaval may well be temporary.

It can be argued that cyclicality has been part and parcel of private capital since its origins. We highlighted in chapter 4 that investors are prone to trend chasing. And as chapter 6 suggested, private capital groups are frequently tempted to raise more funds than are prudent. As a consequence, during periods of rapid growth, investments are made at high prices, often employing high leverage. Once the market conditions deteriorate, the performance of these investments suffers.

The practitioner wisdom about these trends has been corroborated in a line of research that has looked at the performance of investments across market cycles. A strong pattern has emerged: generally, investments made during market peaks (whether of fund-raising or investing) appear to have performed worse. The findings hold at the individual transaction and at the aggregate level, across the various classes of private capital.[1]

This result is perhaps not surprising. If firms completing private transactions at market peaks employ leverage excessively and overpay for transactions, we may expect years and industries with heavy buyout activity to experience more intense subsequent downturns. This is especially so if the effects of this overinvestment are exacerbated by private equity investments putting indirect pressure on rivals not backed by private equity to aggressively invest and leverage themselves. For instance, around the time of the mid-2000s buyout boom (during which one of the largest transactions was the buyout of the Tribune Corporation by Sam Zell), the family owners of the New York Times Company engaged in a debt-fueled orgy of their own, repurchasing several billion dollars of equity from the public markets. (The Tribune filed for bankruptcy in December 2008; the Times staved off distress only by selling off many of their prized assets and accepting a quasi-usurious loan from Mexican billionaire Carlos Slim.) In a more systematic look at this phenomenon, Judy Chevalier showed that in regions where many supermarkets received private equity investments, rivals responded aggressively, entering into the markets and expanding existing stores.[2]

This cyclical pattern may reflect not just leverage but also the probability that the private capital investors themselves are more distracted during boom periods. For instance, Steve Davis and coauthors found that the positive productivity growth at firms undergoing buyouts (relative to controls) varies with industry cycles.[3] The productivity advantage is larger in periods with an unusually high interest rate spread between AAA-rated and BB-rated corporate bonds; that is, periods when risky debt was very expensive, such as the early 1990s and late 2000s. Meanwhile, there was virtually no productivity advantage for private capital–backed firms during periods with low spreads, as was the case during the "go-go" days of the mid-2000s. One interpretation of this pattern is that private equity groups are most committed to adding value to their portfolio during periods when making money through other means (e.g., through leverage and financial engineering) is not feasible, that is, during periods when the debt markets are difficult to access.

Nor are these patterns confined to the years around the financial crisis of the 2000s. Perhaps most dramatic was the crash that followed the buyout wave of the late 1980s. While the overall rate of failure of buyout-backed firms is modest—Steve Kaplan and Per Strömberg show that only 6% of exited deals over the history of the industry worldwide have ended in a bankruptcy or a distressed reorganization—the failure rates appear to be far greater for megadeals concluded at the peak of buyout booms.[4] A study by Steve Kaplan and Jeremy Stein concludes that of the sixty-six largest deals done at the peak of the 1980s buyout boom (i.e., between 1986 and 1988), fully twenty-five (or 38%) experienced financial distress by the end of 1991, which Kaplan and Stein define as default or an actual or attempted restructuring of debt obligations due to difficulties in making payments.[5] Eighteen (or 27%) actually did default on debt repayments, often in conjunction with a chapter 11 filing.

At the same time, it is also important to consider the long-run determinants of the level of private capital, not just the short-run effects. In the short run, as we have highlighted, the ebb and flow of returns and the state of the public markets are likely to be critical. But the types of factors that determine the long-run, steady-state supply of private equity in the economy are more fundamental.

These long-run drivers are likely to include the following:

- The degree of dynamism in the economy as a whole (whether from new innovations, the growth and expansion of companies, or the pace of corporate restructurings), which creates opportunities, for investment firms are more often than not a guiding hand rather than the engine of value creation;
- The ability of private capital investors to systematically add value to portfolio firms by attracting and correctly incentivizing talented professionals capable of selecting, structuring, and overseeing entrepreneurial projects;
- The existence of mechanisms that ensure that institutional investors seeking to invest in private capital can identify and access the best investors; and
- The presence of liquid and competitive markets for investors to sell their investments (whether markets for stock offerings or acquisitions).

However painful the short-run adjustments may be, these more fundamental factors are likely to be critical in establishing the long-run level of patient capital.

By examining these fundamental determinants, a compelling case can be made that there is a continuing and important role for private capital.

A wealth of academic studies suggest that private equity groups add value to the companies in which they invest.[6] Similarly, a variety of works suggest a positive impact of venture capital funds.[7] To be sure, not all aspects of the investment process are rosy—for instance, the work by Steve Davis and coauthors suggests that even though productivity at private equity–backed firms increases substantially, the wages of line employees appear to fall—and studies of the consequences of real asset and real estate funds are harder to come by.[8] But the general picture is far from the media depictions of "barbarians" and "locusts."

Other favorable indicators for the future prospects of the sectors include the increased professionalization of private capital firms that we featured in chapter 5. What was once a cottage industry with very informal practices has been altered fundamentally, as groups systematize their due diligence, portfolio value-added, capital markets, and risk management practices. While we acknowledged a number of weak spots with these funds in chapter 6, the business looks very different from that of two decades ago. Not surprisingly, the willingness of boards of directors to consider the sale of an underperforming asset or company in need of capital to such a fund has increased. The increasing number of professionals and managers accustomed to the employment arrangements offered by private capital–backed companies (such as heavy reliance on stock options) has also been a major shift. Finally, the efficiency of the private capital process has been greatly enhanced by the emergence of other intermediaries familiar with its workings. The presence of such expertise on the part of lawyers, accountants, and others has substantially lowered the transaction costs associated with forming a fund and financing companies or projects.

In short, the increasing familiarity with the private equity process has made the long-term prospects for such investments as attractive as they have ever been, or even more so. It is also worth emphasizing that, despite its growth, the private capital pool today remains a relatively small share of all equity held by institutions. For every $1 of private equity in the portfolio of US institutional investors, there are $6 to $12 of publicly traded equities.[9] The ratios are even more uneven for many overseas institutions: according to the International Monetary Fund, in 2010 this ratio worldwide was about $1 to $58 for asset managers and $1 to $45 for pension funds.[10] Even in Australia, which features many sophisticated institutional investors, the ratio in 2016 was $1 to $36.[11] Similarly, a back-of-the-envelope calculation suggests the ratio of real estate in the form of private funds to the total value of the asset class remains modest. While it is harder to undertake similar computations for real assets such as infrastructure or farmland, the ratio would in all probability be very small. At least to the casual observer, these ratios seem modest when compared to the economic role of new firms, products, processes, and projects in developed economies.

Taken together, these facts suggest that the level of private capital is likely to rebound in the years to come. The fact that the industry has experienced periods of boom and bust is nothing new. The lag in returns in recent years can be understood as a natural part of the historical boom-bust cycle. The private capital model has many inherent strengths, and the maturation of the industry is likely to reinforce these.

DÉJÀ VU ALL OVER AGAIN

The second scenario is rooted in the relatively modest level of, and high degree of disparity in, private capital returns. Taken together, these two facts suggest that for most investors private equity has been—if performance is properly measured—a losing game.

It may well be that the decline in average returns since the financial crisis is not an anomaly but really the consequence of the influx of capital to the industry. Figure 9.2 depicts the amount of capital committed but not invested across the private capital spectrum. If the growth of this dry powder in the private capital industry is indeed depressing returns by introducing hypercompetition, then the current industry structure may not be sustainable. If as a result, the disappointing performance that we discussed in chapter 3 continues, investors may at some point become

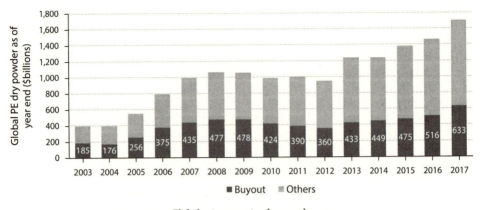

FIGURE 9.2. Global private equity dry powder, 2003–2017.
Source: Compiled by the authors from *Global Private Equity Report 2018*,
Bain & Company, Inc.

disillusioned with private capital. The returns generated by such an investment program may not be worth the trouble associated with managing the effort.

This scenario suggests that over time many investors will decide to exit private equity investing. We might anticipate that the decision to exit would be uneven. We might anticipate that the largest and smallest investors will be among the most likely to exit. Small investors are likely to conclude that they do not have the critical mass to make these investments: that the time and energy associated with these activities are simply too costly. The largest pools of capital may conclude that their choices are too few. Given the amount of huge capital they need to deploy, and the complexity of assessing groups, many large institutions have decided they can only invest in a handful of very large groups at best, a strategy that may not necessarily translate into the best returns. The recruitment and compensation challenges associated with direct investing may also be seen as too daunting.

Thus, this alternative scenario envisions a return to the 1980s, when private capital investing was dominated by midsized, sophisticated investors such as select corporate pensions and endowments. The exit of numerous other investors is likely to be good news for those remaining in the game. There will be less competition from other limited partners to get access to top-tier funds. Returns from fund investing should be higher as well: private capital funds will have less competition from other funds and institutions doing direct deals. Such supply-and-demand dynamics suggest that this environment should see the surviving funds and institutional investors enjoying superior performance.

Indeed, when we look at the world of hedge funds in recent years, we may be seeing the template for private capital. In September 2014, disillusioned by the low returns and high volatility of its hedge fund sector, CalPERS announced its intention to liquidate the program, which at the time consisted of twenty-four funds and six funds-of-funds totaling $4.5 billion.[12] As the largest US pension and one of the first public pensions to launch a hedge fund program (in 2002), the decision was seen as symbolic. Indeed, in subsequent years, pensions including New York City, New Jersey, and Rhode Island, as well as insurers such as MetLife, have followed CalPERS in abandoning or dramatically curtailing their hedge fund programs.[13] Meanwhile, it appears that many endowments are retaining their allocations to this space.

THE LIMITED PARTNERS' DESERTION

The second scenario presented above anticipates that private capital investing does not generate the rate of return that investors expect, and thus by nature is gloomier. In the third scenario, we anticipate that poor returns continue and a problematic organizational structure drives away many investors.

Why might the exit of many limited partners not lead to an improvement of returns, as the second scenario suggested? One possibility is that the wedge between gross and net returns introduced by management fees may be too great to overcome. Even if a shrunken private equity industry leads to gross returns recovering smartly, the net returns that the limited partners receive may still be unsatisfactory.

It is worth pointing out that investors have sought to address high fee levels in the past without success. As we discussed in chapter 7, the

William M. Mercer study of the mid-1990s was motivated by the under-performance that public pensions—many of which had started investing in the mid-1980s, shortly before the meltdown at the end of the decade—had experienced to date. While the report made a number of not unreasonable suggestions regarding compensation, the ideas were dead on arrival, never being taken seriously by the general partners. A similar earlier effort by British limited partners fared little better.

A pessimist might argue that the lack of success of these efforts was not just simply a matter of bad timing or inappropriate arguments. Rather, the issue of compensation of private capital investors may be a fundamentally nonaddressable one. The investor community is fractured across different types of institutions in different geographies. As much as investors espouse solidarity, they are competing among each other to get into top funds. The distribution of fund returns is highly skewed, as seen in chapter 5. The extreme skew in performance makes access to the proper funds critical to success. Moreover, maintaining cohesion among the investor community is difficult when key leaders are frequently lured away to higher-paying positions at funds-of-funds or private equity groups.

All these factors may lead to a dramatic shrinkage in the pool of investors in private capital. General partners may be forced to exit the business or to raise dramatically smaller funds. Investors may increasingly grow impatient with their own direct investing efforts, as turnover and lack of appropriate governance sabotage their success. As a result, entrepreneurs seeking private capital may be forced to turn increasingly to informal sources of capital—for example, family members or angel groups—to support their ventures.

Lest the reader consider this scenario too far-fetched, historical precedents do exist. To cite one example, oil-and-gas limited partnerships were popular among endowments and other forward-thinking limited partners in the 1970s and 1980s. Over time, however, institutions became disillusioned with the low returns from these funds. As one investor explained it to us, most of these oil-patch fund managers of the era appeared to be simultaneously managing wells for the funds that they were managing and investments that they owned individually. Despite the fact that these wells were in close proximity to each other, it somehow always seemed that major finds came from the wells that they owned outright. In the face of these seemingly intractable problems of self-dealing, the investors' allocations to these funds fell sharply.

A BROKEN INDUSTRY

The fourth and final scenario is the most depressing of all. It suggests that while the returns for private capital will be disappointing, the sector may continue to gather substantial amounts of funds. Because of some of the measurement issues associated with private equity, which we explored in chapter 4, as well as the organizational dynamics that are likely to make private capital specialists at many large institutional investment firms unwilling to recommend that the programs be wound down, these groups may continue to raise capital, even if returns are not there. Such a state might continue for a decade or longer.

Again, the skeptical reader may question whether such a scenario could really transpire—after all, it is far removed from the standard notions of market efficiency. But such scenarios are not entirely implausible. After all, despite over five decades of academic studies pointing to the near impossibility of consistently beating the public markets, most equities continue to be held by active managers charging unattractive fees, rather than low-cost index funds.

Closer to home, one example would be corporate venture capital, or the establishment of venture initiatives by large organizations seeking to pursue financial and strategic goals. Beginning in the early part of this decade, the number of such initiatives began rising. The high-water mark came in 2016, when 107 new programs were established.[14]

Yet corporate venturing is far from a new idea. There were waves of activity in the 1960s, 1980s, and late 1990s, corresponding to earlier booms in the independent venture sector. These efforts have, based on an analysis by Thomson Reuters of programs between 1993 and 2013, generated negative financial returns.[15] The often-touted strategic returns have in many cases been difficult to identify as well. All too often, the resistance within the corporations to new ideas, as well as the turnover engendered by the inability of corporations to pay market rates (especially incentive compensation) to their venturing teams, has led to disappointments on this front as well. Our study of the first two waves of corporate venture capital, for instance, found that the median program was abandoned after a little over twelve months.[16]

To be sure, there have been some corporate venture organizations, such as those of Intel and Qualcomm, that have benefited substantially from their programs over extended periods of time. But the willingness of generations of corporate management to pursue the same dream, despite the daunting track record (and in many cases, making the same design mistakes over and over), suggests how problematic investment ideas can persist.

This scenario points to a very unhappy recipe. Limited partners will continue to place money into venture and buyout funds, whether out of stubbornness, self-interest, or misleading data. Yet the returns will not be there. While this might be good news for general partners who can stay in business, it is hard to feel that society as a whole will benefit from such an outcome.

GETTING TO THE UPPER LEFT SCENARIO

In an ideal world, the large pools of capital will be able to successfully invest in projects that boost energy and environmental innovation, address infrastructure needs in the developed and emerging worlds, and promote the sustainable stewardship of natural resources. This outcome is only likely to be feasible if the upper left scenario in figure 9.1 holds.

The previous chapters have highlighted five sets of recommendations that we believe are most likely to lead to the positive scenario. Three of these cut across the investors and private capital funds—those relating to governance, incentives, and measurement—though the emphases in each case differs. Two of these are specific to the individual parties, relating to communications and the flexibility of the partnership structure. In this final section, we review the key areas for change outlined in this book.

Governance

Private capital groups are undoubtedly masters at overseeing the firms in their portfolios. But much of the oversight provided elsewhere in the long-term investment world is deficient, as we have reiterated repeatedly.

We offered a variety of suggestions on how to ensure better oversight, first within the investor groups themselves:

- Move investor board membership from a model where beneficiaries and politicians dominate to one dominated by qualified and knowledgeable individuals. While having "experts" is no cure-all, having a board dominated by board members experienced in the investment world (with rigorous conflict-of-interest rules to avoid self-dealing) is an important step.
- Adopt as many protections as possible, whether structural or based on the board composition, to insulate investors from political pressures.
- At the same time, include on boards a limited number of knowledgeable stakeholder representatives. Training of board members should be a major priority to ensure that everyone is on the same page when addressing these frequently esoteric-seeming issues, as well as encouraging extended terms (with reasonable limits) on boards.
- Frame meetings so that the big picture is front and center, rather than focus on quarterly results, micromanagement of the individual investment decisions, and compliance issues. One approach may be to reduce the frequency of meetings.

We then turned to relationships between the investors and the private capital groups. We acknowledged that the provision of oversight is likely to be limited due to both legal and capacity constraints, as well as more personal considerations. At the same time, the interest in longer-lived funds makes addressing the governance deficiency in long-run investment partnerships even more urgent. We suggested one avenue might be to lower the hurdles for interventions—such as the triggering of the "no-fault divorce" clause—as the fund matures and its condition becomes more readily apparent.

Measurement

The assessment of long-run investment programs is challenging. The process of assigning value—and, consequently, the measurement of risk and return—is challenging for illiquid companies undergoing major transformations over extended periods. While the measurement issues are not quite as baffling as quantum physics—where Erwin Schrödinger's cat could famously be simultaneously dead and alive—there are few easy answers. Moreover, the very process of frequent measurement may distort the behavior of investors.

When we considered the situation of investors, we highlighted three key recommendations:

- Employ whenever possible long-run measurements of performance rather than annual or quarterly numbers. By focusing investment committees, as well as stakeholders, on longer-run measures, the conversation can be framed in a way that maximizes the likelihood of thoughtful decisions rather than reactive ones.
- Focus on a limited number of measures which allow those responsible to understand what is happening to the investments from various perspectives without overwhelming them with too much data. Much of the effort should be on understanding the direction of movements, rather than worrying about (frequently misleading) precision.
- Pause periodically to take a holistic view of the portfolio, looking in greater depth at a select number of challenges and disappointments,

in order to get a fresh perspective on the management of the investment program from multiple dimensions.

On the fund manager side, we highlighted the difficulty of measuring risk and return. In a world where subtle and hard-to-detect changes can allow many groups to present themselves as top tier, we argued that an appropriate remedy would be a nonprofit certification body. This intermediary could get its hands dirty and realistically depict performance in a thoughtful and consistent manner. The world of technology standards, however, has suggested that even not-for-profits can act in problematic ways if competition between certifiers sets in.

Incentives

As in much of human endeavor, rewards are the fuel that drives the behavior of investors. Reflecting the relative youth of professional long-term investing, incentive schemes remain underdeveloped. To cite just one example, many investors have not fully grappled with what kind of incentives are required to recruit and retain a top-notch direct investment team, despite the fact that such investments are increasingly critical to their strategy.

We highlighted three key recommendations for investors:

- If high-caliber staff are to be lured in and retained at an investment firm, they need to be paid differently from traditional civil servants or academic bureaucrats. Educating the investment committee, the stakeholders, and the public at large about this necessity is important.
- Rewards should be strongly linked to actual performance. In an ideal world, investors would adopt a model based in part on the carried interest scheme used by fund managers, as well as on more qualitative considerations. If such open-ended models are infeasible, a bonus scheme where the payouts are based on actual realized returns over three, five, or even longer periods of years should be employed.

- Financial motivations are not the entire story. A strong sense of mission, and of connectedness to the individuals on whose behalf the team is investing, can be a powerful motivator as well—at least for the right team member.

Turning to the fund managers, our concerns stem not from the level of incentives but from the structure of the rewards they receive. In particular, we highlighted how the formulas by which fees are calculated, in combination with the economies of scale of running a fund, have resulted in a world where such payments are a major profit center in their own right. We argued for two changes: annual budgeting to determine fee levels and a higher hurdle rate before profit sharing to reflect the cost of the investors' equity. These could potentially be accompanied by an increase in the profit shares allocated to the fund managers: what is critical is ensuring that everyone does well at the same time.

Communications

The first of our two recommendations that are specific to the individual parties concerns the investors. Investors answer to many masters, including retirees, faculty, ordinary citizens, and the media. In a hypersensitized and polarized world where university administrators can find themselves in the spotlight because the dining hall served insufficiently "culturally sensitive" General Tso's chicken,[17] the challenge is a daunting one. For the task of designing and implementing a successful long-term investment program is a far more complex proposition than properly cooking chicken, in an arena that few fully understand and of which many are suspicious.

We highlighted the need for investors to proactively communicate to two audiences:

- The first involves communication with the stakeholders of the fund. Particularly critical is the need for stakeholders to understand that rough spots with disappointing returns are an inevitable part of the process, and that the appropriate response is not panic selling and course changing. This philosophy rubs against human nature, so conveying it again and again is important.

- Second, potential fund managers must be wooed. While it might be thought that money buys respect and attention, it is not so simple. For most institutions, investors must convince the most attractive private capital fund managers that they should take their money. If the investor has gone to the trouble of developing a thoughtful, long-run approach, making sure that this message is understood is essential.

Flexibility

The second of our party-specific recommendations relates to the structuring of private capital funds. One of the critical themes of this volume has been that private capital is a young industry, with many of the key institutional features being borrowed from other realms in the heat of the moment, rather than designed thoughtfully. Nowhere is this condition truer than when it comes to partnership length, where groups have tended to cluster around a ten-year duration.

While we have seen in the past few years a number of experiments in altering fund life spans, we would like to see (to quote Chairman Mao) "a thousand flowers bloom." Better matching the design of funds to the types of investments should address many of the problematic behaviors we have highlighted. This step will require careful thought to address new issues about compensation, conflicts, and governance that these alternative structures pose, but such time will be well spent.

WRAPPING UP

The outline in this volume is intended to be the starting place for a conversation, rather than the last word. As we have highlighted, the world of long-run investing has been an opaque one, where the motivations and actions of the key actors are often misunderstood. In many cases, this has led to unfair accusations. In other cases, the lack of clarity has disguised behavior inconsistent with growing the size of the overall pie (however its split between investors and fund managers). Our suggestions may be criticized by some as naive, by others as overreaching, and by yet others as underwhelming. But if our ideas can advance this conversation, we will have accomplished our goal.

In addition to the question of whether these are the right recommendations, there remains the issue of how to get there. Some investors may be aware of problematic practices, but to seek to solve them on an individual basis is likely to be a recipe in futility. In fact, the only consequence of such an approach is that it likely establishes a reputation for the investor as a maverick and ultimately scares fund managers away. This seeming dilemma suggests the importance of collective discussions, whether within organizations representing investors or between them and those representing fund managers.[18] These conversations will not be easy or fast, but we are optimistic that the process will yield dividends.

We would like to end with one thought. The world of long-run investing and private capital is complex, with a specialized language and lots of institutional detail. But given the broad consequences of these investments, these issues are too important to leave in the shadows. Our conviction is that greater understanding will yield benefits for investors, fund managers, and society as a whole.

NOTES

CHAPTER 1. THE NEED FOR INVESTING LONG-TERM

1. Laura Secorun Palet, "Spain's 'Ghost Airports': A National Embarrassment?," *Ozy*, August 7, 2014, http://www.ozy.com/acumen/spains-ghost-airports-a-national-embarrassment/33041; European Court of Auditors, "EU-Funded Airport Infrastructures: Poor Value for Money," Special Report no. 21/2014, December 2014, http://www.eca.europa.eu/Lists/ECADocuments /SR14_21/QJAB14021ENC.pdf.

2. See, for instance, Rafael Minder, "In Spain, a Symbol of Ruin at an Airport to Nowhere," *New York Times*, July 18, 2012, http://www.nytimes.com/2012/07/19/world/europe/in-spain -a-symbol-of-ruin-at-an-airport-to-nowhere.html; Rafael Minder, "Revival of 'Ghost Airport' Stirs Hope in Spain," *New York Times*, March 15, 2015, https://www.nytimes.com/2015/03/16 /business/international/revival-of-ghost-airport-stirs-hope-in-spain.html.

3. Andres Cala, "Renewable Energy in Spain Is Taking a Beating," *New York Times*, October 8, 2013, http://www.nytimes.com/2013/10/09/business/energy-environment/renewable-energy -in-spain-is-taking-a-beating.html; Laure Fillon, "Feeding Frenzy in Spain's Renewable Energy Sector," *Phys.Org*, May 1, 2016, https://phys.org/news/2016-05-frenzy-spain-renewable-energy -sector.html; and Jason Deign, "Spain Is a Case Study in How Not to Foster Renewables," *Green Tech Media*, May 5, 2017, https://www.greentechmedia.com/articles/read/spain-is-a -case-study-in-how-not-to-foster-renewables.

4. See, for instance, the discussion in Jon Markoff, "Pentagon Redirects Its Research Dollars," *New York Times*, April 2, 2005, http://www.nytimes.com/2005/04/02/technology/pentagon -redirects-its-research-dollars.html.

5. "OECD.stat," 2017, http://stats.oecd.org/.

6. In making these estimates, we seek to follow the approach outlined in World Economic Forum, *The Future of Long-Term Investing* (Geneva: World Economic Forum, 2011), https://www .weforum.org/reports/future-long-term-investing.

7. Moody's Investor Services, *Government of United States—Government Employee Pension Liabilities Are Moderate Compared to Social Insurance Program* (New York: Moody's, 2016), https://www.moodys.com/researchdocumentcontentpage.aspx?docid=PBC_1018420.

8. See, for instance, Stephanie Landsman, "The One Big Thing Economist Robert Shiller Says Is Preventing a 1929-Like Stock Market Crash," *CNBC*, September 20, 2017, https://www.cnbc .com/2017/09/19/the-one-thing-shiller-says-is-preventing-a-1929-like-crash.html.

9. Yale University Investment Office, *The Yale Endowment* (New Haven, CT: Yale University, 2017).

10. Jean Eaglesham and Coulter Jones, "The Fuel Powering Corporate America: $2.4 Trillion in Private Fundraising," *Wall Street Journal*, April 3, 2018, https://www.wsj.com/article_email/stock-and-bond-markets-dethroned-private-fundraising-is-now-dominant-1522683249-lMyQjAxMTI4MDAwMzIwNTM3Wj/.

11. Craig Doidge, G. Andrew Karolyi, and René M. Stulz, "The U.S. Listing Gap," *Journal of Financial Economics* 123 (2017): 464–487.

12. The cleantech discussion in this and the following paragraph is drawn from numerous press accounts (including those archived at https://www.washingtonpost.com/politics/specialreports/solyndra-scandal/) and various editions of the National Venture Capital Association's *Yearbook*, http://nvca.org/blog/nvca-2017-yearbook-go-resource-venture-ecosystem/.

13. This description is drawn from CalPERS Network, "Discussion of Alternative Private Equity Business Models," July 17, 2017, https://www.youtube.com/playlist?list=PLIKoYJoLyluK59VkASoC0k7w5KU9zFEaG; and Randy Diamond, "CEO Eliopoulos Sees Direct Investment in CalPERS' Future," *Pensions & Investments*, July 17, 2017, http://www.pionline.com/article/20170717/ONLINE/170719840/ceo-eliopoulos-sees-direct-investment-in-calpers-future; Arleen Jacobius, "6 Firms Bid to Partner on CalPERS' Private Equity Portfolio," *Pensions & Investments*, January 24, 2018, http://www.pionline.com/article/20180124/ONLINE/180129924/6-firms-bid-to-partner-on-calpers-private-equity-portfolio.

14. This account is based on, among other sources, Simeon Kerr, "Sleepy Saudi Sovereign Wealth Fund Wakes and Shakes Global Finance," January 28, 2017, https://www.ft.com/content/bd3d7c34-b877-11e6-961e-a1acd97f622d; Kate Kelley and Landon Thomas, "Big Payoff after Blackstone Courted a Saudi Prince," *New York Times*, May 25, 2017, https://www.nytimes.com/2017/05/25/business/dealbook/blackstone-saudi-arabia-investments-infrastructure.html; and Alec Macfarlane and Margherita Stancati, "SoftBank and Saudi Arabia Team Up for $100 Billion Tech Fund," *Wall Street Journal*, October 14, 2016, https://www.wsj.com/articles/softbank-group-launches-investment-fund-1476398189.

15. Victoria Ivashina and Josh Lerner, "Looking for Alternatives: Pension Investment around the World, 2008 to 2017," working paper, 2018.

16. Jacobellis v. Ohio, 378 U.S. 184 (1964).

17. World Economic Forum, *Future of Long-Term Investing*.

18. Dominic Barton and Mark Wiseman, "Focusing Capital on the Long Term," *Harvard Business Review*, January/February 2014, https://hbr.org/2014/01/focusing-capital-on-the-long-term.

19. World Bank, "Stocks Traded, Turnover Ratio of Domestic Shares (%)," http://data.worldbank.org/indicator/CM.MKT.TRNR?locations=US-1W.

20. This history of the iPod is drawn from, among other sources, Walter Isaacson, *Steve Jobs* (New York: Simon & Schuster, 2011); and Brent Schlender and Rick Tetzeling, *Steve Jobs: The Evolution of a Reckless Upstart into a Visionary Leader* (New York: Crown Business, 2016).

21. Brad King and Farhad Manjoo, "Apple's 'Breakthrough' iPod," *Wired*, October 23, 2001, https://www.wired.com/2001/10/apples-breakthrough-ipod/; David Pogue, "Apple's Musical Rendition: A Jukebox Fed by the Mac," *New York Times*, October 25, 2001, http://www.nytimes

.com/2001/10/25/technology/state-of-the-art-apple-s-musical-rendition-a-jukebox-fed-by
-the-mac.html.

22. Sam Costello, "This Is the Number of iPods Sold All-Time," *LifeWire*, March 21, 2017,
https://www.lifewire.com/number-of-ipods-sold-all-time-1999515.

23. Thomas J. Watson, *Father, Son, and Co.: My Life at IBM and Beyond* (New York: Bantam,
1990); Laurence S. Kuter, *The Great Gamble: The Boeing 747: The Boeing—Pan Am Project to
Develop, Produce, and Introduce the 747* (Tuscaloosa: University of Alabama Press, 1973); Joe
Sutter, *747: Creating the World's First Jumbo Jet and Other Adventures from a Life in Aviation*
(Washington, DC: Smithsonian Books, 2006).

24. Jeremy C. Stein, "Efficient Capital Markets, Inefficient Firms: A Model of Myopic Corporate Behavior," *Quarterly Journal of Economics* 104, no. 4 (1989): 655–669.

25. See, for instance, Alon Brav, Wei Jiang, and Hyunseob Kim, "The Real Effects of Hedge
Fund Activism: Productivity, Asset Allocation, and Labor Outcomes," *Review of Financial Studies*
28, no. 10 (October 2015): 2723–2769; and Lucian A. Bebchuk, Alon Brav, and Wei Jiang, "The
Long-Term Effects of Hedge Fund Activism," National Bureau of Economic Research, Working
Paper no. 21227, 2015.

26. Shai Bernstein, "Does Going Public Affect Innovation?," *Journal of Finance* 70 (2015):
1365–1403.

27. The classic treatment of these problems is in Michael C. Jensen and William H. Meckling,
"Theory of the Firm: Managerial Behavior, Agency Costs, and Ownership Structure," *Journal of
Financial Economics* 3 (1976): 305–360.

28. Ilan Guedj and David Scharfstein, "Organizational Scope and Investment: Evidence from
the Drug Development Strategies and Performance of Biopharmaceutical Firms," National Bureau of Economic Research, Working Paper no. 10933, 2004.

29. Bessemer Venture Partners, "Anti-portfolio," http://www.bvp.com/Portfolio/AntiPort
folio.aspx, accessed December 16, 2011.

30. William Kerr, Ramana Nanda, and Matthew Rhodes-Kropf, "Entrepreneurship as Experimentation," *Journal of Economic Perspectives* 28, no. 3 (Summer 2014): 25–48.

31. For a discussion of this point, see S. J. Grossman and O. D. Hart, "Takeover Bids, the Free-
Rider Problem, and the Theory of the Corporation," *Bell Journal of Economics* 11, no. 1 (Spring,
1980). One can also argue that index-linked mutual funds represent long-term investors when
they purchase publicly traded stock and hold it until the company is dropped from the index.
Index funds, however, are less likely to engage in this kind of shareholder activism.

32. The limitations of bank financing are explored in such theoretical and empirical academic
studies as Joseph E. Stiglitz and Andrew Weiss, "Credit Rationing in Markets with Incomplete
Information," *American Economic Review* 71 (1981): 393–409; and Mitchell A. Petersen and
Raghuram G. Rajan, "The Effect of Credit Market Competition on Lending Relationships,"
Quarterly Journal of Economics 110 (1995): 407–444.

33. See, for instance, Larry Neal, "Venture Shares of the Dutch East India Company," in William N. Goetzmann and K. Geert Rouwenhorsts, editors, *The Origins of Value: The Financial
Innovations That Created Modern Capital Markets* (New York: Oxford University Press, 2005),
166–188; and Peter Tufano, "Business Failure, Judicial Intervention, and Financial Innovation:

Restructuring U.S. Railroads in the Nineteenth Century," *Business History Review* 71, no. 1 (1997): 1–40.

34. Josh Lerner and Samuel Kortum, "Assessing the Impact of Venture Capital on Innovation," *Rand Journal of Economics* 31, no. 4 (2000): 674–692; Manju Puri and Rebecca Zarutskie, "On the Life Cycle Dynamics of Venture-Capital- and Non-Venture-Capital-Financed Firms," *Journal of Finance* 67, no. 6 (2012): 2247–2293.

35. Shai Bernstein, Josh Lerner, and Filippo Mezzanotti, "Private Equity and Financial Fragility during the Crisis," National Bureau of Economic Research, Working Paper no. 23626, 2017, http://www.nber.org/papers/w23626; Shai Bernstein and Albert Sheen, "The Operational Consequences of Private Equity Buyouts: Evidence from the Restaurant Industry," *Review of Financial Studies* 29, no. 9 (2016): 2387–2418; Jonathan B. Cohn, Nicole Nestoriak, and Malcolm Wardlaw, "Private Equity Buyouts and Workplace Safety," 2017, https://ssrn.com/abstract=2728704; Steve Davis, John Haltiwanger, Kyle Hanley, Ron Jarmin, Josh Lerner, and Javier Miranda, "Private Equity, Jobs, and Productivity," *American Economic Review* 104, no. 12 (2014): 3956–3990; Josh Lerner, Morten Sørensen, and Per Strömberg, "Private Equity and Long-Run Investment: The Case of Innovation," *Journal of Finance* 66, no. 2 (2011): 445–477. (It should be noted that the Davis et al. paper suggests that the impact of private equity on employment levels and wages is far less benign.)

36. This is based in part on Liz Farmer and Daniel C. Vock, "Alabama's One-Man Pension Show," *Governing*, May 2016, http://www.governing.com/topics/mgmt/gov-alabama-david-bronner.html; Dan Luzadder, "Alabama Pension Fund Plows Millions into Property in Its Own Backyard," *New York Times*, October 27, 2009, http://www.nytimes.com/2009/10/28/reales tate/commercial/28alabama.html; Daniel J. Smith and John A. Dove, "The Economic Consequences of Pension Underfunding: Evidence from the Retirement Systems of Alabama," 2016, SSN Working Paper, https://ssrn.com/abstract=2795692; and Casey Toner, "RSA under Fire: Inside the Latest Battle over Alabama's Pension Powerhouse," AL.com, September 28, 2015, http://www.al.com/news/index.ssf/2015/09/retirement_systems_of_alabama.html.

37. Casey Toner, "RSA's Winners and Losers. Hint: The Golf Courses Are a Drag," AL.com, September 29, 2015, https://www.al.com/news/index.ssf/2015/09/rsas_winners_and_losers _hint_t.html; Cliff Sims, "How an Alabama State Employee Built a Billionaire's Lifestyle in a Taxpayer-Funded Job (Opinion)," *Yellowhammer News*, March 14, 2016, http://yellowham mernews.com/business-2/how-an-alabama-state-employee-built-billionaire-lifestyle/.

38. See the summary of the case in Tom Smith, "Former Plant CEO Indicted in Colbert," *Florence Times Daily*, November 16, 2013, http://www.timesdaily.com/news/local/former-plant -ceo-indicted-in-colbert/article_c6c8695a-4e7e-11e3-9e19-10604b9f6eda.html.

39. Samuel Addy and Ahmad Ijaz, *Economic Impacts of RSA-Owned Investments on Alabama for the Retirement Systems of Alabama*, Center for Business and Economic Research, Culverhouse College of Commerce and Business Administration, University of Alabama, 2008, http://www .rsa-al.gov/uploads/files/RSA_Inv_EI_Final_Report.pdf; Bernie Delinski, "SEDA Board Alters Navistar, FreightCar Incentives," *Florence Times Daily*, February 16, 2016, http://www.times daily.com/seda-board-alters-navistar-freightcar-incentives/article_660ed242-9b4b-5c9d -90bc-0847b8979df5.html.

40. Delinski, "SEDA Board."

41. Kent Faulk, "Alabama Securities Fraud Charges Dismissed against CEO of Canadian Company; RSA to Get $21 Million in Settlement," AL.com, November 14, 2014, http://www.al.com/news/birmingham/index.ssf/2014/11/alabama_securities_fraud_charg.html.

42. David G. Bronner, "RSA Is Making Alabama Better," AL.com, December 18, 2011, http://blog.al.com/press-register-commentary/2011/12/rsa_is_making_alabama_better_i.html.

43. Joshua Rauh, *Hidden Debt, Hidden Deficits: 2017 Edition* (Stanford, CA: Hoover Institution, 2017), http://www.hoover.org/sites/default/files/research/docs/rauh_hiddendebt2017_final_webreadypdf1.pdf.

44. James Barth and John Jahera, *Alabama Public Pensions: Building a Stable Financial Foundation for the Years Ahead* (Birmingham: Alabama Policy Institute, 2015), https://www.alabamapolicy.org/wp-content/uploads/Alabama%E2%80%99s-Public-Pensions-Building-a-Stable-Financial-Foundation-for-the-Years-Ahead.pdf.

45. This account is drawn from Kentucky Retirement Systems, *2016 KRS Comprehensive Annual Financial Reports,* (Frankfort, KY: KRS, 2017), https://kyret.ky.gov/Publications/Books/2016%20CAFR%20(Comprehensive%20Annual%20Financial%20Report).pdf, pp. 62, 96, 122, 145; and Attracta Mooney, "Kentucky, Home to the Worst-Funded Pension Plan in the US," *Financial Times,* June 10, 2016, http://www.ft.com/cms/s/0/a1c5c5d6-2cc9-11e6-bf8d-26294ad519fc.html#axzz4GHOeWaIh.

46. https://pensions.ky.gov/Pages/Overview.aspx, accessed October 26, 2017.

47. PricewaterhouseCoopers, "State Financial Position Index (SFPI) and Competitiveness Posture Report," 2017, http://www.pwc.com/us/en/public-sector/publications/state-financial-position-index.html.

48. John Cheves, "Kentucky Retirement Systems Pays Millions in Fees to Money Managers but Keeps the Details a Secret," *Lexington Herald-Leader,* June 14, 2014, http://www.kentucky.com/news/politics-government/article44493327.html.

49. John Cheves, "Financier Who Stole Millions from Kentucky Retirement Systems Is Sentenced to Prison," *Lexington Herald-Leader,* April 21, 2015, http://www.kentucky.com/news/business/article44595330.html.

50. Ibid.

51. "Fisher Sees Stocks Permanently High; Yale Economist Tells Purchasing Agents Increased Earnings Justify Rise," *New York Times,* October 16, 1929, 8.

52. Paul Samuelson, "Science and Stocks," *Newsweek,* September 19, 1966, 92.

CHAPTER 2. THE MOST IMPORTANT PEOPLE IN THE ROOM

1. The quote and many of the other facts about Keynes's management of the King's College endowment are drawn from David Chambers, Elroy Dimson, and Justin Foo, "Keynes, King's, and Endowment Asset Management," in Jeffrey R. Brown and Caroline M. Hoxby, editors, *How the Financial Crisis and Great Recession Affected Higher Education* (Chicago: University of Chicago Press, 2014). We also relied on David Chambers, Elroy Dimson, and Justin Foo, "Keynes the Stock Market Investor: A Quantitative Approach," *Journal of Financial and Quantitative Analysis* 50 (August 2015): 843–868.

2. David Chambers and Elroy Dimson, "The British Origins of the US Endowment Model," *Financial Analysts Journal* 71 (March–April 2015): 10–14.

3. This discussion is based on "How Larry Tisch and NYU Missed Epic Bull Markets," *Wall Street Journal*, October 16, 1997, http://www.wsj.com/articles/SB876952178231654000; Jonathan Kandell, "Laurence A. Tisch, Investor Known for Saving CBS Inc. from Takeover, Dies at 80," *New York Times*, November 16, 2003, http://www.nytimes.com/2003/11/16/business /laurence-a-tisch-investor-known-for-saving-cbs-inc-from-takeover-dies-at-80.html ?pagewanted=all; and "The Skorina Report: A Look at the New Investment Crew at NYU," *All about Alpha*, July 9, 2015, http://www.allaboutalpha.com/blog/2015/07/09/the-skorina -report-a-look-at-the-new-investment-crew-at-nyu/.

4. "Tsk, Tsk, Larry Tisch," *Fortune*, October 26, 2007, http://archive.fortune.com/magazines /fortune/fortune_archive/1987/10/26/69714/index.htm.

5. Terry Williams, "NYU Remakes Its Endowment," *Pensions & Investments*, March 9, 1998, http://www.pionline.com/article/19980309/PRINT/803090720/nyu-remakes -its-endowment.

6. "Tsk, Tsk, Larry Tisch," *Fortune*.

7. Claude H. W. Johns, *Babylonian and Assyrian Laws, Contracts and Letters* (New York: Charles Scribner's Sons, 1904).

8. This discussion is drawn in large part from Udayan Gupta, "Peter Crisp: Venrock Associates," *Done Deals: Venture Capitalists Tell Their Stories* (Boston: Harvard Business School Press, 2000), 107–112; "Laurance Rockefeller, 1910–2004," *The Rockefeller Family Archive*, 2004, http://rockarch.org/bio/laurance.php; W. David Lewis, *Eddie Rickenbacker: An American Hero in the Twentieth Century* (Baltimore: Johns Hopkins University Press, 2005); David Rockefeller, *Memoirs* (New York: Random House, 2002); and Robin W. Winks, *Laurance S. Rockefeller: Catalyst for Conservation* (Washington, DC: Island Press, 1997).

9. Rupert Cromwell, "Laurance Rockefeller: Conservationist Who Put His Rockefeller Riches to Work," *Independent*, July 12, 2004, http://www.independent.co.uk/news/obituaries/laurance -rockefeller-38820.html.

10. William Elfers, *Greylock: An Adventure Capital Story* (Boston: Greylock Management, 1995), 7.

11. Board of Governors of the Federal Reserve System, "Financial Accounts of the United States," March 8, 2018, Tables L.166 and L.117, https://www.federalreserve.gov/releases/z1/20180308 /html/l117.htm; Commonfund and National Association of College and University Business Officers, *2017 NACUBO-Commonfund Study of Endowments* (Greenwich, CT: Commonfund, 2018).

12. Preqin, *2017 Sovereign Wealth Fund Review* (London: Preqin, 2017) and earlier years.

13. "Norges Bank Investment Management," 2017, https://www.nbim.no/.

14. This account is based on, among other sources, Preqin, *2017 Sovereign Wealth Fund Review*; and International Monetary Fund, "IMF Executive Board Concludes 2016 Article IV Consultation with Kiribati," Press Release 16/400, September 9, 2016, https://www.imf.org/en/News /Articles/2016/09/09/PR16400-Kiribati-IMF-Executive-Board-Concludes -2016-Article -IV-Consultation.

15. "Russian Direct Investment Fund," 2017, https://rdif.ru/Eng_Index/.

16. "About Mubadala," 2017, https://www.mubadala.com/en/who-we-are/about-the-com pany. Of course, in some cases where groups do not have an official mandate other than maximization of risk-adjusted returns, such as the Chinese Investment Corporation (CIC), they may still make investments in industries critical to the nation.

17. The Singapore discussion is drawn from a variety of sources, including Saeed Azhar and Rachel Armstrong, "Singapore GIC Gives Private Equity Firms Run for Their Money," *Reuters*, September 4, 2014, https://www.reuters.com/article/gic-privateequity/going-direct-gic-gives -private-equity-firms-run-for-their-money-idUSL3N0QV1JX20140903; Shirley Koh and Boon-Siong Neo, "Temasek Holdings and Its Governance of Governance-Linked Companies," Nanyang Business School Case no. NTU078, 2016; and Freddy Orchard, "Safeguarding the Future: The Story of How Singapore Has Managed Its Reserves and the Founding of GIC," 2012, http://gichistory.gic.com.sg/.

18. Koh and Neo, "Temasek Holdings," 4.

19. GIC, *Investment Report*, various years, http://www.gic.com.sg/report/report-2015-2016 /investment-report.html.

20. Like many large investors, GIC struggled to match market benchmarks, much less the returns achieved by the top endowments and family offices. According to its *Investment Report*, in the twenty years ended in 2016, GIC generated an annual return of 5.7%. A standard portfolio consisting of a 60% weight on the Wilshire 5000 and 40% on the Barclays Aggregate Bond Index would have returned 7.4% annually.

21. This account is drawn from Canadian Pension Plan Investment Board, *Annual Reports*, Toronto, various years; Felda Hardymon, Ann Leamon, and Josh Lerner, "Canada Pension Plan Investment Board," Harvard Business School Case no. 809-073, 2009 ; and Josh Lerner, Matthew Rhodes-Kropf, and Nathaniel Burbank, "Canada Pension Plan Investment Board: October 2012," Harvard Business School Case no. 813-103, 2013.

22. CPPIB, "Management's Discussion and Analysis," *Annual Report*, 2012, 21.

23. Due to legacy holdings of nontradable bonds, this allocation could never be achieved in reality but served as a target.

24. CPPIB, *2005 Annual Report*, 8.

25. Brad Stone and Claire Cain Miller, "EBay Is Said to Have Deal to Sell Skype," *New York Times*, September 1, 2009, http://www.nytimes.com/2009/09/01/technology/companies /01ebay.html?pagewanted=all.

26. CPPIB, "Investor Group to Acquire Majority Stake in Skype," press release, September 4, 2009, http://www.cppib.ca/files/PDF/Silver_Lake_Press_Release_FINAL.pdf.

27. CPPIB, "Management's Discussion and Analysis," *Annual Report*, 2012, 55.

28. Matthew Rhodes-Kropf, Luis M. Viceira, John D. Dionne, and Nathaniel Burbank, "Texas Teachers and the New Texas Way," Harvard Business School Case no. 9-214-091, 2014.

CHAPTER 3. THE LONG-TERM CONUNDRUM

1. Robert S. Harris and Rüdiger Stucke, "Are Too Many Private Equity Funds Top Quartile?," *Journal of Applied Corporate Finance* 24, no. 4 (2012): 77–89.

2. William Elfers, *Greylock: An Adventure Capital Story* (Boston: Greylock Management, 1995), 162.

3. Howard Marks, "Lines in the Sand," Oaktree Capital Management, April 18, 2017, https://www.oaktreecapital.com/docs/default-source/memos/lines-in-the-sand.pdf.

4. These examples are adapted from Steven Kaplan and Antoinette Schoar, "Private Equity Performance: Returns, Persistence, and Capital," *Journal of Finance* 60, no. 4 (2005): 1791–1823.

5. Robert S. Harris, Tim Jenkinson, and Steven N. Kaplan, "How Do Private Equity Investments Perform Compared to Public Equity?," *Journal of Investment Management* 14, no. 3 (2016): 1–24.

6. This analysis was undertaken for the authors. We thank Nan Zhang for his help.

7. See, for instance, Gregory W. Brown, Oleg Gredil, and Steven N. Kaplan, "Do Private Equity Funds Manipulate Reported Returns?," *Journal of Financial Economics*, forthcoming.

8. Lubos Pastor and Robert Stambaugh, "Liquidity Risk and Expected Stock Returns," *Journal of Political Economy* 111, no. 3 (2003): 642–685.

9. This paragraph is based on Roger Lowenstein, *When Genius Failed: The Rise and Fall of Long-Term Capital Management* (New York: Random House, 2000).

10. Tyler Durden, "Debt-to-EBITDA Ratios Are Now the Highest in History," August 4, 2016, http://www.zerohedge.com/news/2016-08-04/debt-ebitda-ratios-are-now-highest-history, and the S&P Leveraged Commentary and Data database.

11. Preqin, *Preqin 2017 Real Estate Report* (London: Preqin, 2017), 75; Roger Ibbotson, Roger J. Grabowski, James P. Harrington, and Carla Nunes, *Stocks, Bonds, Bills, and Inflation (SBBI) Yearbook* (New York: Wiley, 2017).

12. This analysis is drawn from Cambridge Associates, "10-Year Manager Return Dispersion across Asset Classes: First Quarter 2007–Fourth Quarter 2016 (Trailing 10-Year Period)," 2017.

13. This phenomenon is discussed, for instance, in Jonathan B. Berk and Richard C. Green, "Mutual Fund Flows and Performance in Rational Markets," *Journal of Political Economy* 112, no. 6 (2004): 1269–1295.

14. Arthur Korteweg and Morten Sørensen, "Skill and Luck in Private Equity Performance," *Journal of Financial Economics* 124, no. 3 (2017): 535–562.

15. These performance numbers are from Preqin, as of June 2017.

16. Robert S. Harris, Tim Jenkinson, Steven N. Kaplan, and Rüdiger Stucke, "Has Persistence Persisted in Private Equity? Evidence from Buyout and Venture Capital Funds," Darden Business School, Working Paper no. 2304808, 2014, https://ssrn.com/abstract=2304808.

17. A classic analysis is Mark Carhart, "On Persistence in Mutual Fund Performance," *Journal of Finance* 52 (1997): 57–82.

18. See, for instance, Stephen J. Brown, William N. Goetzmann, and Roger G. Ibbotson, "Offshore Hedge Funds: Survival and Performance, 1989–95," *Journal of Business* 72 (1999): 91–117.

19. Josh Lerner, Antoinette Schoar, and Wan Wong, "Smart Institutions, Foolish Choices?: The Limited Partner Performance Puzzle," *Journal of Finance* 62, no. 2 (2007): 731–764.

20. Josh Lerner, Antoinette Schoar, and Jialan Wang, "Secrets of the Academy: The Drivers of University Endowment Success," *Journal of Economic Perspectives* 22 (Summer 2008): 207–222.

21. "Manifold Effects of Hard Times," *Time Magazine* (December 9, 1974), 40–41; Christopher Shea, "U. of Rochester to Cut Programs, Faculty, and Enrollment," *Chronicle of Higher Education* 42, no. 16 (1995): A33.

22. Harris et al., "Has Persistence Persisted in Private Equity?"

23. Heather Timmons, "Criticism of State-Owned Air India Grows," *New York Times*, May 25, 2011.

24. Philip S. Khinda, Donald E. Wellington, and Ellen S. Zimiles, "Report of the CalPERS Special Review," Steptoe & Johnson and Navigant Consulting, March 2011, https://www.scribd.com/document/214615140/CalPERS-Special-Review-by-Steptoe-Johnson.

25. Ed Timms and Christy Hoppe, "Texas Teacher Pension Fund Gave More in Bonuses Than All Other State Agencies Combined, Analysis Shows," *Dallas Morning News*, April 23, 2011, https://www.dallasnews.com/news/texas/2011/04/23/texas-teacher-pension-fund-gave-more-in-bonuses-than-all-other-state-agencies-combined-analysis-shows.

26. Ibid.

27. Ibid.

28. Ibid.

29. Berk Sensoy, Yingdi Wang, and Michael Weisbach, "Limited Partner Performance and the Maturing of the Private Equity Industry," *Journal of Financial Economics* 112, no. 3 (2014): 320–343.

30. This analysis is taken from Harris et al., "Has Persistence Persisted in Private Equity?"

CHAPTER 4. INVESTING AS IF THE LONG TERM MATTERED

1. Robert H. Hayes and William J. Abernathy, "Managing Our Way to Economic Decline," *Harvard Business Review* (July–August 1980): 67–77.

2. George C. Lodge, *The American Disease* (New York: Alfred A. Knopf, 1984).

3. Yale University Investments Office, *The Yale Endowment: 2017* (New Haven, CT: Yale, 2018) and earlier years.

4. Josh Lerner, "Yale University Investments Office: February 2015," Case no. 815-124 (Boston: Harvard Business School Publishing, 2015).

5. Abby Jackson, "Malcolm Gladwell Unloads on Yale for Reportedly Paying $480 Million to Hedge Fund Managers Last Year," *Business Insider*, August 19, 2015, http://www.businessinsider.com/malcolm-gladwell-attacks-yale-for-its-480-million-payment-to-hedge-fund-managers-2015-8; Warren E. Buffett, "Letter to the Shareholders of Berkshire Hathaway," February 25, 2017, http://www.berkshirehathaway.com/letters/2016ltr.pdf.

6. Lerner, "Yale University Investments Office." The total combines the reduced value of the endowment at the end of the period and the smaller payouts from the endowment that would have happened in the interim, based on the spending rules for university employees.

7. David T. Robinson and Berk A. Sensoy, "Do Private Equity Fund Managers Earn Their Fees? Compensation, Ownership, and Cash Flow Performance," *Review of Financial Studies* 26 (2013): 2760–2797.

8. James B. Stewart, "In College Endowment Returns, Davids Beat the Goliaths," *New York Times*, February 25, 2016, https://www.nytimes.com/2016/02/26/business/in-college-endow

ment-returns-davids-beat-the-goliaths.html. A subsequent correction in the *Times* pointed out that SVU used a nonstandard fiscal year, which encompassed part of the 2015 fiscal year, a more favorable period for equities.

9. National Association of College and University Business Officers, "U.S. and Canadian Institutions Listed by Fiscal Year (FY) 2016 Endowment Market Value and Change in Endowment Market Value from FY2015 to FY2016," NACUBO, 2017, http://www.nacubo.org/Documents /EndowmentFiles/2016-Endowment-Market-Values.pdf.

10. Roger Ibbotson, Roger J. Grabowski, James P. Harrington, and Carla Nunes, *Stocks, Bonds, Bills, and Inflation (SBBI) Yearbook* (New York: Wiley, 2017).

11. This section is drawn from Sean Koh, Josh Lerner, and Alison Tarditi, "PensionDanmark: Direct Infrastructure Investing," in *Innovations in Long-Term Management: The Practitioner's Perspective* (Geneva: World Economic Forum, 2016), 72–79.

12. Australian Centre for Financial Studies, *2016 Melbourne Mercer Global Pension Index Media Release*, 2016, http://www.globalpens,ionindex.com/news/2016-melbourne-mercer -global-pension-index-media-release/.

13. Nicholas Tsafos, "Infrastructure Still Elusive in Pension Fund Asset Allocation," *Pensions & Investments*, March 3, 2014, http://www.pionline.com/article/20140303/PRINT/303039992 /infrastructure-still-elusive-in-pension-fund-asset-allocation.

14. Frederick Blanc-Brude, "Making a Better Match between Institutional Investors and Infrastructure Investments," *Rethinking Infrastructure: Voices from the Global Infrastructure Initiative* (New York: McKinsey & Co., 2014), 13–20, http://www.mckinsey.com/~/media/mckinsey/dotcom /client_service/infrastructure/pdfs/gii%20compendium/rethinkinginfrastructure_gii.ashx.

15. Toby D. Couture and Mischa Bechberger, "Pain in Spain: New Retroactive Changes Hinder Renewable Energy," *Renewable Energy World*, April 19, 2013, http://www.renewableenergyworld .com/articles/2013/04/pain-in-spain-new-retroactive-changes-hinders-renewable-energy.html.

16. Another more recent example of creative expansion into the alternative asset space can be seen in the case of PFA, Denmark's largest private insurance and pension company. For more information, see Victoria Ivashina, Federica Gabrieli, and Jérôme Lenhardt, "PFA Pension: Expansion of Alternatives Portfolio," Harvard Business School Case no. 218-025, 2017.

17. The rest of this chapter owes a substantial debt to Josh Lerner, Antoinette Schoar, and Jialan Wang, "Secrets of the Academy: The Drivers of University Endowment Success," *Journal of Economic Perspectives* 22 (Summer 2008): 207–222, and especially to Ann Leamon, Josh Lerner, and Vladimir Bosiljevac, *Measurement, Governance, and Long-Term Investing* (Geneva: World Economic Forum, 2012). Because of our inability to improve on Ann's prose, many words originally written by her found their way into this chapter.

18. https://www.youtube.com/watch?v=2nf_bu-kBr4.

19. Michael Lewis, *Moneyball* (New York: W. W. Norton & Company, 2004).

20. Advisory Committee on Endowment Management, *Managing Educational Endowments: Report to the Ford Foundation* (New York: Ford Foundation, 1969).

21. Gordon L. Clark and Roger Urwin, "Best-Practice Pension Fund Governance," *Journal of Asset Management* 9, no. 1 (2008): 2–21.

22. Leamon, Lerner, and Bosiljevac, *Measurement, Governance, and Long-Term Investing.*

23. Paul Myners, "Institutional Investment in the United Kingdom: A Review," 2001, http://www.hm-treasury.gov.uk/media/2F9/02/31.pdf, cited in Gordon L. Clark, Emiko Caerlewy-Smith, and John Marshall, "Pension Fund Trustee Competence: Decision-Making in Problems Relevant to Investment Practice," *Journal of Pension Economics and Finance* 5 (2006): 93.

24. Keith Ambachtsheer, Ronald Capelle, and Hubert Lum, "The Pension Governance Deficit: Still with Us," *Rotman International Journal of Pension Management* 1, no. 1 (Fall 2008): 14–21.

25. Pensions Regulator of the U.K., *Code of Practice No. 7: Trustee Knowledge and Understanding*, 2009, accessed February 24, 2012. http://www.thepensionsregulator.gov.uk/docs/code-07-trustee-knowledge-understanding.pdf, 6.

26. Olivia S. Mitchell, John Piggott, and Cagri Kumru, "Managing Public Investment Funds: Best Practices and New Challenges," NBER, Working Paper no. 14078, August 2008, http://www.nber.org/papers/w14078.

27. CalPERS, http://www.calpers.ca.gov/index.jsp?bc=/about/organization/board/home.xml, accessed November 7, 2011. In response to a comprehensive review of its governance practices, CalPERS has reduced the number of board committees and adopted ten governance reforms ("CalPERS Board Adopts Governance Reforms," press release, September 14, 2011, http://www.calpers.ca.gov/index.jsp?bc=/about/press/pr-2011/sept/calpers-board-adopts.xml; and "CalPERS Changes Board Committee Line-Up," press release, February 10, 2012, accessed February 24, 2012, http://www.calpers.ca.gov/index.jsp?bc=/about/press/pr-2012/feb/board-line-up.xml).

28. David Hess, "Protecting and Politicizing Public Pension Fund Assets," *U. Cal-Davis Law Review* 39 (2005): 187–227.

29. Clark, Caerlewy-Smith, and Marshall, "Pension Fund Trustee Competence," 93; Fiona Stewart and Juan Yermo, "Pension Fund Governance: Challenges and Potential Solutions," OECD, Working Papers on Insurance and Private Pensions, no. 18, 2008 (DOI 10.1787/241402256531, http://dx.doi.org/10.1787/241402256531).

30. Aleksandar Andonov, Yael Hochberg, and Joshua Rauh, "Political Representation and Governance: Evidence from the Investment Decisions of Public Pension Funds," *Journal of Finance*, forthcoming.

31. Stewart and Yermo, "Pension Fund Governance."

32. This paragraph is drawn from Canadian Pension Plan Investment Board, *Annual Reports*, Toronto, various years; Felda Hardymon, Ann Leamon, and Josh Lerner, "Canada Pension Plan Investment Board," Harvard Business School Case no. 809-073, 2009 ; and Josh Lerner, Matthew Rhodes-Kropf, and Nathaniel Burbank, "Canada Pension Plan Investment Board: October 2012," Harvard Business School Case no. 813-103, 2013.

33. Hardymon, Leamon, and Lerner, "Canada Pension Plan Investment Board," 1.

34. Clark and Urwin, "Best-Practice Pension Fund Governance."

35. For more, see Martijn Cremers and Antti Petajisto, "How Active Is Your Fund Manager?," *Review of Financial Studies* 22, no. 9 (2009): 3329–3365.

36. Of course, part of this turnover is driven by compensation matters, which we discuss shortly.

37. Leamon, Lerner, and Bosiljevac, *Measurement, Governance, and Long-Term Investing*.

38. Paul A. Gompers, "Grandstanding in the Venture Capital Industry," *Journal of Financial Economics* 42, no. 1 (1996): 133–156.

39. Leamon, Lerner, and Bosiljevac, *Measurement, Governance, and Long-Term Investing.* Some infrastructure funds and a small number of private equity funds, it should be noted, are structured with a longer life to match the asset length. We explore these in more depth in chapter 7.

40. Gregory W. Brown, Oleg Gredil, and Steven N. Kaplan, "Do Private Equity Funds Manipulate Reported Returns?," *Journal of Financial Economics*, forthcoming.

41. Rolfe Winkler, "Andreessen Horowitz's Returns Trail Venture-Capital Elite," *Wall Street Journal*, September 1, 2016, https://www.wsj.com/articles/andreessen-horowitzs-returns -trail-venture-capital-elite-1472722381.

42. Scott Kupor, "When Is a "Mark" Not a Mark? When It's a Venture Capital Mark," *Andreessen Horowitz*, September 1, 2016, http://a16z.com/2016/09/01/marks-offmark/.

43. For a systematic look at the overvaluations that can result in this setting, see Will Gornall and Ilya Strebulaev, "Squaring Venture Capital Valuations with Reality," *Journal of Financial Economics*, forthcoming, https://ssrn.com/abstract=2955455.

44. Loch Adamson, "Sovereign Wealth Funds Starting to Embrace Transparency," *Institutional Investor*, September 15, 2011.

45. Future Fund, "Portfolio Update at 31 March 2017," April 27, 2017, http://www.futurefund .gov.au/-/media/files/futurefund/05---portfolio-updates/portfolio-update-at-31-march-2017 .pdf?la=en&hash=6A0C9979BB7546211E8FA71C4302D33E6CE73E91.

46. Leamon, Lerner, and Bosiljevac, *Measurement, Governance, and Long-Term Investing.*

47. Nicholas Barberis and Richard Thaler, "A Survey of Behavioral Finance," working paper, http://papers.ssrn.com/sol3/papers.cfm?abstract_id=327880.

48. R. Alexander Hetherington, cited in Alison Griswold, "Investments Office Hires Yalies." *Yale Daily News*, October 22, 2010, https://yaledailynews.com/blog/2010/10/22/invest ments-office-hires-yalies/.

49. Hardymon, Leamon, and Lerner, "Canada Pension Plan Investment Board," 12.

50. Teresa M. Amabile, "Motivational Synergy: Toward New Conceptualizations of Intrinsic and Extrinsic Motivation in the Workplace," *Human Resource Management Review* 3, no. 3 (1993): 185–201.

51. Ibbotson et al., *SBBI Yearbook.*

52. Geraldine Fabrikant, "Harvard Endowment Loses 22%," *New York Times*, December 3, 2008, http://www.nytimes.com/2008/12/04/business/04harvard.html.

53. Robert J. Shiller, *Irrational Exuberance* (New York: Random House, Inc., 2005); Werner F. M. De Bondt and Richard Thaler, "Does the Stock Market Overreact?," *Journal of Finance* 40 (1985): 793–808; Werner F. M. De Bondt and Richard Thaler, "Further Evidence on Investor Overreaction and Stock Market Seasonality," *Journal of Finance* 42 (1987): 557–581.

CHAPTER 5. THE GENESIS OF PRIVATE CAPITAL

1. Steven N. Kaplan and Josh Lerner, "It Ain't Broke: The Past, Present, and Future of Venture Capital," *Journal of Applied Corporate Finance* 22 (Spring 2010), 1–12. In doing this calculation, we eliminated IPOs that were not true start-ups—blank-check companies, corporate spin-outs or spin-offs, financial institutions, REITS, and reverse leveraged buyouts.

2. Steve Davis, John Haltiwanger, Kyle Hanley, Ron Jarmin, and Javier Miranda, "The Social Impact of Private Equity over Boom and Bust," working paper, University of Chicago, 2018.

3. This discussion is drawn primarily from Spencer E. Ante, *Creative Capital: Georges Doriot and the Birth of Venture Capital* (Boston, MA: Harvard Business, 2008); David H. Hsu and Martin Kenney, "Organizing Venture Capital: The Rise and Demise of American Research & Development Corporation, 1946–1973," *Industrial and Corporate Change* 14, no. 4 (2005): 579–616; and Tom Nicholas and David Chen, "Georges Doriot and American Venture Capital," Harvard Business School Case no. 9-812-110, 2015.

4. Ante, *Creative Capital*, 112.

5. Hsu and Kenney, "Organizing Venture Capital," 586.

6. Georges Doriot, "Memorandum on Venture Capital," quoted in Nicholas and Chen, "Georges Doriot and American Venture Capital," 8.

7. Gene Bylinsky, "General Doriot's Dream Factory," *Fortune* 76 (August 1967): 104.

8. Ante, *Creative Capital*, 135–136.

9. Patrick R. Liles, *Sustaining the Venture Capital Firm* (Cambridge, MA: Management Analysis Center, 1977). To the best of our knowledge, no one has attempted to do a proper assessment of the ARD's returns during this period (e.g., a tailored public market equivalent analysis that properly controls for risk).

10. This account is especially based on Leslie Berlin, "Draper Gaither and Anderson: First Venture Capital Firm in Silicon Valley," in Bruce Schulman, editor, *Making the American Century: Essays on the Political Culture of Twentieth Century America* (New York: Oxford University Press, 2014); William H. Draper Jr., *The Startup Game: Inside the Partnership between Venture Capitalists and Entrepreneurs* (New York: Palgrave Macmillan, 2011); and "Blue Ribbon Venture Capital," *Business Week* (October 29, 1960): 65–69. It (and the account of 3i) is adapted from this in Josh Lerner, *The Architecture of Innovation* (Boston: Harvard Business School Publishing, 2012).

11. Berlin, "Draper Gaither and Anderson," 4.

12. Though general partners typically try to limit their exposure by using a corporate structure for the general partnership, plaintiffs occasionally have succeeded in extracting settlements or damages. One famous instance involved Hummer Winblad's investment in the notorious file-sharing service Napster (for a thoughtful discussion, see John Ottaviani, "The End is Near— Bertelsmann Settles EMI Claims over Napster," *Technology & Marketing Law Blog*, March 28, 2007, http://blog.ericgoldman.org/archives/2007/03/the_end_is_near.htm).

13. Draper, *The Startup Game*, 26.

14. This account is based primarily on George P. Baker and George D. Smith, *The New Financial Capitalists: Kohlberg Kravis Roberts and the Creation of Corporate Value* (New York: Cambridge University Press, 1998); Brian Burroughs and John Helyar, *Barbarians at the Gate: The Fall of RJR Nabisco* (New York: Harper & Row, 1990); and George Anders, *Merchants of Debt: KKR and the Mortgaging of American Business* (Washington, DC: BeardBooks, 1992).

15. Thomas R. Navin and Marian V. Sears, "A Study in Merger: Formation of the International Mercantile Marine Company," *Business History Review* 28, no. 4 (1954): 291–328.

16. Allan Nevins and Frank Ernest Hill, *Ford: Expansion and Challenge, 1915–1933* (New York: Charles Scribner's Sons, 1957).

17. The deal also used $50 million of preferred stock from banks and other financiers.

18. See, for instance, Steven Davis, John Haltiwanger, Kyle Hanley, Ron Jarmin, Josh Lerner, and Javier Miranda, "Private Equity, Jobs, and Productivity," *American Economic Review* 104 (December 2014): 3956–3990.

19. This history is based primarily on Richard Coopey and Donald Clarke, *3i: Fifty Years Investing in Industry* (Oxford: Oxford University Press, 1995); Felda Hardymon and Ann Leamon, "3i Group PLC—2006," Harvard Business School Case no. 803-020, 2003; Felda Hardymon, Ann Leamon, and Josh Lerner, "3i Group PLC," Harvard Business School Case no. 9-807-006, 2006; Henry Rinjen, "Global Pursuit," *Upside* 12 (October 2000): 90–94; and "3i Drops Early Stage," *European Venture Capital and Private Equity Journal* 150 (March 2008): 15.

20. Dan Gledhill, "3i Has the Balance to Surf the Net's New Wave," *Independent,* February 20, 2000, B7.

21. This is based on Thomson Reuters, "Datastream Database," http://online.thomsonreuters .com/datastream/.

22. Beth Healy, "3i Group: The Biggest Firm You've Never Heard Of," *Boston Globe,* May 6, 2002.

23. Benjamin Wootliff, "Tech Downturn Hits 3i Group," *Telegraph,* May 18, 2001, http://www .telegraph.co.uk/finance/4490768/Tech-downturn-hits-3i-Group.html.

24. Martin Arnold, "3i Quits Early-Stage Investments," *Financial Times,* March 24, 2008, https://www.ft.com/content/b64a1578-f9c6-11dc-9b7c-000077b07658.

25. For all its importance, the history of real estate private equity is not well documented. Two of the best historical discussions of the origins of the asset class are in Peter Linneman and Stanley Ross, "Real Estate Private Equity," Samuel Zell and Robert Lurie Real Estate Center, Working Paper no. 413, Wharton School, University of Pennsylvania, 2003; and Thea C. Hahn, David Geltner, and Nori Gerardo-Lietz, "Real Estate Opportunity Funds," *Journal of Portfolio Management* 31, no. 5 (2005): 143–153.

26. This discussion is drawn in large part on David Carey and John E. Morris, *King of Capital: The Remarkable Rise, Fall, and Rise Again of Steve Schwarzman and Blackstone* (New York: Crown Business, 2012); John Dionne, Josh Lerner, and Amram Migdal, "Blackstone at Age 30," Harvard Business School Case no. 9-816-013, 2015; and Felda Hardymon, Ann Leamon, and Josh Lerner, "The Blackstone Group's IPO," Harvard Business School Case no. 9-808-100, with updates from the Preqin database and https://www.blackstone.com/.

27. Dionne, Lerner, and Migdal, "Blackstone at Age 30," 2.

28. Dionne, Lerner, and Migdal, "Blackstone at Age 30," 3.

29. Hardymon, Leamon, and Lerner, "The Blackstone Group's IPO," 7.

30. Dionne, Lerner, and Migdal, "Blackstone at Age 30," 4.

CHAPTER 6. THE FUND MANAGER'S CHALLENGE

1. This account is drawn from, among other sources, Sarah Buhr, "At Rothenberg Ventures, the Rise and Fall of a Virtual Gatsby," *TechCrunch,* August 18, 2016, https://techcrunch .com/2016/08/18/at-rothenberg-ventures-the-rise-and-fall-of-a-virtual-gatsby/; Matthew

Rhodes-Kropf, Ramana Nanda, and Nathaniel Burbank, "Founder Field Day," Harvard Business School Case no. 815-101 (Boston: Harvard Business Publishing, 2015); and Lauren Smiley and Jessi Hempel, "Trouble in the House of Rothenberg," September 16, 2016, https://back-channel.com/mike-rothenbergs-vc-firm-was-young-splashy-and-loaded-with-cash-now-it-s-all-come-crashing-down-e76fa076c7c5.

2. Rhodes-Kropf, Nanda, and Burbank, "Founder Field Day."

3. See, for instance, Sarah Buhr, "Mike Rothenberg Allegedly Wired $5.2 Million from Silicon Valley Bank without Investor Permission," *TechCrunch*, September 20, 2016, https://techcrunch.com/2016/09/20/mike-rothenberg-allegedly-wired-5-2-million-from-silicon-valley-bank-without-investor-permission/.

4. https://www/sec/gov/news/press-release/2018-160.

5. This account is drawn from, among other sources, Suzanne Andrews, "Won't Someone Please Pay Attention to Teddy Forstmann?," *Institutional Investor*, February 1993, 27–35; Bryan Burrough and John Helyar, *Barbarians at the Gate* (New York: Harper & Row, 1990); "Forstmann Little & Co. History," http://www.fundinguniverse.com/company-histories/forstmann-little-co-history/; Brett Fromson, "Dealmaker of the Decade," *Washington Post*, June 4, 1995, H1, H5; Richard D. Hylton, "How KKR Got Beaten at Its Own Game," *Fortune*, May 2, 1994, 104–107; and Adam Lashinsky, "How Teddy Forstmann Lost His Groove: The Forstmann Little Chief, One of the Greatest Dealmakers Ever, Has Stumbled Badly. Has His Time Passed?," *Fortune*, July 26, 2004, http://archive.fortune.com/magazines/fortune/fortune_archive/2004/07/26/377149/index.htm.

6. A less appealing aspect of Forstmann Little's reliance on mezzanine debt was its implicit requirement that investors in the equity fund had to participate in the mezzanine fund. In these situations, it is natural to wonder whether the mezzanine transactions were done at below-market terms, inflating the returns of the equity fund. For a discussion, see Floyd Norris, "Market Place: Investors Loyal to Buyout Firm," *New York Times*, January 11, 1991, http://www.nytimes.com/1991/01/11/business/market-place-investors-loyal-to-buyout-firm.html.

7. Lashinsky, "How Teddy Forstmann Lost His Groove."

8. The definitive account of the early history of investment partnerships is Guido Astuti, *Origini e Svolgimento Storico della Commenda Fino al Secolo XIII* (Milan: S. Lattes & Co., 1933). The best accounts in English are in Raymond De Roover, "The Organization of Trade," in M. M. Postan, E. E. Rich, and Edward Miller, editors, *The Cambridge Economic History of Europe: Volume III—Economic Organization and Policies in the Middle Ages* (Cambridge: Cambridge University Press, 1963, chapter 2); and Robert S. Lopez and Irving W. Raymond, *Medieval Trade in the Mediterranean World: Illustrative Documents Translated with Introductions and Notes* (New York: Columbia University Press, 1955).

9. Andrew Metrick and Ayako Yasuda, "The Economics of Private Equity Funds," *Review of Financial Studies* 23, no. 6 (2010): 2303–2341.

10. Jessica Davies, "Buyout Shops Rack Up Management Fees," *Private Equity News*, April 24, 2017.

11. Ainslie Chandler, "EQT Offers Investors Their Choice of Carry Formulas," *Bloomberg Brief | Private Equity*, August 6, 2015.

12. Paul Gompers and Josh Lerner, "The Use of Covenants: An Analysis of Venture Partnership Agreements," *Journal of Law and Economics* 39 (October 1996): 463–498.

13. This account is drawn largely from *In the Matter of Fenway Partners, LLC, Peter Lamm, William Gregory Smart, Timothy Mayhew, Jr., and Walter Wiacek, CPA, Respondents*, "Order Instituting Administrative and Cease-and-Desist Proceedings Pursuant to Sections 203(E), 203(F) and 203(K) of the Investment Advisers Act of 1940, Making Findings, and Imposing Remedial Sanctions and a Cease-and-Desist Order," Release no. 4253, US Securities and Exchange Commission, November 3, 2015, https://www.sec.gov/litigation/admin/2015/ia-4253.pdf, and associated documents.

14. Arleen Jacobius, "Zombie PE Funds Draining Investors' Purses," *Pensions & Investments*, January 9, 2012, http://www.pionline.com/article/20120109/PRINT/301099973/zombie-pe-funds-draining-investors-purses.

15. Andrew J. Bowden, "Spreading Sunshine in Private Equity," May 6, 2014, https://www.sec.gov/news/speech/2014--spch05062014cab.html.

16. Ludovic Phalippou, Christian Rauch, and Marc Umber, "Private Equity Portfolio Company Fees," working paper, Said School of Business, Oxford University, 2015.

17. Dan Primack, "I Was Wrong about Private Equity Reform," *Fortune*, February 6, 2015, http://fortune.com/2015/02/06/i-was-wrong-about-private-equity-reform/.

18. Institutional Limited Partners Association, "ILPA Publishes Landmark Guidance on Private Equity Fee Reporting," January 29, 2016, https://ilpa.org/public-industry-news/ilpa-publishes-landmark-guidance-on-private-equity-fee-reporting/.

19. "Texas Teachers OKs More Megasized Checks for Apollo, KKR," *Wall Street Journal*, April 1, 2015, https://blogs.wsj.com/privateequity/2015/04/01/texas-teachers-oks-more-megasized-checks-for-apollo-kkr/; "Blackstone to Get Record $2.5B NJ Investment," *PE Hub*, December 9, 2011, https://www.pehub.com/2011/12/blackstone-to-get-record-25b-nj-investment/.

20. Preqin, *2017 Preqin Global Private Equity & Venture Capital Report* (London: Preqin, 2017) and reports from earlier years.

21. Andrea Rossi, "Decreasing Returns or Mean-Reversion of Luck? The Case of Private Equity Fund Growth," Unpublished working paper, Ohio State University, 2017.

22. At the same time, as Rossi points out, the fact that groups that raise larger funds experience poorer subsequent performance does not mean that the deterioration of performance is entirely due to the increase in fund size. In all likelihood, many of the groups that are most aggressive in raising a larger fund have had a great deal of success in their prior one, partially due to good luck. Due to the fickleness of Lady Luck, these groups are unlikely to have the same success in their next fund.

23. This account is based on that in Josh Lerner, Felda Hardymon, and Ann Leamon, *Venture Capital, Private Equity, and the Financing of Entrepreneurship: The Power of Active Investing* (New York: John Wiley and Sons, 2012), and in turn is based on Alex Hoye and Josh Lerner, "The Exxel Group: September 1995," Harvard Business School Case no. 297-068 (Boston: Harvard Business Publishing, 1997); Alberto Ballve and Josh Lerner, "The Exxel Group: March 2001," Harvard Business School Case no. 9-202-053 (Boston: Harvard Business Publishing, 2001); http://www.exxelgroup.com/site/index.html; and various press accounts.

24. Florencio Lopez-de-Silanes, Ludovic Phalippou, and Oliver Gottschalg, "Giants at the Gate: Investment Returns and Diseconomies of Scale in Private Equity," *Journal of Financial and Quantitative Analysis* 50, no. 3 (2015): 377–411.

25. Cambridge Associates, "Declaring a Major: Sector-Focused Private Investment Funds," Research Note, September 2014.

26. Paul Gompers, Anna Kovner, and Josh Lerner, "Specialization and Success: Evidence from Venture Capital," *Journal of Economics and Management Strategy* 18 (Fall 2009): 827–844.

27. William M. Mercer, *Key Terms and Conditions for Private Equity Investing* (New York: William M. Mercer, 1996).

28. Lisa Keslar, "Private Equity Dust-Up," *Plan Sponsor*, June 1997, http://www.plansponsor.com/MagazineArticle.aspx?id=6442461674.

29. The next several paragraphs are drawn in large part from Victoria Ivashina and Josh Lerner, "Pay Now or Pay Later?: The Economics within the Private Equity Partnership," *Journal of Financial Economics*, forthcoming, 2018.

30. "Venture Lesson," *Crain's Chicago Business*, December 13, 1997, http://www.chicagobusiness.com/article/19971213/ISSUE01/10003805/venture-lesson.

31. "Justin Wender Statement on Quitting Castle Harlan," *PE Hub*, August 6, 2010, https://www.pehub.com/2010/08/justin-wender-statement-on-departure-from-castle-harlan/.

32. "Castle Harlan Stops Fundraising Efforts for Fund VI," *PE Hub*, July 15, 2015, https://www.pehub.com/2015/07/castle-harlan-stops-fundraising-efforts-for-fund-vi/.

33. "Weston Presidio Partners Said to Exit and Firm Cancels New Fund," *Bloomberg Business*, April 30, 2014, http://www.bloomberg.com/news/articles/2014-04-30/weston-presidio-partners-said-to-exit-as-firm-cancels-new-fund.

34. "What Went Wrong at Doughty Hanson?," *Financial News*, April 16, 2015, http://www.efinancialnews.com/story/2015-04-15/douhgty-hanson-private-equity-abandons-fundraising.

35. "Behind the Genteel Facade of the London-Based Private-Equity Firm Lurk Internal Frictions, *Wall Street Journal*, January 5, 2015, http://www.wsj.com/articles/infighting-roils-veteran-british-buyout-firm-1420515182.

36. http://probitaspartners.com/pdfs/emerging_manager_due_diligence_2005.pdf.

37. Based on Katie Benner, "John Doerr to Step Aside and Become Chairman at Kleiner Perkins," *New York Times*, March 31, 2016, https://www.nytimes.com/2016/04/01/technology/john-doerr-to-step-aside-and-become-chairman-at-kleiner-perkins.html; Sarah Mitroff, "Sequoia Capital's Michael Moritz Steps Back Due to Illness," *Venturebeat.com*, May 21, 2012, https://venturebeat.com/2012/05/21/michael-moritz-steps-back/; Alison L. Cowan, "Filling Void at the Top of Clayton & Dubilier," *New York Times*, September 6, 1991, http://www.nytimes.com/1991/09/06/business/business-people-filling-void-at-the-top-of-clayton-dubilier.html; and conversations with executives at these groups.

38. Amar V. Bhide, "McKinsey & Co. (A)—1956," Harvard Business School Case no. 9-393-066, 1992, and follow-on case studies.

39. Karen Richardson and Jason Singer, "Private Equity, Public Offerings Have a History," *Wall Street Journal*, April 2, 2007, C1.

40. For more information on 3i, see Felda Hardymon, Josh Lerner, and Ann Leamon, "3i Group, PLC," Harvard Business School Case no. 803-202, 2004; and Felda Hardymon and Ann Leamon, "3i Group, PLC: May 2006," Harvard Business School Case no. 807-006, 2007.

41. Henry Lahr and Christoph Kaserer, "Net Asset Value Discounts in Listed Private Equity Funds," working paper, http://citeseerx.ist.psu.edu/viewdoc/download?doi=10.1.1.175.6760 &rep=rep1&type=pdf.

42. Blackstone Investor Day Presentation, June 2014.

43. Kevin Dowd, "Private Equity Goes Public: A History of PE Stock Performance," *Pitchbook*, May 20, 2016.

44. Landon Thomas Jr., "Stephen Schwarzman of Blackstone Feels the Agony of Victory," *New York Times*, September 4, 2015.

45. Lopez-de-Silanes, Phalippou, and Gottschalg, "Giants at the Gate."

46. This account is drawn from a variety of media sources, especially Liz Hoffman, Jenny Strasburg, and Sarah Krouse, "SoftBank to Buy Fortress Investment Group for $3.3 Billion," February 14, 2017, https://www.wsj.com/articles/softbank-nears-deal-to-buy-fortress-investment-group -for-more-than-3-billion-1487112978; Kana Inagaki and Arash Massoudi, "SoftBank's Masayoshi Son Surprises with Financial Fortress Deal," *Financial Times*, February 15, 2017, https://www .ft.com/content/26995548-f37b-11e6-8758-6876151821a6; Arleen Jacobius, "SoftBank-Fortress Deal Has Investors' Attention," *Pensions & Investments*, February 20, 2017, http://www .pionline.com/article/20170220/PRINT/302209978/softbank-fortress-deal-has-investors -attention; Bethany McLean, "Over the Hedge," *Vanity Fair*, April 2009, http://www.vanityfair .com/news/2009/04/fortress-group200904-2; and Michael Regan, "Fortress and the Curse of Hedge-Fund IPOs," *Bloomberg View*, October 14, 2015, http://www.sltrib.com/home/3059642 -155/fortress-and-the-curse-of-hedge-fund.

47. www.preqin.com.

48. Based on a compilation by Evercore and news accounts.

49. Chris Witkowsky, "LPs Don't Like When GPs Sell Stakes," *PE Hub*, May 12, 2017, https://www.pehub.com/buyouts/lps-dont-like-when-gps-sell-minority-stakes/.

50. See, for instance, writings such as Eileen Appelbaum and Rosemary Batt, *Fees, Fees and More Fees: How Private Equity Abuses Its Limited Partners and U.S. Taxpayers* (Washington, DC: Center for Economic and Policy Research, 2016); and http://www.nakedcapitalism.com/.

CHAPTER 7. REVISITING THE PRIVATE CAPITAL PARTNERSHIP

1. This section is drawn from William Elfers, *Greylock: An Adventure Capital Story* (Boston: Greylock Management, 1995); Felda Hardymon, Tom Nicholas, and David Lane, "Greylock Partners," Harvard Business School Case no. 9-813-002, 2013; David Hsu and Martin Kenney, "Organizing Venture Capital: The Rise and Demise of American Research & Development Corporation, 1946–1973," *Industrial and Corporate Change* 14 (2005): 579–616; and Charles Waite, "Greylock Management," in Udayan Gupta, editor, *Done Deals: Venture Capitalists Tell Their Stories* (Boston: Harvard Business School Press, 2000).

2. Elfers, *Greylock: An Adventure Capital Story*, 158–159.

3. Greylock Partners, "What Defines Greylock?," http://webcache.googleusercontent.com /search?q=cache:YxZZigzwggwJ:www.greylock.com/what-defines-greylock/+&cd=2&hl=en &ct=clnk&gl=us.

4. Elfers, *Greylock: An Adventure Capital Story*, 49.

5. Greylock Partners, "What Defines Greylock?"

6. While some aspects of Teays River's activities have been discussed in the public domain (for instance, Michael Fritz, "Washington State Investment Board to Weigh $300 Million Outlay to Teays River Investments," *Farmland Investor Letter*, April 9, 2015, http://www.farmlandinves torcenter.com/?p=1403&option=com_wordpress&Itemid=171), many aspects have not. This section is largely based on discussions with the firm's management and investors.

7. This paragraph is derived from various filings with the US Securities and Exchange Commission, and Lloyd L. Drury III, "Publicly-Held Private Equity Firms and the Rejection of Law as a Governance Device," *University of Pennsylvania, Journal of Business Law*, 16 (2013): 57–95, http://scholarship.law.upenn.edu/cgi/viewcontent.cgi?article=1460&context=jbl.

8. Pharmaceutical Research and Manufacturers Association, "Biopharmaceutical Research and Development: The Process Behind New Medicines," (Washington, DC: PhRMA, 2015), http://phrma-docs.phrma.org/sites/default/files/pdf/rd_brochure_022307.pdf.

9. Karlene Lukowitz, "Eight O'Clock Dramatizes the Secrets of Whole Bean Coffee," *Marketing Daily*, February 22, 2016, http://www.mediapost.com/publications/article/269496/eight -oclock-dramatizes-the-secrets-of-whole-be.html; Mobis Philipose and Pallavi Pengonda, "Eight O' Clock Buyout," *Daily News and Analysis India*, June 26, 2006; and other press accounts.

10. This account is drawn from "Atrium Companies' Plan of Reorganization Confirmed by U.S. Bankruptcy Court Company on Track to Emerge from Chapter 11 by April 30," *Business Wire*, April 28, 2010, http://www.businesswire.com/news/home/20100428006336/en/Atrium -Companies%E2%80%99-Plan-Reorganization-Confirmed-U.S.-Bankruptcy; Samuel L. Hayes III and Josh Lerner, "The Fojtasek Companies and Heritage Partners: March 1995," Harvard Business School Case no. 297-046, 1997; Josh Lerner, "The Fojtasek Companies and Heritage Partners: October 1998," Harvard Business School Case no. 200-014, 1999; and numerous press accounts.

11. Francois Degeorge, Jens Martin, and Ludovic Phalippou, "On Secondary Buyouts," *Journal of Financial Economics* 120 (2016): 124–145.

12. This account is drawn from, among other sources, Chris Cumming, "Altas Partners Raises $1 Billion for Longer-Life Private-Equity Fund," *Wall Street Journal*, May 2, 2016, https://www.wsj.com/articles/altas-partners-raises-1-billion-for-longer-life-private-equity -fund-1462190580; Jacqueline Nelson, "Altas Doubles Down on Long-Term Vision with $1–Billion fundraising," *Globe and Mail*, May 2, 2016; Kirk Falconer, "Going Long: Why Altas Partners and OPTrust Invested in St. George's University," *PE Hub.com*, August 25, 2014; and Preqin.

13. Cumming, "Altas Partners Raises $1 Billion."

14. Josh Lerner and Lauren Barley, "Bay Partners (A)" and "Bay Partners (B)." Harvard Business School Case nos. 9-213-102 and 9-213-103, 2013; Dan Primack, "The Best VC Firm You Thought Was Dead and Buried," *Fortune*, August 15, 2014, http://fortune.com/2014/08/15/the -best-vc-firm-you-thought-was-dead/.

15. For a discussion of the "control rule" in the context of private capital, see Christopher Gulinello, "Venture Capital Funds, Organizational Law, and Passive Investors," *Albany Law Review* 70 (2006): 303–365.

16. See, for instance, U.S. Securities and Exchange Commission, "Summary Report of Issues Identified in the Commission Staff's Examinations of Select Credit Rating Agencies," July 2008, https://www.sec.gov/news/studies/2008/craexamination070808.pdf; Efraim Benmelech and Jennifer Dlugosz, "The Credit Rating Crisis," in Daron Acemoglu, Kenneth Rogoff, and Michael Woodford, editors, *National Bureau of Economics Macroeconomics Annual 2009* 24 (2010): 161–207; and Jie He, Jun Qian, and Philip E. Strahan, "Credit Ratings and the Evolution of the Mortgage-Backed Securities Market," *American Economic Review Papers and Proceedings* 101 (May 2011): 131–135.

17. This discussion is based on Josh Lerner and Jean Tirole, "A Better Route to Tech Standards," *Science* 343 (February 28, 2014): 972–973.

18. For an example, see the story of VITA in Thomas O. Barnett, "Business Review Letter: VITA," Antitrust Division, U.S. Department of Justice, October 30. 2006; J. Contreras, "Technical Standards and Ex-Ante Disclosure: Results and Analysis of an Empirical Study," *Jurimetrics* 53 (2013): 163–211; and numerous press accounts.

19. William M. Mercer, *Key Terms and Conditions for Private Equity Investing* (New York: William M. Mercer, 1996), 24.

20. Alison King, "US Chamber Endorses Brown, Attacks Warren," NECN, August 15, 2012, http://www.necn.com/news/politics/_NECN__US_Chamber_Endorses_Brown__Attacks_Warren_NECN-247564861.html.

21. Based on MJ Hudson, *Private Equity Fund Terms Report* (London: MJ Hudson, 2017); and Sarah Unsworth, "Hurdle Rates and Carried Interest for Private Equity Real Estate Funds," *Preqin*, August 10, 2012, https://www.preqin.com/blog/0/5539/hurdle-rates-carried-interest.

CHAPTER 8. THE BEST (OR WORST) OF BOTH WORLDS

1. Preqin, "Private Equity Co-Investment Outlook," *Preqin Special Report*, November 23, 2015.

2. "Record Amounts Pour into Private Equity," *Triago Quarterly*, November 2015, http://www.triago.com/wp-content/uploads/2015/11/Triago-Quarterly_Nov_2015.pdf.

3. Canadian Pension Plan Investment Board, *Annual Reports*, Toronto, various years; Josh Lerner, Matthew Rhodes-Kropf, and Nathaniel Burbank, "Canada Pension Plan Investment Board: October 2012," Harvard Business School Case no. 813-103, 2013.

4. Oliver Gottschalg and Ludovic Phalippou, "The Performance of Private Equity Funds," *Review of Financial Studies* 22 (2009): 1747–1776.

5. Looking across all types of investments (but overwhelmingly publicly traded securities), a CEM Benchmarking survey of nineteen large pension funds found an average expense of 46 basis points (or 0.46%) for external money managers versus 8 basis points for internally managed funds (see Christine Williamson, "More Pension Funds Ponder Going In-House," *Pensions & Investments*, June 29, 2015, http://www.pionline.com/article/20150629/PRINT/306299971/more-pension-funds-ponder-going-in-house). This point is also made by Keith Ambachtsheer

("Maple Revolutionaries," *Economist*, March 3, 2012, http://www.economist.com/node/21548970).

6. Steven Malanga, "The Pension Fund That Ate California," *City Journal* (Winter 2013), https://www.city-journal.org/html/pension-fund-ate-california-13528.html.

7. This account is based on Lori McLeod, "CPPIB Makes Bid for Auckland Airport Official," *Globe and Mail*, December 13, 2007, https://www.theglobeandmail.com/report-on-business/cppib-makes-bid-for-auckland-airport-official/article1091296/; Eric Shackleton, "Auckland Airport, CPPIB Reach Settlement," *Star*, August 18, 2008, https://www.thestar.com/business/2008/08/18/auckland_airport_cppib_reach_settlement.html; and numerous other press accounts.

8. Reputation Institute, "Canada Regains First Place in Reputation Institute's Most Reputable Countries," June 29, 2017, https://www.reputationinstitute.com/CMSPages/GetAzureFile.aspx?path=~\media\media\documents\countryreptrak_pressrelease_2017.pdf&hash=e75265846c7504f2e5318e445ea471dcbd472b3970b7b0b971b034de4bff1df7.

9. This account is drawn from, among other sources, Kyle Pope, "Uneasy Boom: Norway's Oil Bonanza Stirs Fears of a Future When Wells Run Dry—as Output Climbs, Many Say Money Is Being Wasted and a Slump Lies Ahead—a Town's Varying Fortunes," *Wall Street Journal*, October 3, 1995; and Svein Gjedrem, "The Management of Petroleum Wealth," lecture at the Polytechnic Association, November 8, 2005, http://www.bis.org/review/r051116b.pdf.

10. This account is drawn from Seragen's filings with the US Securities and Exchange Commission; the annual reports of the National Association of College and University Business Officers; David Barboza, "Loving a Stock, Not Wisely but Too Well," *New York Times*, September 20, 1998, http://www.nytimes.com/1998/09/20/business/loving-a-stock-not-wisely-but-too-well.html; and Oliver v. Boston University, C.A. no. 16570-NC. (Del. Ch. Apr. 14, 2006).

11. James Iffland, "The Paradox of John Silber," *Chronicle of Higher Education*, October 1, 2012, http://www.chronicle.com/blogs/conversation/2012/10/01/the-paradox-of-john-silber/.

12. Bank of Sweden Prize in Economic Sciences in Memory of Alfred Nobel, "Markets with Asymmetric Information," October 10, 2001, http://www.nobelprize.org/nobel_prizes/economic-sciences/laureates/2001/advanced-economicsciences2001.pdf.

13. This section is based on, among other sources, Juliet Chung and Dawn Lim, "Harvard Endowment to Lay Off Half Its Staff," *Wall Street Journal*, January 25, 2017, https://www.wsj.com/articles/harvard-to-outsource-management-of-its-35-7-billion-endowment-1485363650; Bernard Condon and Nathan Vardi, "How Harvard Investing Superstars Crashed," *Forbes*, February 20, 2009, https://www.forbes.com/2009/02/20/harvard-endowment-failed-business_harvard.html; Kristopher McDaniel, "Harvard Has a Cold," *Chief Investment Officer*, April 9 2012, https://www.ai-cio.com/news/from-the-archives-harvard-has-a-cold/; and Nina Munk, "Rich Harvard, Poor Harvard," *Vanity Fair*, August 2009, https://www.vanityfair.com/news/2009/06/harvard.

14. Michael J. Sandel, *What Money Can't Buy: The Moral Limits of Markets* (New York: Farrar, Straus and Giroux, 2012).

15. Based on Munk, "Rich Harvard, Poor Harvard"; and Christopher Rowland, "How a Hedge Fund Star Lost It All," *New York Times*, August 16, 2007, http://www.nytimes.com/2007/08/16/business/worldbusiness/16iht-hedge.4.7145437.html.

16. Juliet Chung, "Former Harvard Money Whiz Jack Meyer Tries to Regain His Edge: Convexity Capital Management Has Lost $1 Billion of Its Clients' Money over the Last Few Years as Once Reliable Options Trades Backfired," *Wall Street Journal*, April 19, 2017, https://www.wsj.com /articles/under-pressure-ex-harvard-star-jack-meyer-says-its-not-time-to-quit-1492594202.

17. Michael McDonald, "Harvard Called 'Lazy, Fat, Stupid' in Endowment Report Last Year," *Bloomberg Business Week*, October 27, 2016, https://www.bloomberg.com/news/articles/2016 -10-27/harvard-called-lazy-fat-stupid-in-endowment-report-last-year; Daphne C. Thompson, "Management Company Reportedly Described as 'Lazy,' 'Stupid' by Employees in 2015 Review," *Harvard Crimson*, October 28, 2016, http://www.thecrimson.com/article/2016/10/28 /mckinsey-report-on-hmc-bloomberg-report/.

18. This section is based on Felda Hardymon, Ann Leamon, and Josh Lerner, "Canada Pension Plan Investment Board," Harvard Business School Case no. 809-073 (Boston: Harvard Business Publishing, 2009); and Josh Lerner, Matthew Rhodes-Kropf, and Nathaniel Burbank, "Canada Pension Plan Investment Board: October 2012," Harvard Business School Case no. 813-103, 2013.

19. Hardymon, Leamon, and Lerner, "Canada Pension Plan Investment Board," 14.

20. Richard J. Brennen, "$7M Bonus as CPPIB Loses $24B," *Toronto Star*, May 29, 2009, https://www.thestar.com/news/canada/2009/05/29/7m_bonus_as_cpp_loses_24b.html.

21. Ibid.

22. Madison Marriage, "Listed: Highest-Paid Pension Fund CEOs," *Financial Times*, February 7, 2015, https://www.ft.com/content/623683fc-ae16-11e4-919e-00144feab7de.

23. This list is drawn from numerous media accounts.

24. Lily Fang, Victoria Ivashina, and Josh Lerner, "The Disintermediation of Financial Markets: Evidence from Private Equity," *Journal of Financial Economics* 116, no. 1 (2015): 160–178.

25. Jim Edwards, "Uber's Leaked Finances Show the Company Might—Just Might—Be Able to Turn a Profit," *Business Insider*, February 27, 2017, http://www.businessinsider.com/uber-leaked -finances-accounts-revenues-profits-2017-2; Shubham Kalia and Subrat Patnaik, "Uber's Third-Quarter Net Loss Widens to $1.46 Billion: Source," *Reuters*, November 28, 2017, https://www .reuters.com/article/us-uber-results/ubers-third-quarter-net-loss-widens-to-1-46-billion -source-idUSKBN1DT0BQ.

26. This information is derived from https://www.crunchbase.com/organization/uber /funding-rounds and the various pages on that site that are linked to it.

27. Leslie Hook, "SoftBank-Led Group to Acquire $9bn Stake in Uber: Shareholders Agree to Sell 17% of Car-Booking Company at a Discount," *Financial Times*, December 28, 2017, https://www .ft.com/content/33ca6fbc-ec00-11e7-8713-513b1d7ca85a.

28. Reiner Braun, Tim Jenkinson, and Christoph Schemmerl, "Adverse Selection and the Performance of Private Equity Co-investments," working paper, 2017.

29. Josh Lerner, Jason Mao, Antoinette Schoar, and Nan Zhang, "Investing Outside the Box: Evidence from Alternative Vehicles in Private Capital," Working Paper, 2018.

30. This issue is discussed, for instance, in Marc Wyatt, "Private Equity: A Look Back and a Glimpse Ahead," May 13, 2015, https://www.sec.gov/news/speech/private-equity-look-back-and -glimpse-ahead.html.

31. "Just Say No," *Wikipedia*, https://en.wikipedia.org/wiki/Just_Say_No .

CHAPTER 9. THE FUTURE OF LONG-TERM INVESTING

1. See, for instance, Ulf Axelson, Tim Jenkinson, Per Strömberg, and Michael Weisbach, "Borrow Cheap, Buy High? Determinants of Leverage and Pricing in Buyouts," *Journal of Finance* 68 (2013): 2223–2267; and Brad Case, "What Have 25 Years of Performance Data Taught Us about Private Equity Real Estate?," *Journal of Real Estate Portfolio Management* 21 (2015), 1–20.

2. Judith Chevalier, "Capital Structure and Product-Market competition: Empirical Evidence from the Supermarket Industry," *American Economic Review* 85 (1995): 415–435.

3. Steven Davis, John Haltiwanger, Ron Jarmin, Josh Lerner, and Javier Miranda, "Private Equity, Jobs and Productivity," in Anu Gurung and Josh Lerner, editors, *Globalization of Alternative Investments Working Papers Volume 2: Global Economic Impact of Private Equity Report 2009* (Geneva: World Economic Forum, 2009), 25–44. These results were not included in the published paper based on this working paper, but will be explored further in follow-on work.

4. Steven N. Kaplan and Per Strömberg, "Leveraged Buyouts and Private Equity," *Journal of Economic Perspectives* 23 (2009): 121–146.

5. Steven N. Kaplan and Jeremy Stein, "The Evolution of Pricing and Financial Structure in the 1980s," *Quarterly Journal of Economics* 108 (1993): 313–357.

6. Examples include Shai Bernstein, Josh Lerner, Morten Sørensen, and Per Strömberg, "Private Equity and Industry Performance," *Management Science* 63 (2016): 1198–1213; Shai Bernstein and Albert Sheen, "The Operational Consequences of Private Equity Buyouts: Evidence from the Restaurant Industry," *Review of Financial Studies* 29 (2016): 2387–2418; Steve Davis, John Haltiwanger, Ron Jarmin, Josh Lerner, and Javier Miranda, "Private Equity, Jobs, and Productivity," *American Economic Review* 104 (2014): 3956–3990; Steven Kaplan, "The Effects of Management Buyouts on Operating Performance and value," *Journal of Financial Economics* 24 (1989): 217–254; and Josh Lerner, Morten Sørensen, and Per Strömberg, "Private Equity and Long-Run Investment: The Case of Innovation," *Journal of Finance* 66 (2011): 445–477. There are also multiple Harvard Business School cases on this subject by both of us.

7. Shai Bernstein, Xavier Giroud, and Richard R. Townsend, "The Impact of Venture Capital Monitoring," *Journal of Finance* 71 (2016): 1591–1622; Thomas Chemmanur, Karthik Krishnan, and Debarshi K. Nandy, "How Does Venture Capital Financing Improve Efficiency in Private Firms? A Look Beneath the Surface," *Review of Financial Studies* 24 (2011): 4037–4090; Thomas Hellmann and Manju Puri, "Venture Capital and the Professionalization of Start-Up Firms: Empirical Evidence," *Journal of Finance* 57 (2000): 169–197; Samuel Kortum and Josh Lerner, "Assessing the Contribution of Venture Capital to Innovation," *RAND Journal of Economics* 31 (2000): 674–692; Manju Puri and Rebecca Zarutskie, "On the Life Cycle Dynamics of Venture-Capital- and Non-Venture-Capital-Financed Firms," *Journal of Finance* 67 (2012): 2247–2293.

8. Davis et al., "Private Equity, Jobs and Productivity."

9. Greenwich Associates, *2015 United States Institutional Investors Report*, January 2016, https://www.greenwich.com/sites/default/files/files/reports/USII-AssetAllctn-2015-MTG.pdf.

10. International Monetary Fund, *Global Financial Stability Report*, September 2011.

11. Australian Prudential Regulation Authority, "Back Series of Annual Fund-Level Superannuation Statistics," February 2017, http://www.apra.gov.au/Super/Publications/Pages/super

annuation-fund-level-publications.aspx; Australian Bureau of Statistics, "Venture Capital and Later Stage Private Equity, Australia, 2015–16," February 2017, http://www.abs.gov.au/AUS STATS/abs@.nsf/DetailsPage/5678.02015-16?OpenDocument.

12. For more details, see Dan Fitzpatrick, "Calpers to Exit Hedge Funds: Pension Plan to Shed $4 Billion Investment to Simplify Its Assets, Reduce Costs," *Wall Street Journal*, September 15, 2014, https://www.wsj.com/articles/calpers-to-exit-hedge-funds-1410821083; and James B. Stewart, "Hedge Funds Lose Calpers, and More," *New York Times*, September 26, 2014, https://www.nytimes.com/2014/09/27/business/in-calperss-departure-a-watershed-moment -for-hedge-funds.html.

13. Robert Teitelman, "Will Public Pensions Regret Dumping Hedge Funds?" *Institutional Investor*, February 15, 2017, http://www.institutionalinvestor.com/Article/3662075/investors -pensions/will-public-pensions-regret-dumping-hedge-funds.html?ArticleId=3662075#/ .WXSocITyvIV.

14. CB Insights, *The History of CVC: From Exxon and DuPont to Xerox and Microsoft, How Corporates Began Chasing 'The Future,'* 2017, https://www.cbinsights.com/research/report/cor porate-venture-capital-history.

15. Thomson Reuters, "VentureXpert Database," http://vx.thomsonib.com/NASApp/Vx Component/VXMain.jsp.

16. Paul Gompers and Josh Lerner, "The Determinants of Corporate Venture Capital Suc-cess: Organizational Structure, Incentives, and Complementarities," in Randall Morck, editor, *Concentrated Corporate Ownership* (Chicago: University of Chicago Press for the National Bu-reau of Economic Research, 2000), 17–50.

17. Katie Rogers, "Oberlin Students Take Culture War to the Dining Hall," *New York Times*, December 21, 2015, https://www.nytimes.com/2015/12/22/us/oberlin-takes-culture-war-to -the-dining-hall.html.

18. Examples of the former bodies include the Institutional Limited Partners Association and the International Federation of Sovereign Wealth Funds; of the latter, Invest Europe and the American Investment Council.

INDEX